Researching Education Policy

Social Research and Educational Studies Series

Series Editor
Robert G. Burgess,
Professor of Sociology,
University of Warwick

Social Research and Educational Studies Series: 14

Researching Education Policy:
Ethical and Methodological Issues

Edited by

David Halpin
and
Barry Troyna

The Falmer Press

(A member of the Taylor & Francis Group)
London • Washington, D.C.

UK The Falmer Press, 4 John Street, London WC1N 2ET
USA The Falmer Press, Taylor & Francis Inc., 1900 Frost Road, Suite
101, Bristol, PA 19007

First published in 1994

A catelogue record for this book is available from the British Library

Library of Congress Cataloging-in-Publication Data are available on request

ISBN 0 7507 0344 x cased
ISBN 0 7507 0345 8 paper

Jacket design by Caroline Archer

Typeset in 10/12 pt Bembo by
Graphicraft Typesetters Ltd., Hong Kong.

Printed in Great Britain by Burgess Science Press, Basingstoke on paper which has a specified pH value on final paper manufacture of not less than 7.5 and is therefore 'acid free'.

Contents

Contents

Acknowledgments

The chapters in this volume are based on papers delivered by the authors during a series of seminars which we organized at the University of Warwick Institute of Education. We are grateful to the Economic and Social Research Council (ESRC) and the University of Warwick for providing the financial support for the seminars. We would also like to thank Robert Burgess for his helpful advice on editorial matters and Margaret Handy and Donna Jay for their administrative help.

David Halpin and Barry Troyna
University of Warwick Institute of Education

Series Editor's Preface

The purpose of the *Social Research and Educational Studies* series is to provide authoritative guides to key issues in educational research. The series includes overviews of fields, guidance on good practice and discussions of the practical implications of social and educational research. In particular, the series deals with a variety of approaches to conducting social and educational research. Contributors to this series review recent work, raise critical concerns that are particular to the field of education, and reflect on the implications of research for educational policy and practice.

Each volume in the series draws on material that will be relevant for an international audience. The contributors to this series all have wide experience of teaching, conducting and using educational research. The volumes are written so that they will appeal to a wide audience of students, teachers and researchers. Altogether, the volumes in the *Social Research and Educational Studies* series provide a comprehensive guide for anyone concerned with contemporary educational research.

The series will include individually authored books and edited volumes on a range of themes in education including: qualitative research, survey research, the interpretation of data, self-evaluation, research and social policy, analyzing data, action research, the politics and ethics of research.

A recent development in educational research has been the way in which many investigators have focused on policy issues. Much of this work has been devoted to substantive concerns with little attention devoted to methodology beyond descriptive statements about 'policy analysis'. The contributors to this volume focus on key ethical and methodological concerns that have arisen in studies of education policy. Altogether these essays are an essential resource for students, teachers and researchers engaged in developing this style of research.

Robert G. Burgess
University of Warwick

Introduction

David Halpin and Barry Troyna

Background and Context

This book stems from a series of seminars which we convened at the University of Warwick in the early 1990s. The series was supported by the Economic and Social Research Council (ESRC) as part of its 'Research Seminar Competition' established in 1991. The series was called 'Ethical and Methodological Issues Associated with Research into the 1988 Education Reform Act'. A cumbersome title, perhaps, but one which was intended to convey clearly our aim: to provide an opportunity for academics who had been looking at the Act from various angles to reflect on their research activities. Some of the eventual contributors had been involved in empirical research, others in sharpening their methodological tools and applying them to the study of education policy. Whatever the nature of their activity, we encouraged them to reveal and share 'what went on' in the conception, execution and analysis of their research rather than simply delineate 'what they and others had found out'. The focus, then, was very much on process not product.

Another part of the rationale for the series rested on the view that debates about researching policy should not be confined to established academics but should include scholars of varying status within 'the academy' working through different disciplines. Our application to the ESRC indicated that we would open the seminars to scholars at different stages of their careers, in particular graduate students and contract researchers. We reckoned that this constituted one of the merits of the proposal. As one of us suggests later (see Chapter 1), we are now rather more circumspect about this value judgment.

The use of the term 'methodology' in the title of the seminar series hinted at the way in which the enterprise was conceived. The understanding of the term which informed our activities drew heavily on the definition offered by Robert Burgess and Martin Bulmer. They have outlined a useful distinction between the concept 'methodology' and other cognate terms such as 'strategy', 'techniques' and 'methods', arguing that the former 'denotes the systematic and logical study of the principles guiding enquiry' (Burgess and Bulmer, 1981, p. 478). Alvin Gouldner's exposition of the term also proved to be eminently serviceable, For Gouldner, the term 'methodology' is 'infused with ideologically resonant assumptions about what the social world is, and what the nature of the relation between them is' (Gouldner, 1971, pp. 50–1). One of the intentions of the seminars and, by implication, this book, then, was that authors should speak openly and reflectively about the methodological assumptions which underpin the way they approach the study of education policy. Relatedly, we were also concerned to invite them to address some of the ethical issues that arise in the course of undertaking investigations of contentious government initiatives to reform education.

The seminar series complemented two other ventures designed to facilitate discussion between education researchers working on the measures contained in the 1988 Education Reform Act. Not long after the passing of the Act, the British Educational Research Association (BERA) established a number of task groups (including those on the local management of schools, the National Curriculum and assessment), the chief purpose of which was to set new, and consolidate existing, agendas for research in the light of the legislation. The Education Reform Act Research Network (Halpin, 1990), on the other hand, was more concerned to provide a regular forum in which academics working on the Act could discuss the interim outcomes of their research in advance of final publication.

In each case the emphasis was mostly either on propagating fresh ideas or presenting the preliminary findings of ongoing research; in neither was there a declared intention to explicate the theoretical sources and methodological rationale of work in hand. While the importance of the latter was not entirely absent in either the deliberations of the BERA task groups or the seminars coordinated by the Education Reform Act Research Network, it was not central or given much priority. Therefore, in launching the seminar series, we hoped to foster debate that would confer greater significance on this aspect of doing research, not only on the 1988 Education Reform Act, but on education policy generally.

Barry Troyna makes clear in the opening chapter that this book contributes to the growing genre of material which celebrates 'reflexivity' and 'reflectivity'. To that extent it can be usefully read alongside two other books also published by Falmer in its *Social Research and Educational Studies* series. *The Ethics of Educational Research* (Burgess, 1989) focuses on three key areas where *ethical* considerations are involved: data dissemination (questions of confidentiality, reporting back and the use made of research by policy makers); research relations (questions of access, power, deception, harm and secrecy); and research sponsorship (questions about power relations and the way these assist or impede research). Janet Finch's (1986) *Research and Policy: The Uses of Qualitative Methods in Social and Educational Research* promotes the value of *qualitative* research in education policy-making contexts. It also discusses, as do several of the chapters in this collection, some ethical issues in policy-oriented qualitative research, including the political position of the researcher.

Two further volumes, both edited by Geoffrey Walford, also articulate with themes found in this book. *Doing Educational Research* (1991) brings together semi-autobiograpical accounts of the research of thirteen education policy analysts, all of whom were involved in prominent and influential projects. *Doing Research on the Powerful in Education* (1994) provides a set of more focused accounts of how individual researchers gained access to, and obtained data from, respondents working in elite settings. It also reflects on the status of data derived from such enquiries and what, if anything, they add to our understanding of how education policy is first thought of and subsequently implemented.

Organization of Chapters

The chapters in this book are variously interconnected in terms of the issues they address and the theories, research methodologies and ethical controversies they discuss. Consequently, they could have been sequenced in a number of different ways, maintaining a variety of coherent themes and arguments. In the event, however, we allowed the original rationale of the seminar series to dictate largely the organization of the book which is written in three parts with four chapters each.

PART 1 'Theory, Scholarship and Research into Education Policy' includes chapters by Charles Raab, Roger Dale, May Pettigrew and Robert Burgess. Raab's chapter traces the history of education policy analysis as a specialism within British political science, reflecting critically on the 'subject-centrism' of education specialists and their isolation from theory and method in the general policy-studies field. Raab also discusses the limitations of utilizing exclusively either neo-Marxist or neo-pluralist perspectives in the study of education policy and makes a strong plea for the development of research designs that focus on the dynamics of its implementation. Dale's chapter complements Raab's. It comments critically on the 'disciplinary parochialism' and 'ethnocentric assumptions' of some recent studies of education policy. It also argues that the emphasis on 'applied education politics' in these enquiries is leading to a retrograde pre-eminence being placed on 'problem-solving' at the expense of 'critical theory'.

The failure of some education policy research to theorize satisfactorily across and between national and disciplinary cultures, and to shun critique in favour of making things work more efficiently, may have something to do with the conditions under which academics are increasingly forced to work. Certainly, that is what Pettigrew concludes on the basis of her experience of undertaking commissioned research on education policy. Indeed, her chapter offers a somewhat pessimistic account of recent changes in the relationship of government to social enquiry. Specifically, it documents researchers' experience of increasing contractual controls in centrally commissioned social and educational research, including the ability of sponsors to use their power to suppress findings. Burgess, by contrast, adopts a more sanguine attitude. While recognizing that conflicts of interest between sponsors and contract researchers can arise in the course of undertaking sponsored work, he argues these are neither inevitable nor necessary. On the contrary, Burgess concludes that when contract researchers embrace the qualities of the 'good worker', they also take on board the attributes of the scholar in the research community.

PART 2 'The Ethics of Research into Education Policy' includes chapters by Beverley Skeggs, Geoffrey Walford, Stephen Ball and Jenny Ozga and Sharon Gewirtz. In different ways, these contributions highlight the issues associated with incompatibility between the ideological stances of researchers and the subjects of their enquiries. Skeggs exposes as myth the claims of neutrality sometimes made on behalf of recent education policy-making, particularly by its architects. She argues that feminist research is especially well placed, by virtue of its political project and epistemological and methodological orientation, to expose and challenge the contradictions in government policy for education, especially in the areas of curriculum reform, pedagogy and parent power. Walford reflects upon some of the ethical and methodological aspects of a research project he conducted within the first City Technology College. In terms that resonate with Burgess's view of the 'good worker', he argues that political commitment and the search for objectivity need not be incompatible, providing researchers collect, analyse and report their data in honest and rigorous ways.

Ball's chapter is concerned with some interpretational and theoretical difficulties involved in working with data derived from interviews with powerful policy makers. He emphasizes the range of discourses employed by such respondents and the importance of subjecting these to different types and levels of analysis. In similar vein, Ozga and Gewirtz discuss the problems and issues which crop up in the interpretation of interview evidence elicited by women researchers from 'powerful or once-powerful' and 'polished and experienced' male policy makers. Their chapter also reflects on the importance in research design and fieldwork practice of a 'critical-theory' approach in policy research, and some logistic and ethical difficulties to which this can give rise.

PART 3 'Methodological Perspectives on Research into Education Policy' includes chapters by Martyn Hammersley, Rosemary Deem and Kevin Brehony, Gwen Wallace, Jean Rudduck and Susan Harris and Martin Hughes. Hammersley examines the relationship between ethnographic research and education policy-making and practice, arguing that recent education legislation highlights serious problems in conceptualizing the link between them. He suggests that the assumptions behind much of this legislation is fundamentally at odds with the methodological orientation of ethnographers. Equally, Hammersley indicates how sceptical and relativist interpretations of social research may undermine the basis on which ethnographers, and educational researchers generally, can claim relevance of their work to politics and practice.

Deem and Brehony consider some of the methodological issues involved in undertaking a multi-site, ethnographic case study of school governing bodies.

They argue that such an approach is capable of generating theoretically informed analyses of the contradictory aspects of state-education reform. Like Dale, Deem and Brehony conclude with a strong plea for critically informed cross-cultural analyses of education policy.

The chapter by Wallace, Rudduck and Harris discusses the protocols and risks of conducting long-term research in schools in the present climate. It describes ways in which confidence between researchers and schools can be enhanced over an extended period through the 'bearing of gifts', empathic understanding and the establishment of trust. Finally in this section, Hughes outlines some of the methodological issues encountered in the course of undertaking longitudinal research on parents in the context of current educational reforms. In particular, he addresses the difficulty of locating and defining parents and disseminating the findings of such research in the face of urgent demands from the media for up-to-the-minute information and competition from commercial opinion pollsters that are able to provide it to order. In this way, Hughes reminds us of the difficulties faced by researchers who see their work as not simply contributing to knowledge about policy, but also influencing the policy-making process itself in terms of suggesting and propagating alternatives.

The book, however, opens with a chapter by Barry Troyna which examines the problems faced by education policy researchers as they struggle to forge a recognizable academic identity within both education research and mainstream social science. Through a discussion of the process of 'being reflective', the chapter also challenges some of the assumptions we took for granted in our original thinking about the seminar series that gave rise to this book, including the role that non-established researchers could legitimately be expected to play in discussions of the work of tenured academics.

References

BURGESS, R.G. and BULMER, M. (1981) 'Research methodology teaching: Trends and developments', *Sociology*, 15, 4, pp. 447–89.

BURGESS, R. (1989) (Ed) *The Ethics of Educational Research*, London, Falmer Press.

FINCH, J. (1986) *Research and Policy: The Uses of Qualitative Methods in Social and Educational Research*, London, Falmer Press.

GOULDNER, A. (1971) *The Coming Crisis of Western Sociology*, London, Heinemann.

HALPIN, D. (1990) 'The education reform act research network: An exercise in collaboration and communication', *Journal of Curriculum Studies*, 22, 3, pp. 295–7.

WALFORD, G. (1991) (Ed) *Doing Educational Research*, London, Routledge.

WALFORD, G. (1994) (Ed) *Doing Research on the Powerful in Education*, London, University of London Press.

Chapter 1

Reforms, Research and Being Reflexive About Being Reflective

Barry Troyna

Reforms

The debate about educational policy in Britain (and other western democratic societies) is hotting up. It is salutary to recall, for instance, that as recently as the early 1980s certain British academics were lamenting the paucity of policy studies in this country, contrasting this sorry state of affairs with the comparative wealth of literature in the United States. 'The most striking feature of the British literature in this field', wrote Michael Parkinson in 1982, 'is how relatively little of it there is.' He continued: 'As a result the important areas about which we remain ignorant far outweigh those about which we know a little. And the gaps exist at both a theoretical and empirical level' (1982, p. 114).

Although political scientists and sociologists engaged in policy studies still tend to turn a blind eye to the strides made by educationists in exploring this field 'at both a theoretical and empirical level' over the last decade or so (see for instance, Hill, 1993), it is undoubtedly the case that things have improved since Parkinson wrote his review of the literature. This is mostly due to the excitement generated by the plethora of educational reforms introduced by successive Conservative governments since 1979. These reforms are part and parcel of an ideological shift from 'welfarism' to 'neo-liberalism' (Miller and Rose, 1991) and draw inspiration from a conception of democracy framed in terms of individualism. Their impact on the shape and provision of education in England and Wales has been both fundamental and pervasive.

But reforms along these lines have not been confined to these shores. Guided by similar political and ideological imperatives, the move towards self-governing schools, in particular, and the espousal of what Fazal Rizvi calls the 'associated rhetoric of devolution, parent and community participation and school-based decision-making', have also left their indelible mark on the educational landscape in North America, Australasia and parts of mainland Europe (Rizvi, 1993, p. 143). The nature and extent of these reforms indicate that the sphere of education has provided a fertile ground for the cultivation and legislative enactment of these ideologies. Indeed, precisely *why* factions of the Right have been so successful in gaining the ascendancy in education is one of the questions which has dominated the debate about educational policy studies in the 1980s and 1990s (see for instance, Apple, 1993; Dale, 1989; Hall, 1988; Rizvi, 1993). This is how Michael Apple explains the Right's accomplishment:

> The social democratic goal of expanding equality of opportunity (itself a rather limited reform) has lost much of its political potency and its ability to mobilize people. The 'panic' over falling standards and illiteracy, the fears of violence in schools, and the concern with the destruction of family values and religiosity, have all had an effect. These fears are exacerbated, and used, by dominant groups within politics and the economy who have been able to move the debate on education (and all things social) onto their own terrain, the terrain of standardization, productivity and industrial needs. Since so many parents are justifiably concerned about the economic futures of their children — in an economy that is increasingly conditioned by lowered wages, unemployment, capital flight and insecurity — rightist discourse connects with the experiences of many working-class and lower middle-class people. (Apple, 1989, p. 7)

In England and Wales, the 1988 Education Reform Act (ERA) has been emblematic of the political processes to which Apple draws attention. It has also provided the most important shot in the arm to the study of education policy in Britain. Although the ERA constitutes only one of eighteen pieces of legislation on education introduced so far under Conservative rule, it is this package of reforms, comprising 238 clauses and eighteen schedules, which has threatened to bring about the most fundamental reconstitution of the educational system in England and Wales in over forty years. As Jackson Hall noted at the time, the ERA 'was not about the development or reformulation of the 1944 settlement, but about replacing it' (cited in Chitty, 1990, p. 198). Richard Johnson put some flesh on the bones of Hall's comment in what has turned out to be a remarkably prescient observation:

> I believe that the main configurations of formal schooling will be unrecognizable by the mid 1990s in many respects: the powers of local education authorities (LEAs), for example; the balance of public and private provision; the role of the central state . . . The transition will be as fundamental as that of 1780–1840 (the birth of 'mass schooling') or as that of 1865–1880 (the creation of a civic education service). By the end of the century the 'growth' of 1870–1970 may look like a specific historical phase, with its typical educational forms oddly relative to my children's children. (Johnson, 1989, p. 92)

Subsequent legislation, including the 1993 Education Act, has consolidated the ideological rationale for, and extended some of the substantive measures contained within, the ERA. These initiatives have led to a restructuring of the education system along market-led lines. Actually, to use Julian Le Grand and Will Bartlett's more precise term, the education system now has the properties of a 'quasi-market' (Bartlett, 1993). In 'quasi-markets', producers are encouraged to compete against one another and consumers are encouraged to express their preferences, but. . . . no money actually changes hands' (Bartlett, 1993, p. 126).

Allegedly, the reforms have introduced greater diversity of provision. In the school sector this is bound together with a prescribed curriculum, compulsory testing and a formula for funding institutions which rests on a commitment to 'horizontal equity' (Dixon, 1991). Although the Conservatives tend to stress and celebrate the way their reforms have led to deregularization of the system, this is only part of the story. As Andy Hargreaves and David Reynolds point out: 'The rhetoric is consumer choice and diversity. The reality is product standardization. Kentucky Fried Schooling!' (Hargreaves and Reynolds, 1989, p. 10).

It is probably not an exaggeration to say that no stone in this ensemble of legislative initiatives has been left unturned by educational researchers. A quick glance at the relevant shelves in bookshops and libraries and the contents of specialist journals and publishers' catalogues reveals that matters such as the financial and governance implications of school-based management; the provision of Grant Maintained Status to schools; establishment of City Technology Colleges; the National Curriculum and the new modes of testing and assessment have all been subject to rigorous scrutiny. The setting up the ERA Research Network (Halpin, 1990) and various task groups operating under the auspices of the British Educational Research Association (see, for instance, Wallace, 1992), alongside the establishment of new (and dedicated issues of established) academic journals (see Ball and Shilling, 1994; Siraj-Blatchford and Troyna, 1993), have provided educational policy researchers with other conduits for the dissemination of substantive findings based on their inquiries into the Act.

Research

These contemporary educational reforms have also acted as a catalyst for the development of a genre of policy studies which break rank both with empiricist accounts of education policy and with those which rest upon managerialist perspectives on the policy process. Since the early 1980s, there has been a burgeoning of education policy studies which give centre stage to social scientific interpretations of the antecedents, production and orientation of education policy. These studies, according to Gerald Grace (1984), constitute 'policy scholarship'. In his view they contrast favourably with studies undertaken by what he calls 'policy scientists'. Research structured along these latter lines approximates to what C.W. Mills (1959) referred to as 'abstracted empiricism'. That is to say, it is reactive and infatuated with the description and evaluation of organizational reform, management improvement and implementation strategies and procedures.

Some researchers contest Grace's distinction within this field of enquiry, arguing that it is at best divisive, possibly even illusory. They prefer to place their studies in the self-proclaimed discourse of 'education policy sociology' (see, for instance, Ball, 1990a). Jenny Ozga reckons that this genre of research is 'rooted in the social science tradition, historically informed and drawing on qualitative and illuminative techniques' (Ozga, 1987, p. 14). Like Grace's categories, 'education policy sociology' is a controversial, possibly imprecise, more likely inaccurate, appellation (see Troyna, 1994). However, like the term, 'policy scholarship', 'education policy sociology' gives some clues to the 'more theoretically sophisticated and historically informed approach' to policy studies which has arisen in the last few years (Grace, 1989, p. 88). Of course, this is not to suggest that these recent studies, whatever they are called, have made a clean break with the earlier, atheoretical, apparently value-free and objective, stance on policy studies. On the contrary, it is Ozga's concern that certain studies of ERA and post-ERA developments continue along the 'policy-science' road by sacrificing the elaboration of theory on the altar of (abstracted) empiricism. In her view, these studies are more concerned with the accumulation of information about particular issues than with positioning their analyses in the 'bigger picture' of the role of the State in education policy making (Ozga, 1990).

Despite Ozga's critique, some of the current theoretical and empirical explorations of educational policy show a healthy disregard for managerialist and bureaucratic conceptions of the policy process. In fact, this corpus of research reveals influences from an impressive array of theoretical and disciplinary sources. Some are embedded in Marxist frameworks (Cultural Studies, 1991; Dale, 1992; Hatcher and Troyna, 1994), while others draw on pluralist approaches (Ball, 1990a; Kogan, *et al.* 1984; McPherson and Raab, 1988) and feminist perspectives (Blackmore and Kenway, 1993; Hughes, 1992). It is also possible to discern the influence of various (mainland European) theorists on studies of contemporary education policy. These include Foucault (Ball, 1990a; Bowe, Ball and Gold, 1992; Kenway, 1993), Baudrillard (Bowe, Gewirtz and Ball, 1992), Bourdieu and Offe (Codd, 1992) and Barthes (Bowe, Ball and Gold, 1992; Maguire, 1991; Rosie, 1992). There are also significant differences in the way education policy 'scholars' (to use Grace's appellation) have operationalized their research designs. Some, such as McPherson and Raab (1988), have relied almost entirely on interviews; others, like Salter and Tapper (1981), have emphasized primary source documentation; while Bowe, Ball and Gold (1992), Deem and Brehony (1993) and Walford and Miller (1991), among others, have adopted a 'partial' ethnographic approach. Researchers working along these lines in Britain have also derived their empirical evidence from a range of research sites: Whitehall, schools, local education authorities, private residencies and governing bodies. All in all, then, it seems that what Janet Finch (1985) called 'methodological eclecticism' reigns supreme in this subfield of education policy studies.

Being Reflective

It is our expectation that the book (like the seminar series on which it was based) would contribute to that emerging body of literature which challenges the idealized conceptions of social research found in traditional research-methods textbooks. Technicist conceptions of research, which focus purely and simply on 'how to do' empirical projects, continue to dominate the research literature (see for instance, Bell, 1987; Cohen and Manion, 1980; Moser and Kalton, 1957). However, in their determination to lay bare the allegedly logical and sequential phases of the conception, execution and dissemination of social research, these interpretations of the activity help to sanction and reproduce the 'myth of objectivity' (Medawar, 1963). In contrast, *Researching Education Policy* was conceived from a perspective in which research is not construed as something pristine but as something 'carried out by flesh and blood figures who are engaged in real life activities' (Jacubowicz, 1991, p. 5). To reiterate the point made earlier: its purpose is to highlight the ways in which academics working in the field of educational policy grapple with the theoretical, ethical and political dramas associated with their research.

This genre of writing is often labelled 'reflexive', a diffuse concept which is used by academics in a bewildering number of ways. In some contexts, it seems to denote an allegiance to particular epistemological stances; in others, to methodological practices. Different again are those contexts where the two meanings are conflated — or confused (see Bonnett, 1993; Hammersley, 1983; Steier, 1991; Woolgar, 1988 for discussion). Some writers characterize their work as 'reflexive' but make no attempt to define the term (e.g., Nias, 1991) while others avoid the word entirely. Then again there are those who prefer to label accounts drawn in this fashion as 'reflective', 'first-hand', *'post hoc'*, 'autobiographical', or some such variant. Meanwhile, there are those who see the exercise as bordering on catharsis. They use phrases such as 'confessional' or 'warts and all' to characterize the exposés on their research. Raymond Lee reckons that accounts such as these often assume the status of 'heroic tales' in which the diligence, cleverness and artifice of the researcher is very much to the fore (Lee, 1993, p. 121). However, as Alastair Bonnett notes, these 'heroic tales', or auto-critique as he calls the process, tend to efface the social location of authors 'even as they subject themselves to a seemingly rigorous exercise in self-criticism' (Bonnett, 1993, p. 165).

Whatever the nomenclature, this perspective is now beginning to question the hegemonic status of technicist and prescriptive approaches to research in the social sciences. Even within the continued proliferation of manuals which stress the technicalities of so-called 'data collection', tentative steps have been taken to acknowledge that research is a social activity, which intrudes on peoples' lives. The result: to a greater or lesser extent, the technicalities of research are no longer artificially detached from the political, ethical and social arena.

In the rest of this chapter I want to do two things. First, I want to document briefly how reflective writings on research have become increasingly fashionable in the last few years. Second, I want to cast a critical eye over this approach and tease out and discuss some of its epistemological, strategic and political problems. My involvement in *Researching Education Policy* testifies to the fact that I do not want to deny entirely the efficacy or value of 'reflectivity' in educational research. However, it is in the spirit of the exercise that I should be reflexive about 'being reflective' — a stance which, according to Hammersley and Atkinson, is all too rarely taken in '*post hoc*' accounts. They say that it 'is no good being reflexive in the course of planning and executing a piece of research if one is only to abandon that reflexivity when it comes to writing about it' (1983, p. 209).

Being Reflexive

Being reflective has a long tradition in accounts of sociological and social anthropological research in the United States. Its classic expression, of course, is to be found in William Foote Whyte's appendix to his ethnographic study, *Street Corner Society* (1955). But it is only in the last couple of decades that it has figured in the research methodology literature in Britain. Even now it is most commonly found in feminist accounts of research (see for instance, Cook and Fonow, 1986; Cotterill and Letherby, 1993; Roberts, 1981; Stanley and Wise, 1983). 'Reflective' accounts of educational research in Britain have an even shorter history, for one reason or another, and are to be found in a relatively limited range of publications (e.g., Adelman, 1984; Burgess, 1984; 1985; 1989; Walford, 1987; 1991).

On the face of it, social and educational researchers seem to be united in their conviction that exposés of the research process are a good thing, largely for two reasons. First, they function as aids to the socialization of novice researchers. Second, they constitute a corrective to the view of the researcher as a mere technician. Consider the view of Colin Bell and Howard Newby, for instance. They helped to establish the genre in Britain with their edited volume, *Doing Sociological Research* (1977). Although the volume failed to include either feminist or antiracist perspectives on the research process the authors contended that 'accounts of doing sociological research are *at least* as valuable, both to students of sociology and to its practitioners, as the exhortations to be found in the much more common textbooks on methodology' (1977, p. 9). They went on to say that they saw their book serving political, philosophical and practical purposes (1977, p. 10). Geoffrey Walford

who, along with Robert Burgess, has played a major part in encouraging educationists to put into print their reflections on doing research, also commends
this approach. Walford claims that the contributions to his edited collection,
Doing Sociology of Education (1987), like others in the genre, are 'revelatory'
and 'get beneath the surface' of the research process. He contrasts them with
conventional research accounts which he thinks provide only superficial and
contrived records. 'Reflectivity', then, provides 'a further perspective' in which
research is shown to centre 'around compromises, short-cuts, hunches and
serendipitous occurrences' (Walford, 1987, p. 1). Even Martyn Hammersley
and Paul Atkinson, who are more sceptical than most about this genre of
writing, have recognized its value within the ethnographic tradition. 'Such
first-hand accounts', they have suggested:

> often have something of a confessional tone to them, whereby the
> problematic, incomplete, mistaken, dubious, unethical or uncomfort-
> able aspects of the work are allowed to emerge. (Hammersley and
> Atkinson, 1983)

However, they mention some important caveats:

> Yet these problems are rarely allowed to intrude directly on much of
> the ethnographic text. They are often kept at a safe distance from the
> main 'findings', in an appendix, or in a separate paper. (ibid., p. 229)

I have other reservations about 'reflectivity', of which there are three in
particular. To begin with, these accounts tend to suffer from delusions of
grandeur. The reason is that they are only selective reconstructions of the
research process. They no more 'tell it like it is' than the normative 'cook
books' against which they are favourably compared. Indeed, for those who
question a social realist epistemology, 'reflective' essays may do more harm
than good in helping to legitimate the view that there exists 'somewhere out
there' an uncontested 'it' that can be captured in an account and diffused to a
wider audience.

The exchange between William Foote Whyte and W.A. Marianne Boelen
about the 'reality of Cornerville' represented in *Street Corner Society* is testi-
mony to this assumption. In a special issue of the *Journal of Contemporary
Ethnography* (*JCE*) (Adler *et al.*, 1992), Boelen tells us that she revisited
'Cornerville' twenty-five times between 1970 and 1989 and met some of the
same people that Whyte had encountered, observed, interviewed and portrayed
in his book some forty years earlier. She criticizes Whyte for offering incor-
rect or inappropriate interpretations of life in 'Cornerville' and for factual
misrepresentations (Boelen, 1992). Not surprisingly, Whyte (1992) contests
Boelen's arguments and repudiates her claims, as does Orlandella (1992), one
of Whyte's original respondents.

This is not the first occasion where there have been disputes between practitioners who have visited the same research site and emerged with different findings and interpretations. However, what is exceptional about the *JCE* debate is Norman Denzin's contribution. He reorients the discussion by arguing that the 'combatants' are locked in a positivist, social realist epistemology. Denzin recognizes that, while this epistemology is probably still pre-eminent in social science research discourses, it is no longer sacrosanct. Writing from a poststructuralist perspective, Denzin challenges the realist agenda to which both Whyte and Boelen have subscribed. In effect, he pours scorn on their claims to have 'told it like it is'. There is no 'it', no 'obdurate social world', according to Denzin. 'There are only different tellings of different stories', and these are 'organized under the heading of the same tale'. He continues:

> This position runs counter to the theory that structures the Boelen–Whyte debate. As a countertheory, it justifies treating each document as a separate story. It also renders fruitless their debates over who got the facts right. There are few facts: concrete occurrences with single, shared interpretations. Instead, there are only facticities or concrete social experiences given different meanings by the same and different individuals over the course of time. Boelen got one set of facticities, Whyte another. (Denzin, 1992, p. 125)

This trenchant critique has implications for, and even challenges, what is often the taken-for-granted rationale for 'reflectivity'. Taking Denzin's arguments to their logical conclusion, all that this genre of research writing can provide is an individualized, even idiosyncratic, account of a researcher's experiences. A narrative structured along these lines may be of social, historical and intellectual interest; it may also demystify a researcher's particular experiences in the framing, execution or dissemination of a study. As Frederick Steier notes the imperative in this scenario is that as researchers 'we understand and become aware of our own research activities as *telling ourselves a story about ourselves*' (1991, p. 3). To repeat, this is interesting, But, whether it is — or ever can be — of *methodological* significance must not be taken for granted.

The second of my concerns is that this genre of writing tends to be confined to a limited range of members of the research community. Commenting on this pattern, Walford (1991) points out that it is sociologists, rather than psychologists who are most likely to engage in first-hand accounts of their research. In fact, the boundaries are drawn even more sharply. As the list of players represented in the 'reflective' literature shows, it is sociologists who favour qualitative over quantitative research methodologies who tend to open their work up for scrutiny. Although there are some conspicuous exceptions to this trend (see for instance, Steedman, 1987; Sammons, 1989) it is nonetheless true that 'reflectivity' is hardly pervasive in social science research discourses. As Judith Aldridge observes:

many aspects of social science writing remain untouched by concern to make explicit the mechanisms by which academic research and writing are accomplished. Especially in quantitative research, all trace of the production and producer has traditionally been expected to be wiped from research account writing. In spite of historical social scientific precedent to attend to epistemological issues, writers of quantitative research accounts for the most part proceed as though epistemological concerns are either implicitly unproblematic, or irrelevant to their task. (Aldridge, 1993, p. 54)

Stephen Ball suggests that ethnographers should always engage in 'reflective' practices. Indeed, he asserts that it should be 'the requirement for methodological rigour that every ethnography be accompanied by a *research biography*, that is a reflexive account of the conduct of the research' (Ball, 1990b, p. 170). I appreciate the spirit of Ball's argument and agree that the inclusion of a research biography might improve the presentation of ethnographic accounts which still, unfortunately, tend to be rather sanitized. Against this, I am not convinced by his claim that, by 'baring their souls', ethnographers (and others working within the qualitative tradition) necessarily enhance the rigour of their research. In fact, as Mary Maynard points out in her review of Patti Lather's *Getting Smart*, such accounts often degenerate into 'vanity ethnography' where too much emphasis is placed by the researcher in 'reflexively locating herself in her work' (Maynard, 1993, p. 329). Nor do I believe that it strengthens the credibility of the methodology. In the conservative 1980s and 1990s the allegedly 'softer' research methodologies are probably taken less seriously than ever by researchers working in other paradigms, and by lay people (including policy makers) who question any research other than that based on a logical positivistic epistemology. The routine inclusion of a research biography in ethnographic accounts does not seem to me to provide a way to assuage these concerns.

But my concern with Ball's recommendation goes even deeper. The standard insertion of a 'research biography' into qualitative (but not necessarily quantitative) research accounts might, unwittingly perhaps, further consolidate a view which is already entrenched and circulating widely in the populist circles; namely, that qualitative research is subjective, value-laden and, therefore, unscientific and invalid, in contrast to quantitative research, which meets the criteria of being objective, value-free, scientific and therefore valid. Howard Becker is, of course, correct in saying that the epistemological problems faced by qualitative educational researchers are 'no worse than those of social scientists working on any other kind of social organization' (Becker, 1990, p. 235). But the question of credibility is one which, unfortunately, cannot be wished away.

Ball's exhortation to qualitative researchers leads on to my third and final reservation about 'reflective' research; namely, its articulation with power relations within the research community. Let me explain. I noted earlier the repertoire of terms used to characterize this genre of writing. 'Self-appraisal' was not among them. Yet, it could be argued that this concept provides the most incisive and accurate description of the enterprise. After all, by opening up the research process to reflective analysis, the researcher is allowing himself or herself to be scrutinized by peers within the research community. I want to contend that for those with established positions and reputations within this professional community the process of public self-appraisal (and, as a corollary, public surveillance) is nowhere near as threatening as it is for those on the fringes of that community such as, postgraduate students; contract researchers; and others at relatively early stages of their careers. Therefore, 'reflectivity' has the potential to inscribe the differential power relations between different and competing research paradigms. But more than this, it might also operate as a policing mechanism; contributing to the enforced marginalization and subordination of those researchers who write confessional, *post hoc* accounts of their research.

Carrie Paechter (1993) has mounted a similar argument. She draws on a Foucauldian perspective, emphasizing in particular the idea of panoptic observation to sustain her argument that the rise of 'confessional writing' in social and educational research constitutes one of the (insidious) ways in which the regulation of research and its practitioners is enacted and secured. She claims that 'as pressure increases to include such writing as a regular feature of accounts of research, such confessions, at least from the point of view of the least powerful within the community, lose their voluntary nature and become, at least to some extent, coerced' (1993, p. 8). Perversely, perhaps, 'openness' in accounts helps to consolidate 'closure' within research, given that this professional community encompasses and reflects differential power relations. Against this background, then, I am no longer convinced that David Halpin and I should have seen the encouragement of contract researchers and postgraduate students in the seminar series as one of the 'merits' of our application to the ESRC.

Conclusion

'Reflexivity' according to Hammersley and Atkinson requires 'explicit recognition of the fact that the social researcher, and the research act itself, are part and parcel of the social world under investigation' (1983, p. 234). In this opening chapter I have adopted a reflexive stance on the enterprise which gave rise to this book.[1] In this process I find that it is with some reservations (and trepidation) that I help to bring this book into the public domain. Let me repeat what I said earlier. Being reflexive about the way in which Halpin and I conceived and put into operation this book should not be taken as a signal that we wish to deny its usefulness or our affiliation to it. On the contrary, the purpose of this chapter has been to provide a critical (self) appraisal of the enterprise and to question some of the taken-for-granted assumptions which tend to inform the way in which 'being reflective' is generally represented in the research methodology literature.

Note

1   I am grateful to Wendy Ball, Martyn Denscombe and Martyn Hammersley for talking through with me some of the points raised in this chapter.

References

ADELMAN, C. (1984) (Ed) *The Politics and Ethics of Evaluation*, Beckenham, Croom Helm.

ADLER, P.A. *et al.* (1992) 'Street Corner Society revisited: New questions about old issues', *Journal of Contemporary Ethnography*, (special issue) 21, 1, pp. 3–10.

ALDRIDGE, J. (1993) 'The textual disembodiment of knowledge in research account writing', *Sociology*, 27, 1, pp. 53–66.

APPLE, M. (1989) 'Critical introduction: Ideology and the state in education policy', in DALE, R. *The State and Education Policy*, Milton Keynes, Open University Press.

APPLE, M. (1993) *Official Knowledge: Democratic Education in a Conservative Age*, London, Routledge.

BALL, S. (1990a) *Politics and Policy-Making in Education*, London, Routledge.

BALL, S. (1990b) 'Self-doubt and soft-data: social and technical trajectories in ethnographic fieldwork', *International Journal of Qualitative Studies in Education*, 3, 2, pp. 157–71.

BALL, S. and SHILLING, C. (1994) 'At the cross-roads: Education policy studies', *British Journal of Educational Studies* (Special Issue), 42, 1, pp. 1–6.

BARTLETT, W. (1993) 'Quasi-markets and educational reforms', in LE GRAND, J. and BARTLETT, W. (Eds) *Quasi-Markets and Social Policy*, London, Macmillan.

BECKER, H. (1990) 'Generalizing from case studies' in EISNER, E.W. and PESHKIN, A. (Eds) *Qualitative Inquiry in Education: The Continuing Debate*, New York, Teachers' College.

BELL, J. (1987) *Doing Your Research Project*, Milton Keynes, Open University Press.

BELL, C. and NEWBY, H. (1977) (Eds) *Doing Sociological Research*, London, Allen and Unwin.

BLACKMORE, J. and KENWAY, J. (1993) (Eds) *Gender Matters in Educational Administration and Policy*, London, Falmer Press.

BOELEN, W.A.M. (1992) 'Street Corner Society revisted', *Journal of Contemporary Ethnography*, 21, 1, pp. 11–51.

BONNETT, A. (1993) 'Contours of crisis: Anti-racism and reflexivity', in JACKSON, P. and PENROSE, J. (Eds) *Constructions of 'Race', Place and Nation*, London, UCL Press.

BOWE, R., BALL, S. and GOLD, A. (1992) *Reforming Education and 'Changing' Schools*, London, Routledge.

BOWE, R., GEWIRTZ, S. and BALL, S. (1992) *Captured by the Discourse? Issues and Concerns in Researching 'Parental Choice'*, Paper presented at CEDAR, University of Warwick, 9 November.

BURGESS, R.G. (1984) (Ed) *The Research Process in Educational Settings: Ten Case Studies*, Lewes, Falmer Press.

BURGESS, R.G. (1985) (Ed) *Issues in Educational Research: Qualitative Methods*, Lewes, Falmer Press.

BURGESS, R.G. (1989) (Ed) *The Ethics of Educational Research*, Lewes, Falmer Press.

CHITTY, C. (1990) *Towards a New Education System: The Victory of the New Right?* London, Falmer Press.

CODD, J. (1992) *Contractualism, Contestability and Choice: Capturing the Language of Educational Reform in New Zealand*, Paper presented at the AARE/NZARE conference, Geelong, Deakin University, 22–6 November.

COHEN, L. and MANION, L. (1980) *Research Methods in Education*, London, Routledge and Kegan Paul.

COOK, J.A. and FONOW, M.M. (1986) 'Knowledge and women's interests: Issues of epistemology and methodology in feminist sociological research', *Sociological Inquiry*, 56, pp. 2–29.

COTTERILL, P. and LETHERBY, G. (1993) 'Weaving stories: Personal auto-biographies in feminist research', *Sociology*, 27, 1, pp. 67–80.

CULTURAL STUDIES (1991) *Education Unlimited*, London, Hutchinson.

DALE, R. (1989) *The State and Education Policy*, Milton Keynes, Open University Press.

DALE, R. (1992) 'Whither the State and Education Policy? Recent work in Australia and New Zealand', *British Journal of Sociology of Education*, 13, 3, pp. 387–95.

DEEM, R. and BREHONY, K. (1993) 'Reforming School Governing Bodies: A Sociological Investigation', Unpublished report to the Economic and Social Research Council.

DENZIN, N. (1992) 'Whose Cornerville is it anyway?', *Journal of Contemporary Ethnography*, 21, 1, pp. 120–32.

DIXON, R. (1991) 'Repercussions of LMS', *Educational Management and Administration*, 19, 1, pp. 52–61.

FINCH, J. (1985) 'Social policy and education: problems and possibilities of using qualitative research', in BURGESS, R.G. (Ed) *Issues in Educational Research*, Lewes, Falmer Press.

GRACE, G. (1984) 'Urban education: policy science or critical scholarship?', in GRACE, G. (Ed) *Education and the City*, London, Routledge and Kegan Paul.

GRACE, G. (1989) 'Education policy studies: developments in Britain in the 1970s and 1980s', *New Zealand Journal of Educational Studies*, 24, 1, pp. 87–95.

HALL, S. (1988) 'The toad in the garden: Thatcherism among the theorists', in NELSON, C. and GROSSBERG, L. (Eds) *Marxism and the Interpretation of Culture*, Urbana, University of Illinois Press.

HALPIN, D. (1990) 'The Education Reform Act Network: an exercise in collaboration and communication', *Journal of Curriculum Studies*, 22, 3, pp. 295–7.

HAMMERSLEY, M. (1983) 'Introduction: reflexivity and naturalism in ethnography', in HAMMERSLEY, M. (Ed) *The Ethnography of Schooling*, Driffield, Nafferton Books.

HAMMERSLEY, M. and ATKINSON, P. (1983) *Ethnography: Principles in Practice*, London, Tavistock Books.

HARGREAVES, A. and REYNOLDS, D. (1989) 'Decomprehensivization', in HARGREAVES, A. and REYNOLDS, D. (Eds) *Education Policies: Controversies and Critiques*, Lewes, Falmer Press.

HATCHER, R. and TROYNA, B. (1994) 'The "Policy Cycle": A Ball by Ball account', *Journal of Education Policy*, 9, 2, pp. 155–70.

HILL, M. (1993) (Ed) *The Policy Process: A Reader*, Herts, Harvester/Wheatsheaf.

HUGHES, M. (1992) '"The shrinking sisterhood": women as educational policy-makers', *Gender and Education*, 4, 3, pp. 255–72.

JACUBOWICZ, A. (1991) *Race Research and Ethnic Relations in Pluralist Societies*, Research and Policy Papers, No. 1, The Race Relations Unit, University of Bradford.

JOHNSON, R. (1989) 'Thatcherism and English education: breaking the mould or confirming the pattern?' *History of Education*, 18, 2, pp. 91–121.

KENWAY, J. (1993) 'Feminist theories of the state: to be or not to be?', in MUETZELFELDT, M. (Ed) *Society, State and Politics in Australia*, New South Wales, Pluto Press.

KOGAN, M. *et al.* (1984) *School Governing Bodies*, London, Heinemann Educational Books.

LEE, R.M. (1993) *Doing Research on Sensitive Topics*, London, Sage Books.

MAGUIRE, M. (1991) *Education and Qualitative Research: Teaching, Learning and Educational Change*, Paper presented at the St Hilda's conference, University of Warwick, September.

MAYNARD, M. (1993) 'Feminism and the possibilities of a postmodern research practice', *British Journal of Sociology of Education*, 14, 3, pp. 327–31.

MCPHERSON, A. and RAAB, C. (1988) *Governing Education: A Sociology of Policy Since 1945*, Edinburgh, Edinburgh University Press.

MEDAWAR, P. (1963) 'Is the scientific paper a fraud?', *The Listener*, 12 September.

MILLER, P. and ROSE, N. (1991) 'Programming the poor: Poverty, calculation and expertise', in LEHTO, J. (Ed) *Deprivation, Social Welfare and Expertise (Report 7)*, Helsinki, National Agency for Welfare and Health Research.

MILLS, C.W. (1959) *The Sociological Imagination*, New York, Oxford University Press.

MOSER, C. and KALTON, G. (1957) *Survey Methods and Social Investigation*, London, Heinemann.

NIAS, J, (1991) 'Primary teachers talking: A reflexive account of longitudinal research', in WALFORD, G. (Ed) *Doing Educational Research*, London, Routledge.

ORLANDELLA, A.R. (1992) 'Boelen may know Holland, Boelen may know Barzini, but Boelen "doesn't know diddle about the North End"', *Journal of Contemporary Ethnography*, 21, 1, pp. 69–79.

OZGA, J. (1987) 'Studying education through the lives of policy-makers', in BARTON, L. and WALKER, S. (Eds) *Changing Policies, Changing Teachers*, Milton Keynes, Open University Press.

OZGA, J. (1990) 'Policy research and policy theory: A comment on Fitz and Halpin', *Journal of Education Policy*, 5, 4, pp. 359–62.

PAECHTER, C. (1993) *Power and research methodology*, Paper presented at the symposium 'Methodology and Epistemology in Educational Research', University of Liverpool.

PARKINSON, M. (1982) 'Politics and policy-making in education', in HARTNETT, A. (Ed) *The Social Sciences in Educational Studies*, London, Heinemann.

RIZVI, F. (1993) 'Williams on democracy and the governance of education', in DWORKIN, D.L. and ROMAN, L.G. (Eds) *Views From the Border Country: Raymond Williams and Cultural Politics*, London, Routledge.

ROBERTS, H. (1981) (Ed) *Doing Feminist Research*, London, Routledge and Kegan Paul.

ROSIE, A.(1992) *Policy Presentation and Representation: School-Based Teacher Training*, Paper presented at the CEDAR International Conference, University of Warwick, 10–12 April.

SALTER, B. and TAPPER, T. (1981) *Education, Politics and the State: The Theory and Practice of Educational Change*, London, Grant McIntyre.

SAMMONS, P. (1989) 'Ethical issues and statistical work', in BURGESS, R.G. (Ed) *The Ethics of Educational Research*, Lewes, Falmer Press.

SIRAJ-BLATCHFORD, I. and TROYNA, B. (1993) 'Equal opportunities, research and educational reform: Some introductory notes', *British Educational Research Journal (special issue)*, 19, 3. pp. 223–6.

STANLEY, L. and WISE, S. (1983) (Eds) *Breaking Out: Feminist Consciousness and Feminist Research*, London, Routledge and Kegan Paul.

STEEDMAN, J. (1987) 'Longitudinal survey research into progress in secondary schools, based on the National Child Development Study', in WALFORD, G. (Ed) *Doing Sociology of Education*, Lewes, Falmer Press.

STEIER, F. (1991) 'Introduction: Research as self-reflexivity, self-reflexivity as social process', in STEIER, F. (Ed) *Research and Reflexivity*, London, Sage.

TROYNA, B. (1994) 'Critical social research and education policy', *British Journal of Educational Studies*, 42, 1, pp. 70–84.

WALFORD, G. (1987) (Ed) *Doing Sociology of Education*, Lewes, Falmer Press.

WALFORD, G. (1991) (Ed) *Doing Educational Research*, London, Routledge.

WALFORD, G. and MILLER, H. (1991) *City Technology College*, Milton Keynes, Open University Press.

WALLACE, G. (1992) (Ed) *Local Management of Schools*, Clevedon, Multilingual Matters.

WHYTE, W.F. (1955) *Street Corner Society*, Chicago, University of Chicago Press.

WHYTE, W.F. (1992) 'In defence of Street Corner Society', *Journal of Contemporary Ethnography*, 21, 1, pp. 52–68.

WOOLGAR, S. (1988) 'Reflexivity is the ethnographer of the text', in WOOLGAR, S. (Ed) *Knowledge and Reflexivity*, London, Sage.

Part I

Theory, Scholarship and Research into Education Policy

Chapter 2

Where We Are Now: Reflections on the Sociology of Education Policy

Charles D. Raab

Education Policy and Academic Research

The transformations that have been in train in British education since the 1970s have discredited many of its most deeply-held values and have altered many familiar characteristics. For long stretches of post-war history, assumptions or myths about bureaucratic and professional control, about the role of politics and ministers, about 'partnership', and about the very integrity or boundedness of the systems themselves had been sustained by policies and practices, albeit often with difficulty. Recent criticisms and changes in these dimensions of power are not merely events in the education system alone: they are major occurrences in society and in the politics and government of Britain.

This is because education claims a large share of public expenditure and is centrally important to so many cultural, social and economic processes and institutions of government. Therefore, radical departures in education policy and governance are likely to have strong repercussions elsewhere. However, those departures were themselves instigated in part by social, economic or cultural pressures and policies originating outside the education system but mediated through political processes. The restructuring of government and the State entails political and managerial ideologies of general application that also shape the particular form that educational change takes. Moreover, these are developments not only in the affairs of a single country, but in the politics and policy of many countries from whom lessons are learnt and policy ideas are borrowed. The academic study of these phenomena has entailed the development of new approaches to recording and analysing change. This chapter does not review this burgeoning literature, but seeks to comment upon the intersection of political science and educational studies in the formation of perspectives upon education policy, and to take stock of current approaches.

Charles D. Raab

Moving Beyond Description

Many researchers have been attracted to study the substance, processes and implications of these changes. The vast scope of the 1988 Education Reform Act (ERA) alone, reaching into so many areas of education policy and practice in England and Wales, has provided an array of research possibilities that is likely to continue to absorb the energies of investigators drawn from widely differing social-scientific disciplinary traditions. More recent legislation, together with implementation, policy modification and reversal, as well as related developments in Scotland and in Northern Ireland, offer still more opportunities for study; moreover, they enable and even require comparative analysis in order to make sense of change.

Recent developments are broad in scope; they are likely to be deep in effect and long in their period of influence upon education. They are echoed in the proliferation of descriptive and evaluative studies. The sheer scale of government initiatives in education may encourage the feeling that the world cannot be stopped whilst analytical tools are sharpened. An argument might be that when education is being so rapidly transformed, and when there is so much to be studied, is connoisseurship of models and methods not an unaffordable luxury? On the other hand, the understandable temptation simply to describe everything and anything can too easily become mindless empiricism, contributing relatively little to knowledge and serving no science. Long before the coming of new policy initiatives, Karabel and Halsey (1977, p. 75) disparagingly observed that, within educational sociology, 'small-scale empirical studies continue to pile up while questions of broader theoretical interest remain unexplored'. They had particularly in mind atheoretical quantitative studies, but one might see equal danger in qualitative micro-studies that failed to engage with wider theoretical issues. Depressingly, so many years later, in various ways Ozga (1990), Dale (1992a, 1992b), Power (1992) and Ball and Shilling (1994) have seen fit to warn against premature, unanalytical reactions and to bemoan the theoretical poverty of the profuse post-1988 education policy literature; *plus ça change.*

To escape this, various instruments are being taken up to look at the 'impact', effects or consequences of policy, to get inside its language or 'discourse', or to explain its provenance and processes. In addition, there is a heightened consciousness of analytical strategies, for the waves of new policies broke on the shores of academic disciplines just as theoretical and methodological presuppositions were being questioned. Deep-seated social scientific issues remain to be resolved. These include the relationship between structure and agency as well as the macro–micro divide. There are other important gaps as well, but these might be more easily bridged: between the study of politics and the study of education, and between up-dated versions of Marxism and of pluralism.

Political Science and Educational Studies

In British academic discourse, there is a large gap between the study of politics and education. Writing without particular reference to Britain, Karabel and Halsey (1977, p. 367) observed that 'political scientists have failed to produce a serious body of research in the politics of education', but they saw a spark of hope in Kogan's (1975) then recent publication of a study of policy-making. As Ozga (1987) observes, the field of education policy was occupied largely by non-sociologists until the 1970s, before which it was the province of specialists in educational or social administration and in social policy. The extent to which it 'found a space within . . . government and politics' (Ozga, 1987, p. 138) is highly debatable, apart from Kogan's indispensable and prominent work (e.g., Kogan, 1975, 1978). His investigations and those of others, whether political scientists or not (e.g., Coates, 1972; Fenwick, 1976; Jennings, 1977; Pattison, 1980; Ranson, 1985; Regan, 1979; Ribbins and Brown, 1979; Salter and Tapper, 1981; Tapper and Salter, 1978), contributed in diverse ways to the description, understanding and analysis of education politics, government and policy.

However, that did not mark any firm establishment of education politics and policy as a significant field of specialization within British political science; nor does it so exist today. For the most part, political scientists have eschewed education as a substantive field or sector, whether on a descriptive level or as a terrain on which to develop or adapt theories of power, conflict, consensus, ideology or other political or governmental phenomena, from either Marxist or non-Marxist perspectives. The main journal of the discipline, *Political Studies*, founded in 1950, has published almost nothing in this specialism, and only infrequently has research come to light in the pages of non-field-specific British periodicals that are likely to be read by policy-oriented students of politics (e.g., Geen, 1981; Raab, 1982; Moon and Richardson, 1984; Ranson, 1985).

General 'policy studies' is a distinct specialism, typically combined with public administration or with studies of current politics, and not confined to any substantive sector. It has developed its own conceptual armoury as well as a literature that draws upon the broader study of politics, government and the State. In addition, it is enriched by organizational sociology and by other social science disciplines. However, education policy only occasionally features in its literature as a field of application. For example, education policy is included in a book exploring the contribution of the New Right to public policy (Jordan and Ashford, 1993) and is accorded a chapter in the third edition of a prominent textbook on British politics (Dunleavy *et al.*, 1990), only to be excluded from the latter's fourth edition. Despite the prominence of education policy and the ERA in the politics of the 1980s, it merited neither a chapter nor an index listing in a book claiming to provide an audit of the implementation of policies during the Thatcher period (Marsh and Rhodes,

1992), nor is there an account of education in a previous collection of papers on implementation in the first Thatcher administration (Jackson, 1985). On the other hand, another source on the Thatcher years does include a chapter on education policy (Savage and Robins, 1990).

In the light of education's centrality to states, societies and individuals and as a principal site of cultural production, transmission and reproduction, such neglect is both unfortunate and highly ironic. For Scotland, one should add to this centrality education's institutional prominence as a distinguishing feature of civil society and culture. Along with the Church and the Law, it has for long enjoyed a place close to the heart of Scottish identity, however shrouded in myth have been its traditional values and relative quality (McPherson, 1983; McPherson and Raab, 1988). Yet here, too, the education policy and politics of Scotland's separate system has mixed fortunes in the political science literature, and most of what there is originates outwith that field. Discussion of education is conspicuously absent or barely present in prominent politics texts on Scottish government (Keating and Midwinter, 1983; Midwinter *et al.*, 1991), although it does figure in another (Kellas, 1994). McPherson and Raab (1988) contribute to the study of politics and public policy as well as to sociology, and Humes (1986) has also discussed the way Scottish education is governed. Adler *et al.*'s (1989) social-policy study of parental choice adds much to the understanding of policy and its implementation. Other works written from the perspective of social policy or educational studies have often figured in annual volumes of *The Scottish Government Yearbook* (e.g., Macbeth, 1983; Munn, 1992; Raffe, 1983). Whilst these have usually tended to be descriptive, they have cast light on the politics and government of education.

Thus, on both sides of the Border, the politics of education, or of education policy, has not until recently occupied centre stage as 'high politics' in the way that the economy or foreign policy has done, and thus never 'high political science'. It is possible that a certain academic disdain has left research on education, and perhaps particularly on schooling, mainly to the 'mere' teachers and their educators who were steeped in its practice, placing it out of contention as 'serious' political science. Although education is now an issue area of the first rank on governmental and party agendas, and in public debate, it remains the case that few political scientists with an inclination to policy studies have it clearly in their sights.

There is a counterpart to this neglect on the educationists' side, where a lamentable subject-centrism has kept education-research specialists from direct contact with the developments of theory and method that have taken place within the general policy studies field, or for that matter within other applied fields such as housing, health or social security. Dale (1992b, p. 3) deplores this 'disciplinary parochialism' that restricts the analytical focus to the education sector alone in research on the ERA, and in previous work. But this is to overlook an influential trend in the 1970s and 1980s: the incorporation into educational studies, not of the orthodox social sciences, but of a critical and sometimes politically committed sociology, including new perspectives on the sociology of knowledge, and of debates about the necessity and possibility of change (e.g., Apple, 1985; CCCS, 1981; Dale, 1989; Young, 1971; Young and Whitty, 1977). Adherents ignored or rejected 'mainstream' political science and policy-studies perspectives that were deemed positivist or wedded to powerful controlling interests.

Such critical, conflict-oriented approaches breathed new life into the subject and can now be seen to have formed the crucible from which emerged the research perspectives of many investigators of the ERA and its successors. Drawing on Harvey (1990), Troyna (1994) seems to suggest that, in the issues it tackles and in its analysis, education policy sociology is very like critical social research *sans* political commitment. In any case, in bringing to bear upon education policy conceptions of the State and its relation to education that are rooted in various tendencies within Marxist thought, as well as radical stances concerning knowledge and the curriculum, critical research has important methodological implications apart from its radical or liberationist tendencies. It provides rationales for both 'micro' research into classroom processes and practices, and for research on the wider, 'macro' structures of the society, economy and polity. The relationship between the two, and a specific focus upon the nature of the State, has been seen as an important priority on the research agenda by Dale (1983, 1992a) and Ozga (1990); the implications of this focus and its relation to policy-network theory has been discussed in another place (Raab, 1994).

The complementary value of 'bourgeois' social science, ethnographic study, statistical and historical analysis, and macro-political theorizing has rapidly become realized by many whose starting-points vary considerably. Researchers of whatever provenance seem less fascinated by functions than by processes, and by getting inside institutions, relationships and discourses in order to understand the exercise of power (e.g., Ball, 1990a). Interestingly, when Karabel and Halsey (1977) lamented political scientists' neglect of education, they attributed it to the myth that schools are not political institutions. However, from within the sociology of education rather than political science, Ball's (1987) micro-political study of organization and power in schools is a prominent British contribution to understanding both the politics of education and the sociology of organizations, using a conflict perspective.

Marxism, Pluralism and Beyond

Even before the ERA itself, conceptual reformulations pointed towards a new research agenda and body of method. This development implicitly held out prospects of moving the Marxist tradition closer to other avenues of social (and political) science, although this was certainly not its purpose. Any such approximation might only have been made possible through the flexibility afforded by the neo-Marxist idea of the relative autonomy of the State. That notion superseded grand-theory constructs that were more determinist and more resistant to the necessities of empirical study of the relationship between states and social or educational processes. Theorizing the relative autonomy of the State in education, and indicating relevant research strategies, has opened a path to a new empiricism that is enriched by (neo-)Marxist understandings but is not imprisoned or blinkered by them. In this, it edged nearer to a form of (neo-)pluralism which, it has elsewhere been argued (Raab, 1990) is not necessarily antagonistic to it, and which is free from the post-war transatlantic simplicities that have been attributed to this family of models.

It should be emphasized, however, that the deficiencies of the tradition of pluralist analysis in political science have often led those who have read little of it at first-hand to suppose that it was permanently frozen into one-dimensional naiveties of American self-congratulation about the distribution of power and influence. Rhodes (1990, p. 300) aptly complains about the 'grosser misrepresentations of pluralist theory, too many of which verge on caricature and seem to presuppose that the proponents of the theory are suffering from terminal brain damage'. Remarks in a similar vein have been made elsewhere (Raab, 1990) about Dale's (1981) borrowed distortion of pluralism in regard to the politics of education. The grounds upon which pluralism, in any of its various old or new forms, has been dismissed in such work are highly suspect.

However, the further development of general neo-pluralist and policy network theory (see Dunleavy and O'Leary, 1987, ch. 6; Jordan and Schubert, 1992), of neo-Marxist analysis of education (Apple, 1985; Dale, 1989), and of empirical education policy sociology (Ball, 1990a; Bowe, Ball and Gold, 1992) makes debate between Marxist and pluralist versions less gladiatorial and more fruitful. If Marxists are no longer so inclined to read off education policy and political action from the nature of capitalism and the class structure, so pluralists do not read them off from either the configuration of interest-group relationships or from the ought-statements of democratic theory, American style. Marxist researchers now find it necessary to handle psychological and human-agency variables seriously, whilst a legacy of the 'new' sociology of education of the 1970s is the attention paid to processes and to actors' meanings in intimate settings.

Reciprocally, research in the non-Marxist tradition may be framed in terms of the institutional or network structures of the State and the biases or inequalities they bring to bear on policy processes and outcomes (e.g., McPherson and Raab, 1988). If, as Smith *et al.* (1993) assert, some interest-group pluralists ignored research into the 'black box' of the State in explaining public policy, so too did Marxists, for whom the activity inside the 'box' held far less interest than did the position of the 'box' within the capitalist system. Dale (1992b, p. 20), for example, now strongly insists upon the necessity of studying institutions, which have hitherto been neglected: they 'have an effect on what policies can be made and on how and how likely they are to be put into practice . . . the ways that they matter have been consistently underestimated and overlooked . . .'. This seems to open up new avenues for the sociology of policy.

Enter 'Policy Sociology'

Although it is not a sociology of *government* policy, Ball's (1987) study concerns intra-school conflicts over *school* policy. The 'micro' reference of its title is not to the school — which, as an organization, is at the 'meso' level (Ball, 1987, p. 23) — but to the actors and their conflicts within the organization. But at whatever analytical or concrete level, the action, processes and concepts involved in this kind of educational sociology are the familiar fare of students of politics and policy as well.

For Ozga (1987, p. 144), policy sociology is 'rooted in the social science tradition, historically informed and draw[s] on qualitative and illuminative techniques'. What 'tradition' this is, and whether there is a singular tradition or many, are questions that are left unanswered, but Ozga's formulation implies that there is nothing exclusively 'sociological' about education policy sociology, as Troyna (1994) has approvingly pointed out. The social sciences are conceptually, empirically, ideologically and internationally diverse. So, too, are sociology and policy studies. Drawing on qualitative techniques does not, and ought not, preclude drawing on quantitative techniques that are likewise located in the traditions of social science, sociology and policy studies. For example, a cross-LEA survey of the attitudes of teachers, school governors, and headteachers towards devolved school management would represent policy sociology just as much as would, say, a study of classroom practices involving the National Curriculum or of the links between manufacturing industry and New Right educational think-tanks. Counting, *verstehen* and critical theory are all within the sociological, and social-scientific, pale.

Despite its uncertain theoretical grounding, education policy sociology may therefore represent, to some degree, a convergence of perspectives, although its strength lies in its catholicity and experimentalism. These could become weaknesses if 'anything goes' under a newly-fashionable label and if, moreover, policy sociology in education fails to connect with similar research in other fields. However, 'policy sociology' does attempt to forge a new approach through linkages and reformulations of existing ones.

There is no clearly distinctive approach under this label. Payne *et al.* (1981) use the term to refer to a kind of sociology applied to policy in which, through involvement as advisers and consultants on the 'inside', sociologists bring their knowledge to bear in policy-making and thus gain some influence over it. This conception differs fundamentally from that envisaged more recently by Ozga (1987) and by, for example, McPherson and Raab (1988) and by Ball (1990a). Although methods and subjects vary, policy sociologists examine the relationship between process and product, and between motive and action. In each case, however, knowledge of the former is to be gained empirically and not on the basis of inference from the latter or by deduction from grand theory. Hence the importance of going beyond the public pro-nouncements of 'policy makers' and actually talking to them, for meanings and 'assumptive worlds' are essential parts of the policy process and require to be understood if action itself is to be understood.

McPherson and Raab's (1988) 'sociology of policy', to quote its subtitle, atempted to cast light upon the relationship between structure, process and policy in Scottish secondary schooling, over a long stretch of time, largely through the use of oral-history interviews with persons in a fairly tight policy network (or community), and sought to theorize the nature of the policy system which the evidence yielded. Ball's (1990a) study of Conservative edu-cation policy in the 1980s is also explicitly conceived as 'policy sociology'. Its exploration of power and policy combines lengthy interview material with forms of analysis, including a concentration upon discourse, to make sense of the 'unwieldy and complex' making of Thatcherite policy, including its '[d]iscontinuities, compromises, omissions and exceptions' (Ball, 1990a, p. 3). A less well-known and undeclared 'sociology of policy' study is Maclure's (1984) analysis of educational school building in England from 1945 to 1973, which illustrates the possibility of explaining the building programme and the blueprinted specifics of the schools it built in terms of the ideas and interac-tions of a policy network of administrators, architects and others over thirty years, using a variety of complementary research techniques.

What is important in these perspectives is the sense of 'policy' as process and not merely as substance. Ball (1990a, p. 185) puts this well when he writes that policy is not

> something that happens and then is over and fixed . . . In effect, the ERA is a half-written text, a story outline; its detail, meaning and practice lie in on-going struggles related to the interpretation of its key components. (Ball, 1990a)

As discussed elsewhere (Fitz *et al.*, 1994; Raab, 1994), implementation and its discourses are essential data for explanations of policy. In education, but not uniquely so, this implies a very long time span for study because of the nature of policy implementation, as Sabatier (1986) and Deem (1988) remind us. Curricular innovations, for example, are likely to take ten or more years from conception to full permeation of schools and classrooms; even at that, as British experience since 1988 amply testifies, the pudding eaten is a far cry from the original recipe.

In addition, the policy process in education embraces a vast range of sites of action and discourse, from central-government machinery through to places where practice is arbitrated. This is a long and elaborate implementation chain, or rather, thousands of them, each corresponding to a school or a classroom, say, and each passing through a local education authority. Whether in its political or its educational culture, none of the points on the chain is a clone of any other at the same level. Halpin (1990) emphasizes that the National Curriculum provides much scope for alternative policies and strategies, and does not just enjoin dutiful, top–down implementation upon practitioners. It therefore provides a field of action, or of struggle, in which policy is powerfully shaped by practice and is even deflected from its legislated intentions.

This means that 'human agency' must be taken seriously in explanations of policy. But so, too, must the context of action within structures and processes located at other sites, or enveloping all of them, and providing the constraints and opportunities for action. Policy sociologists of all stripes may agree on this framing of the subject; where they are likely to disagree is on how to construe 'human agency' to, what contexts are relevant to an explanation, and the configuration of possibilities and constraints.

Some Problems of Conceptualization

The perception that the policy process in education is complex, fragmented, multi-organizational and conflict-ridden would not strike policy-studies specialists as any new discovery about the nature of government, the State, or policy. It follows that its study will not yield much to the *grands simplificateurs* of flat-earth versions of either pluralism or Marxism. But emerging conceptions in policy studies generally, embodying structurally disaggragated, policy-network conceptions of public-policy processes (Jordan and Schubert, 1992; Raab, 1994) are close to the complexities and relative autonomies that policy sociology, as it has developed outside political science-based work, also discerns and theorizes. Yet conceptual problems remain.

Commenting upon Ozga's (1987) delineation of research approaches, Ball (1990b) questions her exclusion, from the social science project, of a concern with a specific policy problem or its implementation. He wishes to include study of the effects of policy, but concedes that this could incorporate virtually all of social science unless one relates these effects coherently to the policy process. This form of policy sociology therefore tries to deal simultaneously with both policy and practice, and to incorporate both 'macro' and 'micro' dimensions. Devising the procedures for this endeavour and embedding the analysis in understandings of culture and history is, however, a formidable theoretical project, as Hargreaves (1985), Archer (1987) and Shilling (1992) have illustrated. In parallel fashion, conceptualizing the relationship between the 'formulation' and the 'implementation' of education policy is also beset with problems (Dale, 1992a; Fitz *et al.*, 1994; Raab, 1994).

Hargreaves (1985) points out confusions concerning what 'macro' and 'micro' have been taken to mean in educational sociology as a result of the application of these terms to different pairs: theory and evidence, two levels of theory itself, and school and society. In a similar way, Raab (1992, pp. 75–9) has queried some policy-network theorization for failing to distinguish between concrete and analytical dimensions of micro-analysis and for therefore eschewing the study of policy actors' personal interactions. He also points out the ambiguity in that literature's use of 'macro', 'micro' and 'meso'; it should be noted that the use of these labels cannot clearly be read across to their use in education policy sociology. Dale (1992a) has noted other confusions between levels of abstraction (e.g., explanation; description) and of analysis.

Criticizing the gulf between ethnographic studies of classrooms or schools and the unempirical speculations of grand theory about society, Hargreaves (1985) argues against the confinement of interactionist analysis only to one type of setting. He urges its extension to, say, County Hall or the central government department. Interviews and written documents would be used, and studies would be linked in order to understand more precisely the impingement of context upon setting or of structure upon action in ways that avoid an unilluminating resort to abstractions for explanation. Hargreaves (1985) says:

> It is a mistake, then, to regard educational policy as belonging exclusively to the world of macro theory . . . not just because classroom teachers have policies too . . . , but also because even outside the school, policy still has to be negotiated and implemented through interaction, be this face to face, on the telephone or via correspondence. (Hargreaves, 1985, p. 43)

However, Shilling (1992) has disparaged this approach to bridging the macro–micro gap for side-stepping the structure-agency problem and for failing to theorize 'structuration'. This concept, developed in recent sociological theory (e.g., Abrams, 1982; Giddens, 1984), reformulates the meaning of structure and agency in terms of their mutual entailment and of structures' duality as 'rules and resources which are both the medium and outcome of social interaction' (Shilling, 1992, p. 83) and thus as not to be construed merely as external constraints.

These problems of levels and of structure-and-agency have long been on the agenda in the sociology of education, as Ball (1987, p. 3) somewhat wearily reminds us, but they are not easily skirted; nor, however, can they easily or permanently solved. But to the extent that they involve matters of power and policy, no discipline can claim exclusive custodianship of the conceptual and methodological issues involved. The importance of investigating ethnographically what happens inside the State rather than dogmatically asserting what 'must' be the case amongst policy elites is by now well understood in the sociology of policy. Also, to use a particular research method across widely differing settings is to imply that at least one gap is based on a misconception. As has been similarly argued elsewhere (Raab, 1992), interactions, exchanges and trust should not only be seen as constitutive properties of interpersonal social relations but as inherent in the 'larger' structural contexts of policy networks as well. In addition, by construing the concept of 'policy' in a way that liberates it from any particular setting, Hargreaves (1985) has mooted a policy sociology of some sophistication, one that is capable of encompassing practice as well as 'big decisions' within the scope of the study of education policy.

Conclusion

In any case, that field of study now seems to be more firmly positioned within the social sciences as a branch of policy studies, and therefore shares its problems as well as its prospects. Precisely because the ERA and its legislative and practical aftermath go beyond conventional policy-making to lay the ground for a new system of education, they transform the terrain upon which research is conducted. Investigators have no shortage of empirical material with which to deal in improving or in testing theoretical tools of a wide variety, and in explaining the world. Explanations are likely to be sufficiently different from each other as to sustain critical debate, but in policy sociology there may be hopeful signs that those concerned will at least be talking to, and not past, each other. The variety may have less to do with definitional problems than with the diverse package of policy initiatives that have emerged in the 1980s and 1990s, and the large number of, and characteristically differentiated, sites in which implementation is attempted. It may reflect more deeply-seated differences concerning the nature of politics and the State, although these may be less than is supposed and it is arguable that their bases might be eroding (Raab, 1990, 1994). On the other hand, academic orthodoxy has its dangers; fortunately, it seems that there is little danger of that orthodoxy emerging.

Walford (1987) aptly notes that

> [a]cademic subject areas are not static monolithic entities, but shifting amalgams of sub-groups and traditions. The frontiers of the discipline are stretched. . . . [d]isputes arise as to what should be included . . . [c]hanges in the external environment raise new questions, new methods, new theoretical frameworks . . . (Walford, 1987, p. 1)

Where we are now is perhaps best described not so much as a roundabout with many poorly-signposted exits, but as a round table whose participants confront a world of policy in common, with the possibility of converging on ways of understanding it. What may well emerge is not orthodoxy but a common academic discourse, if education policy sociology shares premises and methods with policy studies within political science and its cognate disciplines. Some may intend to go beyond discourse and research into management practice, or into the *praxis* of resistance and change. These differences should not be minimized, but they are beyond the scope of the present chapter.

Charles D. Raab

References

ABRAMS, P. (1982) *Historical Sociology*, Shepton Mallet, Open Books.
ADLER, M., PETCH, A. and TWEEDIE, J. (1989) *Parental Choice and Educational Policy*, Edinburgh, Edinburgh University Press.
APPLE, M. (1985) *Education and Power*, Boston, London, Ark Paperbacks.
ARCHER, M. (1987) 'The problems of scope in the sociology of education', *International Review of Sociology*, New Series, No. 1, pp. 83–99.
BALL, S. (1987) '*The Micro-Politics of the School*, London, Methuen.
BALL, S. (1990a) *Politics and Policy Making in Education*, London Routledge.
BALL, S. (1990b) 'Review essay: The sociological implications of the Education Reform Act', *British Journal of Sociology of Education*, 11, 4, pp. 485–91.
BALL, S. and SHILLING, C. (1994) 'Guest editorial: At the cross-roads: education policy studies', *British Journal of Educational Studies*, 41, 1, pp. 1–5.
BOWE, R., BALL, S. and GOLD, A. (1992) *Reforming Education and Changing Schools*, London, Routledge.
Centre for Contemporary Cultural Studies (CCCS) (1981) *Unpopular Education*, London, Hutchinson.
COATES, R. (1972) *Teachers' Unions and Interest Group Politics*, Cambridge, Cambridge University Press.
DALE, R. (1981) *Society, Education and the State*, Unit 3, E353, Milton Keynes, Open University Press.
DALE, R. (1983) 'Review essay: The political sociology of education', *British Journal of Sociology of Education*, 4, 2, pp. 185–202.
DALE, R. (1989) *The State and Education Policy*, Milton Keynes, Open University Press.
DALE, R. (1992a) 'Review essay: Whither the state and education policy? recent work in Australia and New Zealand', *British Journal of Sociology of Education*, 13, 3, pp. 387–95.
DALE, R. (1992b) 'What do they know of England who don't know they've been speaking prose?', Paper presented to the ESRC Research Seminar on Methodological and Ethical Issues Associated with Research into the 1988 Education Reform Act, University of Warwick, 29 April.
DEEM, R. (1988) 'The Great Education Reform Bill 1988: Some issues and implications', *Journal of Education Policy*, 3, 2, pp. 181–9.
DUNLEAVY, P., GAMBLE, A. and PEELE, G. (Eds) (1990) *Developments in British Politics 3*, Basingstoke, Macmillan.
DUNLEAVY, P. and O'LEARY, B. (1987) *Theories of the State*, London, Macmillan.
FENWICK, I.G.K. (1976) *The Comprehensive School 1944–1970: The Politics of Secondary School Reorganization*, London, Methuen.
FITZ, J., HALPIN, D. and POWER, S. (1994) 'Implementation research and education policy: Practice and prospects', *British Journal of Educational Studies*, 42, 1, pp. 53–69.
GEEN, A. (1981) 'Educational policy making in Cardiff, 1944–1970', *Public Administration*, 59, 1, pp. 85–104.
GIDDENS, A. (1984) *The Constitution of Society*, Cambridge, Policy Press.
HALPIN, D. (1990) 'The sociology of education and the National Curriculum', *British Journal of Sociology of Education*, 11, 1, pp. 21–35.
HARGREAVES, A. (1985) 'The micro-macro problem in the sociology of education', in BURGESS, R. (Ed) *Issues in Educational Research: Qualitative Methods*, London, Falmer Press.
HARVEY, L. (1990) *Critical Social Research*, London, Unwin Hyman.
HUMES, W. (1986) *The Leadership Class in Scottish Education*, Edinburgh, John Donald.
JACKSON, P. (Ed) (1985) *Implementing Government Policy Initiatives: The Thatcher Administration 1979–1983*, London, Royal Institute of Public Administration.

JENNINGS, R. (1977) *Education and Politics*, London, B.T. Batsford Ltd.

JORDAN, A. and ASHFORD, N. (Eds) (1993) *Public Policy and the Impact of the New Right*, London, Pinter Publishers.

JORDAN, A. and SCHUBERT, K. (Eds) (1992) *European Journal of Political Research*, 21, 1–2, Special Issue: Policy Networks.

KARABEL, J. and HALSEY, A. (1977) 'Education research: A review and an interpretation', in KARABEL, J. and HALSEY, A. (Eds) *Power and Ideology in Education*, New York, Oxford University Press.

KEATING, M. and MIDWINTER, A. (1983) *The Government of Scotland*, Edinburgh, Mainstream.

KELLAS, J. (1994) *The Scottish Political System*, 4th ed., Cambridge, Cambridge University Press.

KOGAN, M. (1975) *Educational Policy-Making*, London, Allen and Unwin.

KOGAN, M. (1978) *The Politics of Educational Change*, Manchester, Manchester University Press.

MACBETH, A. (1983) 'The government of Scottish education: Partnership or compromise?', in MCCRONE, D. (Ed) *The Scottish Government Yearbook 1984*, Edinburgh, Unit for the Study of Government in Scotland, University of Edinburgh.

MACLURE, S. (1984) *Educational Development and School Building*, London, Longman.

MARSH, D. and RHODES, R. (Eds) (1992) *Implementing Thatcherite Policies*, Buckingham, Open University Press.

MCPHERSON, A. (1983) 'An angle on the geist: persistence and change in the Scottish educational tradition', in HUMES, W. and PATERSON, H. (Eds) *Scottish Culture and Scottish Education 1800–1980*, Edinburgh, John Donald.

MCPHERSON, A. and RAAB, C. (1988) *Governing Education*, Edinburgh, Edinburgh University Press.

MIDWINTER, A., KEATING, M. and MITCHELL, J. (1991) *Politics and Public Policy in Scotland*, London, Macmillan.

MOON, J. and RICHARDSON, J. (1984) 'Policy-making with a difference? The Technical and Vocational Education Initiative', *Public Administration*, 62, 1, pp. 23–33.

MUNN, P. (1992) 'Devolved management of schools and FE colleges: A victory for the producer over the consumer?', in PATERSON, L. and MCCRONE, D. (Eds) *The Scottish Government Yearbook 1992*, Edinburgh, Unit for the Study of Government in Scotland, University of Edinburgh.

OZGA, J. (1987) 'Studying education policy through the lives of the policy-makers: an attempt to close the macro–micro gap', in WALKER, S. and BARTON, L. (Eds) *Changing Policies, Changing Teachers*, Milton Keynes, Open University Press.

OZGA, J. (1990) 'Policy research and policy theory: A comment on Fitz and Halpin', *Journal of Education Policy*, 5, 4, pp. 359–62.

OZGA, J. (1992) 'Review essay: education management', *British Journal of Sociology of Education*, 13, 2, pp. 279–80.

PATTISON, M. (1980) 'Intergovernmental relations and the limitations of central control: Reconstructing the politics of comprehensive education', *Oxford Review of Education*, 6, 1, pp. 63–89.

PAYNE, G., DINGWALL, R., PAYNE, J. and CARTER, M. (1981) *Sociology and Social Research*, London, Routledge.

POWER, S. (1992) 'Researching the impact of education policy: Difficulties and discontinuities', *Journal of Education Policy*, 7, 5, pp. 493–500.

RAAB, C. (1982) 'Mapping the boundaries of education policy systems: The case of Scotland', *Public Administration Bulletin*, 39, pp. 40–57.

RAAB, C. (1990) 'Review symposium: The state and education policy', *British Journal of Sociology of Education*, 11, 1, pp. 87–91.

RAAB, C. (1992) 'Taking networks seriously: Education policy in Britain', *European Journal of Political Research*, 21, 1–2, pp. 69–90.

RAAB, C. (1994) 'Theorising the governance of education', *British Journal of Educational Studies*, 42, 1, pp. 6–22.

RAFFE, D. (1983) 'Youth unemployment and the MSC 1977–1983', in McCRONE, D. (Ed) *The Scottish Government Yearbook 1984*, Edinburgh, Unit for the Study of Government in Scotland, University of Edinburgh.

RANSON, S. (1985) 'Contradictions in the government of educational change', *Political Studies*, 33, 1, pp. 56–72.

REGAN, D. (1979) *Local Government and Education*, 2nd ed., London, Allen and Unwin.

RHODES, R. (1990) 'Policy networks — a British perspective', *Journal of Theoretical Politics*, 2, 3, pp. 293–317.

RIBBINS, P. and BROWN, R. (1979) 'Policy making in English local government: The case of secondary school reorganization', *Public Administration*, 57, 2, pp. 187–202.

SABATIER, P. (1986) 'Top–down and bottom-up approaches to implementation research: A critical analysis and suggested synthesis', *Journal of Public Policy*, 6, 1, pp. 21–48.

SALTER, B. and TAPPER, T. (1981) *Education, Politics and the State*, London, Grant McIntyre.

SAVAGE, S. and ROBINS, L. (Eds) (1990) *Public Policy Under Thatcher*, Basingstoke, Macmillan.

SHILLING, C. (1992) 'Reconceptualising structure and agency in the sociology of education: Structuration theory and schooling', *British Journal of Sociology of Education*, 13, 1, pp. 69–87.

SMITH, M., MARSH, D. and RICHARDS, D. (1993) 'Central government departments and the policy process', *Public Administration*, 71, 4, pp. 567–94.

TAPPER, T. and SALTER, B. (1978) *Education and the Political Order*, London, Macmillan.

TROYNA, B. (1994) 'Critical social research and education policy', *British Journal of Educational Studies*, 42, 1, pp. 70–84.

WALFORD, G. (1987) 'Introduction: The research process', in WALFORD, G. (Ed) *Doing Sociology of Education*, London, Falmer Press.

YOUNG, M. (Ed) (1971) *Knowledge and Control*, London, Collier-Macmillan.

YOUNG, M. and WHITTY, G. (Eds) (1977) *Society, State and Schooling*, London, Falmer Press.

Chapter 3

Applied Education Politics or Political Sociology of Education?: Contrasting Approaches to the Study of Recent Education Reform in England and Wales

Roger Dale

The many recent changes to the system of compulsory education in England and Wales have provided ample research opportunities for sociologists of education interested in education policy, especially since several of them have been successful in obtaining research funding from the ESRC. The source of this funding is significant at a time when the difficulty of getting any kind of research funding, on the one hand, and the instrumental, practical, sometimes apparently confirmatory expectations of funding bodies with even a remote 'applied' interest in the outcomes of the research, on the other, are both increasing. It creates the legitimate hope and expectation that research funded by a body with a 'pure' research mission may be enabled to proceed in relative freedom from those pressures and be relieved from the obligation to produce work whose immediate practicality and relevance are expected to be paramount. In particular, we might look to the ESRC funded projects to be relatively well insulated against the various academic and political pressures that inevitably tend to lead educational researchers to an excessive and premature concentration on the short-term consequences of policies, or their success in the terms laid down by the sponsoring body.

More broadly, and even more importantly, the ESRC funded research on the Education Reform Act might be enabled to escape or avoid the assumptions that underlie what seems to be the central paradigm in the sociology of education. Very briefly, what I mean by the central paradigm arises not only as a response to the discipline's recent funding difficulties but, more importantly, from a combination of two crucial factors. One of these is what might be called the dominant project of the sociology of education, which essentially includes a commitment to changing rather than merely analysing education. The other is the professional working conditions experienced by sociologists of education. One aspect of these conditions is their institutional location in departments of education and other places where the presence of teacher education as the main or sustaining activity ensures that questions of short-term, practical application constantly threaten to displace theoretical questions at the top of the agenda. This is a feature of sociology of education in many countries. The other aspect is more confined to contemporary England, though not to sociology of education is the pressure both to amass the publications and to win the research contracts on which the future funding of their institutions has been made increasingly to depend by government policy.

This combination produces what amounts to a selection principle that forms the discipline's central paradigm — its problematic and the appropriate modes of addressing that problematic. That is, it identifies not only the appropriate subject matter of the sociology of education but also its appropriate meta-theoretical assumptions, theories and methodologies. The way that this principle has been framed has given precedence to the subject's putative public impact and relevance rather than to the wider adequacy and comprehensiveness of the analyses it provides. (For an elaboration of the concept and the nature of the central paradigm see Dale, 1992 and 1993a). One consequence of the dominance of this paradigm has been a narrowing of the scope of theoretical work, particularly that which seems not to be immediately germane to informed commentary on, or amelioration of, educational policy and/or practice.

It will be my argument here that the dominance of the central paradigm appears to have overridden the possibilities for escape from it that the presence of 'pure' research funding might be thought to have enabled. I will suggest that aspects of the dangers and consequences of the 'premature application' that the central paradigm inherently encourages can be seen in four features in particular of recent work on education policy. These four features are disciplinary parochialism, ethnocentrism, an emphasis on education politics rather than the politics of education and a problem-solving rather than a critical orientation to theory. These four features are clearly related to each other; they might even be said to 'imply' each other. They jointly comprise a particular problematic, a particular conception of the appropriate delineation of, and approach to, 'education policy sociology' that might best be described as 'applied education politics'.

Disciplinary Parochialism

The central paradigm, both in itself and through the medium of the search for immediate relevance and application that it encourages, contains strong pressures to disciplinary parochialism. This manifests itself in a narrowing of theoretical focus that is apparently based on the assumption that if education policy cannot be comprehensively explained in terms of accounts and theories of the education sector alone, then it certainly can be so explained adequately for immediate purposes. The pervasiveness of this disciplinary parochialism is clearly evident in the lists of references, bibliographies and footnotes of a great deal of the work, recent and not so recent, carried out on education policy. Few of the articles or books contain many references to work in journals or books that are not primarily or exclusively concerned with education, or written by people whose major interests are in education; indeed, it is sometimes very difficult to find references to articles or books that do not have 'education' in the title, or do not appear in journals or books that have 'education' in the title. To take just one instance, in an account summarizing a major ESRC-funded project on the ERA (Halpin, Fitz and Power, 1993), out of forty-four items included in the bibliography only two are not directly education-related.

This disciplinary parochialism appears to rest on an unstated assumption of the uniqueness of education policy (and in a particular national context, as I shall point out below); in effect it prioritizes the distinctiveness of 'education' over the generality of 'policy'. Of course, education does have a distinctiveness, but that which constitutes that distinctiveness has to be demonstrated and elaborated rather than merely being asserted; taking for granted both that education is 'different' and that the parameters of that difference are either obvious or irrelevant is to pass over a quite crucial dimension both of what education policy actually is and of what is involved in beginning to understand it. This encapsulates the fundamental objection to disciplinary parochialism; it leads us to look only where it sheds most light and to leave unilluminated areas that may be indispensable to an adequate understanding of education policy. This might not matter so much if there were not such a clear *prima facie* case that other disciplinary perspectives have much to offer us in the analysis of education policy; I have in mind here such work as that of Claus Offe, Christopher Hood, Anna Yeatman, Michael Pusey, Gosta Esping-Andersen — in fact, a whole range of theorists whose work enables us to frame a more adequate understanding of the politics of education, rather than to elaborate over more finely detailed accounts of education politics. Of course, there are references in much, if not most, of the work recently produced on education policy to 'non-educational' work but its use tends to be restricted; there is a pervasive impression of moving from the 'inside out', of calling in, and calling on, such work for particular limited purposes rather than regarding it as indispensable or even considering the possibility of its broader and more extensive value. That is, such work is typically selectively incorporated into the 'educational' approach rather than being used to expand it. Hence, its use confirms and deepens disciplinary parochialism rather than challenging it.

Ethnocentric Assumptions

Though not necessarily associated with disciplinary parochialism the ethnocentric assumptions of work on education policy in England have somewhat similar consequences. It is important to draw attention to these assumptions because they are so prevalent and elusive and because their consequences are so far-reaching.

It might be argued that there is nothing wrong with theoretical ethnocentrism; because we have learned to expect it and to take account of it we can continue to draw full benefit from the theory by recognizing and, as it were, allowing for its ethnocentric basis, biases and assumptions. This is what we have done for as long as I can remember with much of the American material we have encountered. To take just one example, schools we know may not have provided the precise kinds of counselling services that Cicourel and Kitsuse (1966) wrote about, but their work did give us greater insight into the processes of intra-school selection in schools we did know about.

There are, though, two further points to be noted here. First, we do not invariably and unfailingly recognize and allow for any ethnocentric biases and assumptions in theoretical work. One very useful illustration of this (though not as directly relevant as might first appear) can be found in the work of Margaret Archer. She argues that the work of both Bernstein and Bourdieu is characterized by a set of implicit assumptions about the nature of education systems that are based on features of the education systems that the two theorists are most familiar with (Archer, 1989). For Bernstein and Bourdieu, she suggests, 'certain characteristics of the English and French systems are treated as *normal* and are incorporated, respectively, into the two theories.' (Archer, 1989, p. 251) Not only this, but their work also ' "normalizes" each national system by underestimating its distinctive aspects, thus *making* it more like others' (ibid., p. 253) Now it may be debatable how far Archer is able to substantiate the specific critiques of Bernstein and Bourdieu (she refers to no work either of them have published since 1975); it is certainly the case that the value of both theorists' work does not depend on the specific national contexts from which they draw their assumptions (see, for instance, Bourdieu's introduction to the English edition of *Distinction*, where he addresses this point directly). However, in a sense, that reinforces the importance of the general point being made; for those whose work does depend on the specific national contexts from which they draw their assumptions it is crucial to attempt to recognize and take them into account. Here the points Archer makes about the 'treating the education system as normal' and 'normalizing the education system' are useful. In one sense it is neither possible nor desirable to treat the particular education system on which we are concentrating as anything but 'normal'; it is, after all, our intention to make sense of that system. This does not mean, however, that we have to 'normalize' the system, in the sense of proceeding on the assumption that the way the system is now is how it 'has to be', or how it is 'naturally'. Taking for granted in this way both the mandate and the capacity of an education system entails taking the system's 'normality' as unproblematic, as a point of departure of, rather than a destination of, the analysis. When such assumptions are incidental it may be possible to take them into account in assessing the theory in question. However, when the system itself is the focus of the analysis it is essential to make especially strenuous efforts to avoid 'normalizing' it.

The second point we can take from Archer concerns the importance of education systems. Though she does not refer to any work that does focus on education systems, such as that of Kogan, McPherson and Raab and so on, she does once again emphasize that '(the) differences in structure (between state education systems) make the greatest difference to the processes of change available, to who has access to these and to their outcomes' (ibid., p. 259). We do not have to accept this list as exhaustive or to follow Archer's own elaboration of it to recognize the importance of focusing closely on the structure and process of state-education systems — 'nationwide and differentiated collection(s) of institutions devoted to formal, whose overall control and supervision is at least partly governmental, and whose component parts and processes are related to one another' (Archer, 1979, p. 54). Again, one example may suffice to illustrate the importance of recognizing when we are making assumptions and the assumptions we are making. It concerns the status of the teacher unions as interest groups in English education. Prior to their summary expulsion from the corridors of educational power and influence, it might have been assumed that they were there as of right; it was only that expulsion which made it clear that their presence, like that of any other interest group, was dependent on government decision. Being required, as a result of that event, to revise our assumptions about the granting of interest group status, can only have enriched our understanding of education policy.

Politics of Education and Education Politics

One quite central characteristic of most recent work on education policy has been an emphasis on education politics at the expense of the politics of education. Very broadly, by the politics of education I mean the agenda for education and the processes and structures through which it is created. By education politics I mean the processes whereby this agenda is translated into problems and issues for schools, and schools' responses to those problems and issues. The essence of my argument is that education politics cannot be understood or explained without a more or less explicit reference to, and appreciation of, the politics of education — and those references and appreciation have been very largely absent from most of the recent work on education policy. An exclusive concentration on education politics rests on, and reinforces, the assumption that 'education can be explained from within education' — and, it sometimes seems, in the terms and categories used by those involved in education politics. Where education politics is the dominant focus there is an inevitable tendency to take the boundaries of education as settled and the agenda of education largely for granted. The constitution, as opposed to the content, of the agenda is rarely regarded as a matter of great significance or deserving of close attention. There may be some attention paid to any more obviously 'educational' aspects of that constitution process, or some reference to broader background features (such as 'the decline of the welfare state', or 'the rise of the "New Right" '), but little beyond this. A good example of what I am referring to is to be found in Stephen Ball's very important study *Politics and Policy Making in Education*. The basis of this study is a large number of interviews with key individuals associated with the design and implementation of the ERA. However, though we are nowhere told how those interviewees were selected, it is clear that they were all or nearly all associated in some way with the administration of education. Now it may be that that selection could be defended theoretically. The crucial point is that it has to be; the relative importance and relevance of those interviewed should be made explicit rather than being left to be assumed. In this respect, if in no other, Ball's book bears some resemblance to Maurice Kogan's 1975 study *Education Policy Making*. What is notable is the similarity not only of methodology but of theoretical assumptions about which were the key constituencies and individuals to include in the study (though the link between the two is much more explicit in Kogan). These similarities are all the more striking given not only the major political changes that took place in the period between the publication of the two books, but the clear and explicit differences of theoretical approach between the authors. I would suggest that these similarities do seem to point to the existence of a set of common assumptions about the appropriate approach to studying education policy that transcend a number of more apparent differences among writers in the field, and that these assumptions are rooted in, and inform an emphasis on, education politics at the expense of the politics of education.

Such a claim probably obliges me to set out in somewhat more detail what might be entailed by a more appropriate balance between education politics and the politics of education. Fundamentally, the politics of education is the process and structures through which macro-societal expectations of education as an institution are identified and interpreted and constituted as an agenda for the education system. Somewhat more concretely (perhaps!), these 'macro-societal expectations' may be regarded as the outcome of the specification and ordering of what I have referred to as the 'core problems' of the State in capitalist society, the support of the accumulation process, the maintenance of a social context not unamenable to the continuation of that accumulation process and the legitimation of the system (see Dale, 1989). The specification and ordering of these problems comes about essentially as a response to the 'objective' problems confronting the State at any given moment as a result of its location within the world economy. Such responses are not determined by the nature of the problems or by the contexts in which they arise; they have to be translated into 'problems' of a kind that can be addressed by means of institutional structures and traditions that are already available nationally. (A good example is Olsen's account of how the burgeoning oil industry was incorporated into the governmental institutions of Norway; see Olsen, 1991).

This tends to bring education into prominence since both macro-social expectations and the claims of professional educators have been prone to point to what sometimes has approached a panacea status for education in respect of social and economic problems. However, and this is crucial, the problems thus identified are no more 'objectively' given to education, or beyond interpretation, than are the broader problems confronted by the State. They, too, have to be constructed to a considerable degree by means of, and on the basis of, already existing institutions and discourses, to be formulated through the prism of available forms and structures. And it is these processes of interpretation, formulation and specification that are at the core of the politics of education. It should be noted too that these processes themselves, as well as what they are processing, are shaped and constrained by the more macro-level interpretations of problems, responses and resources.

Essentially, the terrain of the politics of education is that identified most recently and effectively as a result of those critiques of the 'correspondence principle' that pointed to the failure to specify how the needs of the economy were translated into an agenda for schools. Perhaps the main response that this critique produced was the emphasis on the role of the State in education policy. That did represent an advance in the understanding of education policy, but by no means a solution to it. The focus on the State helped define the problematic of the politics of education but it did not, and could not in itself, provide definitive accounts of the politics of education, if only because the State is an extremely complex concept. This focus did, however, lead to at least an implicit recognition of the location and importance of the politics of education, albeit a recognition that tended to reduce the politics of education to a considerably oversimplified notion of the State. I have referred to this process elsewhere as 'theoretical painting by numbers', where the terrain of the politics of education is filled in in a relatively unreflective and undertheorized way by whatever happens to be the currently fashionable concept. Thus, 'the State' replaced 'pluralism' in this space and is itself now in the process of being replaced by equally undertheorized concepts of 'the market' or the 'New Right'.

There appear, then, to be three main ways that the relationship between macro-social processes and education policy and practice are conceived. The first, which is implied by an exclusive focus on education politics, involves effectively ignoring anything that happens outside a more or less narrowly defined conception of education policy. A second way of relating macro-social processes and education policy is to assume that the former maps directly on to the latter, that education policy is a more or less unmediated response to the requirements of the national economy and/or polity. Such accounts, that parallel the correspondence principle, can be found presently especially in accounts with a 'post-' prefix; post-fordist and postmodernist accounts of wider societal changes are linked to conceptions of what might be expected in the post-fordist or postmodern school. An excellent critique of this kind of work has been provided by Peter Watkins (1993) who points both to the broad range of different approaches and assumptions subsumed under the rubric of 'post-Fordism' and to their different implications for education.

What tends to be neglected in these accounts is the effect of the 'macro' changes (post-Fordism, etc.) on the mechanisms through which they are translated into educational practice. This was, of course, a central criticism of the correspondence approach, but it is one to which more recent accounts of the relationship seem equally vulnerable. For instance, the nature of the central–local relationship post-ERA seems to have received relatively little attention; certainly, there appear to be few, if any, contenders to replace 'partnership' in this slot. And perhaps the clearest indication of the lack of interest in this area is the absence of work on what is in many ways the most remarkable feature of the education reforms, the abolition of the ILEA.

All this indicates the importance of the third alternative, which is obviously to take seriously the politics of education. There has been some recognition of the importance of this mediating level but it has received little sustained attention. Having pointed to the gaps I perceive in existing work it is probably incumbent upon me to offer some alternative suggestion. Since my space here is distinctly limited, and since I have indicated elsewhere in more detail what that alternative approach to the politics of education might look like (see Dale, 1993b, Dale and Jesson, 1993) I shall confine myself here to a rather brief and schematic account.

What is required is, in essence, a more rigorous attempt to locate 'the State' and to disaggregate the concept. This involves two fundamental moves. First, we need to do more to build on theoretically the recognition of the increasing importance of 'the market' in education, and the widespread encouragement to various forms of the devolution or decentralization of education. This might be done most effectively by developing what has long been understood but not so far much used theoretically, certainly in the sociology of education, that the State has never been the sole means through which education (or any other social service) has been coordinated and de-livered. This work has always been done through particular combinations of the State, the market and what is variously referred to as 'the community', 'social networks' or 'civil society'. So, the point is not to seek to establish which one of these sets of institutions and practices and their associated modes of social coordination is in operation in the education sphere at any given time. It is rather to recognize that all three are always present in different combinations and to seek to discover the nature of the current form of that combination, the factors affecting it and its implications for education policy and practice.

In a similar way we need to recognize that each of these three sets of institutions and practices can affect education policy and practice through any one of, or any combination of, the three essential (but distinct) components of the government of education, i.e., in its funding, provision or regulation. It is perhaps useful to point out at this juncture that what is entailed in the reduction of the politics of education to 'the State' is the assumption that the State alone funds, provides and regulates education policy and practice; it is to be hoped that the limitations of this approach and the value of the increased complexity suggested for the politics of education are evident — and that the crucial importance of a focus on the politics of eduction in the study is also clarified by this example.

The difference between education politics and the politics of education, then, lies in the attention each pays to the ways that the agenda that confronts education policy, and eventually schools, is constructed, and in the importance they place on the nature and consequences of that process. Either ignoring that process or peripheralizing it by 'reading off' education politics directly from changes at the macro-social level inevitably sets limits to the kind and the value of the analyses produced.

Problem-solving or Critical Theory?

The final feature of the 'applied-education politics' problematic that I wish to mention relates mainly to its metatheoretical assumptions. It can be described very succinctly by drawing on the distinction made by Robert Cox between what he calls problem-solving and critical theory. The former, he says,

> takes the world as it finds it. With the prevailing social and power relationships and the institutions into which they are organised, as the given framework for action. The general aim of problem-solving is to make these relationships and institutions work smoothly by dealing effectively with particular sources of trouble. Since the general pattern of institutions and relationships is not called into question, particular problems can be considered in relation to the specialized areas of activity in which they arise. Problem-solving theories are thus fragmented among a multiplicity of spheres or aspects of action, each of which assumes a certain stability in the other spheres (which enables them in practice to be ignored) when confronting a problem arising in its own. The strength of the problem-solving approach lies in its ability to fix limits or parameters to a problem area and to reduce the statement of a problem to a limited number of variables which are amenable to relatively close and precise examination. (Cox, 1980, p. 129)

Critical theory, by contrast,

> stands apart from the prevailing order of the world and asks how that order came about. [It] does not take institutions and social and power relationships for granted but calls them into question by concerning itself with their origins and how and whether they might be in the process of changing. It is directed towards an appraisal of the very framework for action, or problematic, which problem-solving theory accepts as its parameters. Critical theory is directed to the social and political complex as a whole rather than to the separate parts. As a

matter of practice, critical theory, like problem-solving theory, takes as its starting point some aspect or particular sphere of human activity. But whereas the problem-solving approach leads to further analytic subdivision and limitation of the issue to be dealt with, the critical approach leads towards the construction of a larger picture of the whole of which the initially contemplated part is just one component, and seeks to understand the processes of change in which both parts and whole are involved. (ibid., p. 130)

That distinction summarizes some of the most important differences between 'applied-education politics' and the political sociology of education. It is not that we should not be seeking to solve problems — there is very little point in theory for its own sake — but that we should be conscious of what we are doing, of what we are including and excluding and why, and of what our assumptions are, when we are seeking to understand and solve the problems of education policy. It is not that research on education policy necessarily or even typically has as its aim making things work more smoothly — often quite the opposite! — but that the limitations it sets and accepts for itself are the same as if that were the case. This may have a somewhat restrictive effect on what such work can achieve; for the point is, of course, that the self-imposed limitations of a problem-solving approach severely curtail its ability to solve problems.

Conclusion

In conclusion, I wish only to mention what seem to me two of the more important consequences of the prevalence of the 'applied-education politics' approach. First, the combination of the four elements I have identified as making up the problematic of 'applied-education politics' tends to lead to a kind of 'serial adhocery' at a theoretical or conceptual level. I have already referred to the phenomenon of 'painting by numbers' in this area, and it does seem to be an inherent problem of the parochialism, ethnocentrism and problem-solving orientation that I have referred to. The danger has been neatly summed up by Giovanni Sartori in a discussion of what he calls parochialism; this 'refers to single-country studies *in vacuo* that purely and simply ignore the categories established by general theories and/or by comparative frameworks of analysis, and thereby unceasingly invent, on the spur of the moment, an *ad hoc*, self-tailored terminology.' (Sartori, 1991, p. 247)

The second danger of the dominance of this problematic is that it may impede the emergence of constructive alternatives, whose identification has been a central feature of the dominant paradigm of the sociology of education (see Dale, 1993a). Where what is made problematic about education policy remains firmly within a national focus, where the attempts to come to terms with it are restricted to the understandings available within the discipline of education and where the constitution of the educational agenda is taken largely for granted there is a danger that constructive analysis will be replaced by various forms of 'political hostility' that may be as difficult to substantiate as they are undertheorized.

While only the briefest outline of an alternative approach has been provided here, I hope that the critique it contains and on which it is based may be recognized as indicating constructive alternative approaches in the crucially important work of understanding education policy.

References

ARCHER, M. (1979) *Social Origins of Education Systems* London, Sage.

ARCHER, M. (1989) 'Cross-national research and the analysis of education systems', in KOHN, M.L. (Ed) *Cross National Research in Sociology*, Newbury Park, Sage.

BALL, S.J. (1991) *Politics and Policy Making in Education* London, Routledge.

CICOUREL, A. and KITSUSE, J. (1966) *The Educational Decision Makers* Chicago, Bobbs Merrill.

COX, R.W. (1980) 'Social forces, states and world order', *Millenium* 10, 2, pp. 126–55.

DALE, R. (1989) *The State and Education Policy*, Milton Keynes, Open University Press.

DALE, R. (1992) 'Recovering from a Pyrrhic Victory?: Quality, relevance and impact in the sociology of education', in ARNOT, M. and BARTON, L. (Eds) *Voicing Concerns: Sociological Perspectives on Contemporary Educational Reform*, Wallingford, Triangle Books.

DALE, R. (1993a) 'The Dominant Paradigm in the Sociology of Education and its Consequences', Paper presented to seminar at La Trobe University, Department of Education, September.

DALE, R. (1993b) 'Circumscribing the State, Marketing the Market and Making Civil Society Less Civil and Less Social', Paper presented to first comparative education policy seminar, Uppsala University, April.

DALE, R. and JESSON, J. (1993) ' "Mainstreaming" Education: The Role of the State Services Commission', in MANSON, H. (Ed) *Annual Review of Education in New Zealand, No.2* Wellington, Victoria University Press.

ESPING-ANDERSEN, G. (1990) *Three Worlds of Welfare Capitalism* Cambridge, Polity Press.

HALPIN, D., FITZ, J. and POWER, S. (1993) *The Early Impact and Long term Implications of the Grant Maintained Schools Policy: Warwick Papers in Education Policy Number 4*, Stoke-on- Trent, Trentham Books.

HOOD, C. (1991) 'De-Sir Humphreyfying the Westminster model of bureaucracy: A new style of governance?' *Governance* 3, 2, pp. 205–14.

KOGAN, M. (1975) *Education Policy Making*, London, Longman.

MCPHERSON, A. and RAAB, C. (1988) *Governing Education: A Sociology of Policy Since 1945*, Edinburgh, Edinburgh University Press.

OFFE, C. (1985) *Contradictions of the Welfare State*, Cambridge, MA, MIT Press.

OLSEN, J.P. (1991) 'Political science and organisation theory: Parallel agenda but mutual disregard', in CZARDA, R. and WINDHOFF-HERETIER, A. (Eds) *Public Choice: Institutions, Rules and the Limits of Rationality*, Frankfurt-am-Main, Campus.

PUSEY, M. (1992) *Economic Rationalism in Canberra*, Sydney, Cambridge University Press.

SARTORI, G. (1991) 'Comparing and miscomparing', *Journal of Theoretical Politics*, 3, 3, pp. 243–57.

WATKINS, P. (1993) 'The Fordist/post-Fordist debate: The educational implications', in KENWAY, J. (Ed) *Economising Education: The Post-Fordist Directions*, Geelong, Deakin University.

YEATMAN, A. (1991) *Bureaucrats, Femocrats, Technocrats*, Sydney, Allen and Unwin.

Chapter 4

Coming to Terms with Research:
The Contract Business

May Pettigrew

This chapter is about researcher experience of undertaking government-sponsored educational research and about how the terms under which such research is commissioned, conducted and reported have been changing over recent years. It is based upon the work of an ESRC funded research project (EAR) which has been exploring the contemporary conditions of applied research and evaluation across the social sciences (see appendix for a description of the nature and scope of the research).[1]

Boom Times or Bad Times?

> I have been in educational research for 25 years now, and these have been boom times, and they've been very good. Clearly they are not going to continue because the searchlight is going to move onto something else, but the last 5 years have been very very good. (EAR interviewee)

It seems odd, does it not, to think of the last few years of upheaval in the education system as also boom times for educational research, but opportunities for educational researchers to obtain commissions for applied research and evaluation have indeed grown. Government commissioning of research has been increasing over the last twenty years with particular activity manifest in education over the last ten. (Cabinet Office, 1993). Most of this opportunity has come from contracting to government departments and agencies such as the National Curriculum Council (NCC), the Schools Examinations and Assessment Authority (SEAC), the Health Education Authority (HEA), the Employment Department (ED), the National Council for Vocational Qualifications (NCVQ) the Department of Trade and Industry (DTI) and the Department for Education (DFE) to name but a few. With the most fundamental changes to the education system in Britain since the 1944 Education Act still in process, 'the searchlight' is on education but is the research it mobilizes generating more heat than light?

Sponsor Control

Paul Black as chairman of the TGAT group, charged with drawing up the proposals on national assessment criteria for the National Curriculum in 1988 has had more experience of working within the ERA reforms than most. In 1992 he voiced some of his concerns thus:

> The changes might be defended if they were to be accompanied by thorough and independent evaluation so that the programmes could be monitored and lessons learnt from the only experience that matters, that of pupils in classroom. My own experience in the National Curriculum Council was that comprehensive programmes for monitoring were cut back by Ministers, who have retained to themselves direct control over any research or evaluation activities of that Council. All that were allowed were programmes with modest budgets aimed to explore tightly defined questions. In consequence, evidence that the reforms as a whole might contain serious flaws cannot be forthcoming. (Black, 1992)

Paul Black was no doubt referring to the three major, two-year, evaluations of the National Curriculum, commissioned by the NCC in September 1991, and conducted by teams from the University of Liverpool (science), University of Warwick (English) and Kings College (maths). He noted the tightly defined question brief and alluded to ministerial control of research. In fact, these evaluations were conducted under conditions of considerable constraint upon both the process and products of research. Through the terms of the contract agreement for these evaluations, the NCC assumed the power of direct management of the research. The clause to this effect stated: 'NCC shall from time to time nominate in writing a person from whom the Evaluator shall take instructions in respect of day to day matters arising from this Agreement and who will be responsible for overseeing the Evaluator's undertaking of the Project.' These contracts also gave the NCC right of access on an ongoing basis, to 'copies of all materials generated in connection with the Project including (without limitation) questionnaires, data, interview, schedules and analysis'. The contract also prohibited publication, press releases, the delivery of lectures 'for academic or any other purpose' without prior written approval of the NCC during and after the completion of the studies. The submission of reports to the NCC was also governed by strict conditions which gave the NCC rights to withhold approval. The contract further stated that, 'Where such approval is withheld the NCC Chairman and Chief Executive shall indicate in writing the reasons for withholding approval and, in general terms, the changes necessary to any items in order for them to be acceptable.'

Such contractual conditions reflect the 'down side' of the expansion of educational research. These are times in which social research in general and educational research in particular, have come to be dominated by the short-term, proscribed requirements of policy makers and have been subject to explicit controls over the conduct and reporting of enquiries (Pettigrew and Norris, 1992). The NCC evaluation contracts may represent an extreme case, and it is important to note that these studies have now been published. How-ever, most if not all contracts from government contain clauses which vest ownership of copyright and control over publication and dissemination in the sponsor. It appears that with the exception of contracts from the Scottish Office Education Department and the Scottish Home and Health Department, all government and agency contracts can prohibit publication both during and any time after completion of the commissioned study. Many contracts, in-cluding those of the DFE, the Department of Health (DH) and SEAC, give the sponsor rights of access to data.[2] A particularly worrying trend is towards contracts containing moral-rights waivers. These are terms which remove the authors' rights to be credited with authorship of studies and to object to prejudicial alteration or mutilation of reports. Moral-rights waivers are now standard in the contracts of the ED, the HEA and the Department of Envi-ronment (DoE). Some contracts even contain terms, somewhat similar to those of the NCC described previously, which allow the sponsor to assume complete control of the enquiry process. This is the case with standard con-tracts from the DoE and the HEA.

The terminology of contracts and tenders from government employ the language of trade, conveying the reduction of research to a simple market transaction bought and owned by the customer. Researchers may be 'provid-ers' (HEA) supplying 'goods' (NCC) or 'services' (SEAC). The specifications are technical as if, said researchers interviewed for this study, 'the department was contracting for ten tons of aggregate' or 'buying a fridge'. Time-scales for negotiating the tender and conducting the research tend now to be compressed to fit in with rapidly changing policy contexts and the need for feedback on implementation of programmes. Such pressured, short-term work can lead to what has been described to us as 'inefficiencies' or as 'push-ing you into hunchy judgements and corner cutting' resulting at worst in, 'shoddy work'.

In some cases the methodology and the timetabling of the research may be prescribed in such detail that, in one interviewee's words: 'when you come to write the project bid, you think, "what have I got left to write except put the names in of who is going to do what?" There is almost no discretion — not only in terms of what the project is about, but how it is to be done . . . for me that is an enormous change over the last 10 years . . . On all three of those counts, the what, the how and the accountability, the scope for the exercise of our professionalism has been almost entirely removed. So we are, if you like, paid lackeys. It's proletarianisation. I think that will result, certainly, with the lowering of the quality of the research.'

Methodological constraints of this sort may be imposed by departments who, 'want to know how many, what, what penetration; give us numbers, give us a percentage'. In short-term studies with a broad remit or where early interim reporting is required to inform policy decisions, demands for hard data can put severe pressure on researchers in their efforts to maintain proper standards of rigour and validity: 'So we've been pushed into providing — the word that's used is 'crunchy' — crunchy results are wanted at every stage — we've had some indications from certain sorts of data, so actually we haven't been happy about writing the sorts of reports that are wanted in terms of hard conclusions. In fact we haven't agreed to write them.'

Enquiries may be abruptly terminated (as in the case of the SEAC Key Stage 3 development work in 1991 or the earlier Department of Employment, New Job Training Scheme) or policies or programmes abandoned before the research which was intended to inform decision-making has reported. However, even where researchers have the opportunity to complete their research brief, however limited the problem definition they are required to explore, the high political visibility of educational programme and policy making can induce self-imposed constraints. So, for example, reports may have to be highly guarded in their wording so that 'sound bites' cannot be picked off by ministers or the press and misrepresented out of context.

Most worrying are attempts by government sponsors to suppress or change research findings. There have been numerous reports of, 'efforts by civil servants to exercise control over the content and wording of what was published'. (Mays, 1989). Descriptions of such interference vary. One researcher in describing work for the Department of Health, had this to say: 'The process of submitting drafts in advance has been there for quite a long time but it was a formality. About three years ago you started to get comments back, from "there should be a full stop there" to "take that out, it is contrary to government policy". So that was coming directly down from on top.'

Mary James in her account of the evaluation of the Pilot Records of Achievement in Schools initiative (PRAISE) (1989) is more low-key in her comments, 'We encountered a few situations where we were under pressure, usually from senior management of schools or pilot schemes, but sometimes from the DES, to amend or abandon reports.' The evaluation team, however, had employed an effective methodological strategy to counter anticipated attempts to suppress reports. At the outset, they negotiated ethical protocols for the conduct of the evaluation which included participant validation, 'which made provision for a dialogue to validate and "clear" findings with participants', in effect a kind of 'controlled leaking'.

The publication of the PRAISE B report was delayed for some months after ministerial approval in 1991 — another frequent occurrence in the biography of centrally commissioned studies. Often reports appear to be timed for release when the public's interest lies elsewhere or in some cases not published at all. When the Language in the National Curriculum Project, directed by Professor Ron Carter at Nottingham University, reported in June 1991, government ministers refused to publish the LINC materials, despite the investment of £20.4 million to develop them and resource training in their use. The Government's reasons for the ban were given by Tim Eggar, Minister for Education:

> There is useful material in the LINC units for in-service training: the material specifically related to grammar . . . But there is a lot more which is a distraction from the main task of teaching children to write, spell and punctuate correctly. A number of fashionable secondary agendas have pushed into the foreground. An obvious example is the unit on 'Accent, dialect and Standard English' most of which is in fact concerned with non standard English. (*TES*, 28 June 1991)

His point in essence was that the LINC materials were 'not suitable for teaching national curriculum English to children'. Yet, as Professor Carter has been at pains to point out, (*TES*, 21 June 1991) the LINC model of English teaching was based upon the officially approved work of the Kingman and Cox Committees — both accepted at the time by the government as the foundation of the National Curriculum.

The continuing high profile of educational policy making makes the work of educational researchers particularly vulnerable to control by the State. The mood, we are all aware, is 'back to basics' and 'market choice', a curious, if not oxymoronic coupling. Research or development that collides with these two dictats is viewed as unhelpful and subject to rejection or suppression, or where funded outside government, ridicule and hostility. Hence Kenneth Clarke's response as Secretary of State for Education to the findings of Halpin and Fitz that grant-maintained schools were not particularly innovative. He said:

> I didn't commission that research. The public sector is obsessed with academic research. I don't know of any other large organization that would ask academics in education to advise them on management . . . The only conclusion researchers ever reach is that more research is needed. (*TES*, 27 March 1992)

Their research project is one of a number presently being funded by the ESRC on effects of the Education Reform Act and is thus free of publication restrictions. However, as noted earlier government-commissioned evaluations in education are subject to strong control both in terms of remit and reporting. Such conditions favour leaks to the press as happened in the case of two interim reports by the Warwick team conducting the NCC English evaluation. Researchers argue that this is hardly an adequate means of satisfying the needs of teachers and rights of the public generally, to information about publicly funded educational programmes. Indeed, where there is no guarantee that research work will be available for peer and public scrutiny, quality control may lie with civil servants and managers whose impartiality and knowledge of the discipline of research may well be in short measure. This not only places constraints upon the credibility, trustworthiness and validity of research but also its longer-term ability to generate accumulated understandings.

Efforts by BERA

The British Educational Research Association has been alive to these issues for some time. Since at least the mid 1980s there have been numerous warnings from educational researchers about the threats that sponsor control poses to educational research. These concerns have been presented to BERA by a succession of presidents of the association. (e.g., David Hamilton 1985, Patricia Broadfoot 1988, Michael Bassey 1992). In 1992 the BERA president, Caroline Gipps, in her address to the conference, urged the educational research community to work together within BERA to 'move forward in a hostile climate'. Citing the occurrence of increasing intervention and restrictions on reporting of centrally funded research, she concluded that, 'If we do not insist on bringing research findings (which may be politically inconvenient) into the public arena, we contribute to the erosion of democracy' (Gipps, 1993). Over the last few years, BERA Executive has tried to bring to the attention of its research community, the importance of monitoring restrictive contractual terms (as has UCET) and the need to work with members to negotiate a code governing the practice of research. However, John Elliott, who was instrumental in organizing a BERA seminar on sponsor control in 1988 and in drawing up a draft code of practice for educational research, observed in his 1990 presidential address that there had been a 'lack of response, on the part of senior academics in education, to BERA's draft code of practice' (Elliott, 1991). Perhaps this is not surprising given the upheaval that university departments of education have had to cope with in recent years, such as, meeting the requirements of CATE, the National Curriculum and changes in the organization and funding of initial teacher training. In addition to all of these, of course, university-based academics are faced with demands to improve their departmental research ranking (or risk cuts in base funding) and this includes securing research contracts. BERA has now published an agreed set of ethical guidelines in respect of the research work of its members. These will no doubt go some way to support the efforts of researchers in securing fairer terms of research. However, in her comments on this BERA code Helen Simons noted that, 'Compared with the positive ethics that have evolved over the past twenty years, guidelines today are driven by more negative considerations.' (Simons, 1993). This, she went on to suggest, is evident in the tenor of the wording of the BERA guidelines: 'In many respects they start from a deficit. It is not a question of establishing the most promising conditions for research but rather one of trying to establish that researchers have rights at all; rights to work independently, rights to be treated fairly, rights to protect participants in research, rights to get research published.'

The University Context

With pressures on universities to keep external income coming in, researchers are caught between the rock of further funding and the hard place of falling out of favour. The need to keep contract workers in employment is a prime consideration that often has to take precedence over refusing contracts that seem unfair or unreasonable. Contract researchers represent a highly vulnerable and growing pool of expertise — research staff in the university sector on fixed-term contracts rose from 8,000 in 1976 to over 17,000 in 1990 (CVCP/ AUT, 1990). Maintaining them in employment and holding on to their expertise is a problematic priority. Almost every research project leader interviewed for this research, has expressed concerns in this respect.

However, there are other reasons why contract research, even though it may be governed by constraints, may appeal to researchers. It is an important source of research training and provides opportunities to develop a track record in new and interesting fields. It can be a means of creating research teams and bringing outsiders into a department which has become intellectually tired. The extra money generated is clearly a significant dimension in freeing up resource blockages as well as providing bridging arrangements for temporary staff.

Power, Politics and Methodology

So there is another side to the relations between government sponsors and researchers. Research conditions are not altogether unfavourable as noted above. Indeed some educational researchers indicate that they experience little difficulty in conducting and publishing centrally funded work, and imply that there is a large gap between the rhetoric of contractual terms and realities of the practice of research. This may reflect institutional or individual credibility and history of research relationships with the sponsor as well as the degree of political sensitivity of the research. However, what researchers construe as 'reasonable conditions' will ultimately depend on their values with regard to the purposes of research and acceptability of limits to academic autonomy. Fundamentally, though, these issues are also about the differential power relations that exist between the individual or their organizations and central sponsors. Steven Lukes (1974) suggests that 'normal times' are those of submission and intellectual subordination and he is concerned to know, 'what the exercise of power prevents people from doing, and sometimes even thinking. Hence we should examine how people react to opportunities — or, more precisely, perceived opportunities — when these occur, to escape from the subordinate positions in hierarchical systems.'

The forms that resistance may take to positions of subordination will depend on how effective powerful agents have been in influencing the climate of what counts as 'normal'. In the case of government contractual terms for example, few researchers will argue against restrictive copyright clauses, 'They have just gone by the board now and we don't even try to argue about them.' The threshold that activates opposition incrementally edges upwards or rather, as another interviewee put it, 'In a sense we have become used to working with what we are allowed to work within.' So the ways in which resistance is expressed may become oblique or focus on some personal values rather than others. Restrictive contracts may be acceptable for example, 'if there is a degree of academic freedom and it is possible as researchers to retain integrity and do under that heading . . . at least some of the work you consider important.' Indeed subordination can be, in a sense, its own opportunity structure which can be used creatively. The researcher just quoted went on to say that: 'there has always been a distinction between the formal arrangement, the formal project title, the formal thing on paper and what people do. Some of the most innovative work, in fact almost by definition innovative work has to be of that nature because you can't get it funded because nobody recognises it, . . . it doesn't fit the model. So you do something that fits the model on paper and you do it differently in practice.'

When it comes to dissemination, publication and presentations may be barred but a value of open reporting can be expressed through word of mouth: 'I think it is the case that some of the employees in government agencies adopt . . . the same sort of personal rules — that they feel much freer about talking to groups of teachers about information that is technically confidential, but obviously they wouldn't dream of putting it on paper. So I think there is a kind of oral culture in which these things are circulating now.'

But perhaps most important of all with regard to the issue of power is its micro-dynamics in terms of the nature of the relationships that can be built up over time. This has been expressed to us in numerous ways such as, 'The contracts may not be terribly good but it is the ongoing relationship that counts. If you can get the rapport right the research conditions in practice are reasonable.' Such cooperation is an acknowledgment that lack of conflict is in the interests of both parties. Also implicit here is the asymmetry of power that exists and is manifest in the legally binding terms of contracts. Good relationships depend on trust. But trust is also complicit with power, for relations of trust contain obligations to justify their continuation. Those obligations are similarly asymmetrical. The engagement of researcher and government official in the work of a contract may be friendly and cooperative. Yet as one researcher pointed out in referring to his work for a government agency: 'One could find oneself blacklisted, there is a clear understanding that one wouldn't do the dirty on them.'

Just as trust is related to power, so is methodology. There is an authority vested in quantification that extends beyond scientific orthodoxy and concerns the sublimation of people into things. Persons; descriptions of them and their complexities, bring up the problems that pluralistic values pose to singular political decisions. The greater the number of values and interests that are exposed and legitimated, the greater the demand upon the State to resource their expression. In this respect, numbers may be much less politically consequential than the studies of real people and institutions. One interviewee argued this point on the basis that research which generates what are considered to be facts, can be appropriated by different interest groups to suit their purposes: 'Empirical facts are the oil of consensus — once you've got a fact, people have got to adapt their positions to incorporate that fact. Its more difficult to cite a qualitative fact as you would a statistic.'

Researchers who conduct quantitative studies appear to experience fewer problems. Is this because numbers are indeed less threatening to policy makers or is there a tendency for some researchers to view quantification as part of a practice of science with its own integrity; a field outside of the world of politics and accountability? One researcher who described the last five years as 'boom times for educational research', went on to say: 'Where we are dealing with a matter of truth about the world, I can't see that this process of suppression going on or being very effective. Now if it's relating to interpretations of the world then that seems to me fair game.' and concluded by saying, 'so in just the same way that opinion poll organisations carry out work which is published in the newspapers but also carry out work for political parties, we would, providing it was an enjoyable piece of work to do, it came within our area of competence and it paid sufficiently we'd be perfectly happy to carry out work that wasn't going to be published.'

However, it is also evident from the comments by researchers earlier, that civil servants favour quantitative studies or are under pressure from above to demand them. For example, guidelines on policy evaluation prepared by the Treasury for use by government departments conducting or commissioning evaluative studies (HM Treasury, 1988), advise civil service managers that, 'whenever possible, an evaluation should look for exact measures and, if they are not obtainable, for indicators which throw light on those aspects which are not easily measurable.' The stress in these guidelines is upon input–output studies to evaluate the economy, efficiency and effectiveness of policies and programmes and ultimately their value for money. Trends within the applied research and evaluation community towards pluralistic and stakeholder models of evaluation or those that view evaluation as a form of persuasion rather than objective judgment (House, 1980), have tended to be ignored by government. The basic assumptions have been positivistic and Henkel (1991) on this point has argued, 'The government had itself not only weakened pluralism and the institutional arrangements on which it was based. It had also confronted the epistemology underpinning it.' (Henkel, 1991).

Changing the Terms — Some Practical Advice

Researchers may agree to restrictive contracts because they do not appreciate the implications of the terms for their work. It is evident too, that many feel their room for manœuvre is minimal and that attempts to change the rules will threaten successful bidding in the future. Researchers may also be told by the officials with whom they are negotiating that: 'Regrettably, our contracts are drawn up by our legal department and we have no say in their wording.' However, the advice the EAR project has received is that gentle persistence can be effective especially if mediated through the university contracts office. While some terms of contract would appear to be non-negotiable such as clauses vesting copyright with the sponsor, many can be altered in favour of the researchers. These include standard terms covering staffing, termination of the contract and protocols regarding publication. For example in the standard contract of one government agency the clause relating to publication states: 'No publication of information by any means shall take place without the prior written consent of the (Sponsor's) Project Officer.' In the renegotiated agreement with this sponsor the university concerned secured the following additional clause:

> The [Sponsor] recognises that under policy of the [Researcher's Institution] the results of the Project should be publishable and agree that the Researchers engaged in the Project shall be permitted to present at symposia, national, or regional professional meetings, and to publish in journals, theses or dissertations, or otherwise of their own choosing, methods and results of the Project, provided, however that the Sponsor shall have been furnished copies of any proposed publication or presentation at least one month in advance of the submission of such proposed publication or presentation to a journal, editor, or other third party *provided*, however, that (a) funding shall have been acknowledged and (b) the Sponsor shall have one month, after receipt of said copies to object to such proposed presentation or proposed publication. In the event that the Sponsor makes such objection, the said Researchers shall refrain from making such publication or presentation.

It hardly needs to be said that this extra clause makes important concessions to the research team. The sponsor still holds the power to veto publication but the agreement that publication is to be expected, shifts the issue significantly in the researchers' favour.

It is clear that significant restrictive terms can be renegotiated as in the example above. The CVCP report *Sponsored University Research: Recommendations and Guidance on Contract Issues* is a particularly useful source of support in negotiations over contract terms (CVCP, 1990). The CVCP has made it quite clear that 'under no circumstances should the university allow the sponsor the right to delay publication for an unrestricted period of time.' It also cautions researchers against agreeing to terms which permit the sponsor to withhold payment until a report to the satisfaction of the sponsor has been submitted. Such terms can bind researchers into redrafting reports until the wording finds favour with the sponsor and it is important that these be changed to: reports will be submitted 'in a format acceptable to the sponsor'. It is also worth invoking the arguments put forward by the Office of Science and Technology (OST) with regard to ownership and exploitation of intellectual property arising from sponsored research (Cabinet Office, 1992). These guidelines are intended to support the commercial exploitation of research though their recommendations have more general implications. They urge sponsors to recognize that 'restrictions on publication of research results, although often necessary for commercial, security or other reasons, strike at the heart of the academic ethos and could have implications for the Charitable status of HEIs (Higher Education Institutions)' (p. 39). This latter point has been noted by the Inland Revenue who have recently held discussions with the Committee of Vice-Chancellors and Principals. In future, commissioned research which has not resulted in publication within two years may be audited by the Inland Revenue with a view to reclaiming tax. As a consequence we are likely to see greater efforts by university contracts officers to secure terms of contract which grant researchers the rights to publish.

The OST guidelines drew heavily upon the work of an earlier interdepartmental committee chaired by Philip Cooper (The Cooper Report, 1989) which concluded that on balance, ownership of IPR should remain with HEIs. In essence, the OST guidelines favour this solution in the longer-term and state that 'if HEIs developed expertise in IPR management, one would expect them to have a stronger case for retaining ownership of IPR.' Moreover, the OST guidelines argue that 'HEIs and sponsors should be free to negotiate without presumption all matters relating to ownership, licensing and exploitation of IPR.' In other words, the draft contract issued by the sponsor should be considered the starting position for negotiations over terms, not the end point.

Conclusion

This chapter has been concerned with the terms under which educational research is commissioned by government and with researchers' responses to increasing constraint upon their work. The research upon which it is based is not yet complete and I expect to return to these and other issues in future. I have made no attempt here for example, to explore the wider policy context nor changing demands within government and their influence upon the culture of research. In this respect it will be important to look at the history of social research in relation to government perceptions of its utility. Without this, the argument so far is rather one-sided. Certainly, times and conditions of contract research have changed. But it is important to remember that good relationships between sponsors and researchers can mediate bad contractual conditions. There are still spaces for creative work and there are still sponsors who offer fair terms outside of government. However government is a major sponsor of educational research and its influence upon the market and climate of research sponsorship is profound. Ten or fifteen years ago standard contracts from government departments implicitly assumed that research was a public service, conducted independently, and whose processes and products were the concern of the professional researchers commissioned to do the work. Going back to 1978, we can see this reflected in the terms of contract issued by the Department of Education and Science which had this to say on matters relating to publication: 'A final report shall be submitted to the Department. It should include a concise statement of the objectives, method, results and conclusions, with a critical appraisal of the project, its limitations, possible uses and interested bodies. The report should make reference to the publications which have emerged or are likely to emerge from the project.' (Form P2 1978).

Currently the powers that government has to control research it commissions, whether or not it choses to use them, are extreme. What is at stake for researchers, is the warrant for their work, its credibility and ultimately the development of the disciplinary field of social research.

Notes

1 I am grateful for the assistance of Nigel Norris, my colleague in this research and for the support of the ESRC who have funded our work.
2 SEAC and the NCC merged to form the School Curriculum and Assessment Authority (SCAA) in October 1993. At the time of writing no evidence is available on the new authority's terms for commissioned research.

References

BLACK, P. (1992) *The Shifting Scenery of the National Curriculum*, Presidential Address to the British Association, Science Festival, August.

BROADFOOT, P. (1988) 'Educational research: Two cultures and three estates', *British Educational Research Journal*, 11, 1, pp. 3–11.

BASSEY, M. (1992) 'Creating education through research', *British Educational Research Journal*, 18, 1, pp. 3–16.

CABINET OFFICE/OFFICE OF PUBLIC SERVICE and SCIENCE/OFFICE OF SCIENCE AND TECHNOLOGY (1992) *Intellectual Property in the Public Sector Research Base*, HMSO, London.

CABINET OFFICE/OST (1993) *Yearbook of Research and Development*, London, HMSO.

CARTER, R. (1991) 'Caught out on a point of grammar', *Times Educational Supplement*, 21 June, p. 20.

CVCP GUIDANCE (1990) *Sponsored University Research: Recommendations and Guidance on Contract issues*, London, Committee of Vice-Chancellors and Principals, June.

CVCP/AUT (1990) *Recommendations on Codes of Practice for the employment of Research Staff on fixed term contracts*, London, Committee of Vice-Chancellors and Principals.

EGGAR, T. (1992) 'Correct use of English is essential', *Times Educational Supplement*, 28 June, p. 14.

ELLIOT, J. (1991) 'A model of professionalism and its implications for teacher education', *British Educational Research Journal*, 17, pp. 309–18.

GIPPS, C.V. (1993) 'The profession of educational research', *British Educational Research Journal*, 19, 1, pp. 3–16.

HACKETT, G. (1992) 'A bluff boy turns coy-Kenneth Clarke', *Times Educational Supplement*, 27 March, p. 4.

HAMILTON, D. (1985) 'Bread and Circuses: Some challenges to educational research in the 1980s', *British Educational Research Journal*, 11, 1, pp. 3–11.

HENKEL, M. (1991) *Government, Evaluation and Change*, Jessica Kingsley, London.

HM TREASURY (1988) *Policy Evaluation: A Guide For Managers*, HMSO, London.

HOUSE, E.R. (1980) *Evaluating with Validity*, Sage, London.

JAMES, M. (1989) Evaluation for policy: Rationality and political reality: The paradigm case of PRAISE?, Paper presented at an international invitation conference on 'Evaluation for Policy' at CEDAR, University of Warwick.

LUKES, S. (1974) *Power: A Radical View*, London, Macmillan.

MAYS N. (1989) The DHSS Contract of Research, Paper delivered to the Society of Low Temperature Biology, October.

PETTIGREW M. and NORRIS N. (1992) Expand and Contract — the conditions of government sponsored social research, Unpublished report, CARE, University of East Anglia, Norwich.

SIMONS, H (1993) *The Politics and Ethics of Educational Research*, Paper delivered to the annual meeting of the American Educational Research Association, Atlanta, Georgia, April.

REPORT OF THE INTERDEPARTMENTAL INTELLECTUAL PROPERTY GROUP (1989) *Intellectual Property Rights in Collaborative R&D Ventures with Higher Education Institutions* (the Cooper Report), September.

Chapter 5

Scholarship and Sponsored Research: Contradiction, Continuum or Complementary Activity?

Robert G. Burgess

The terms scholarship, research, sponsorship and in turn contract research are all contested concepts. They are the subject of discussion and debate among researchers in higher education. In part, the debate relates to the social and political context in which higher education institutions, not only in the UK, but also worldwide are now located. Furthermore, in Britain debates about research have been fuelled by discussions from the funding councils on research selectivity and the way in which research is to be assessed for the purposes of grant allocations to institutions. In these discussions some distinctions have been drawn between basic, strategic and applied research with a hierarchy being implied through the use of these terms in different contexts. In these circumstances, one question that arises, is the appropriateness of this terminology for social and educational research. In part, the title of this chapter is taken from a series of conversations that I have had with colleagues over the last year or so. One of my colleagues always makes the point 'I'm not a scholar, I'm a researcher'. A statement that signals (at least for him) a distinction between these activities. A further colleague also in conversation with me, outlined a similar distinction when he remarked: 'I have a postgraduate who has few opportunities of getting a job so I suppose she will have to go into contract research. She will be doing contract research during the day and working as a scholar, writing social theory in the evening.' Such comments leave researchers in little doubt that distinctions are made about the activities in which they are involved. This has been highlighted recently in the field of political science where Allison (1993) has suggested that the word research has taken on a talismanic power. In particular, he argues:

> Given the financial pressures that academic institutions are under, what counts as research is whatever an outside body is prepared to pay for . . . So we now have a system of incentives which rewards those who spend the most public money and penalises those who do not spend any. (Allison, 1993)

Indeed, he goes on to state that much funded research in the humanities and the social sciences involves 'Questions of relatively local interest whose answers have relatively short sell by dates'. This overstates the case. All research in higher education is funded by public money. However, it does raise questions about the relationship between funding, scholarship and research.

We can begin by asking: how far do these comments on scholarship, research and contract research apply to social and educational research? In recent years there have been discussions in the field of education about the opportunities that exist for researchers to engage in research and evaluation supported by a range of sponsors including government departments (Taylor, 1985). However, given the scale of change that has occurred consequent upon the passing of the Education Reform Act in 1988, there have been opportunities not only for researchers to pose their own questions, but requests from a variety of national and local organizations for researchers to engage in examining, monitoring and evaluating change consequent upon the legislation. It is some of these issues that will be examined in this chapter with reference to funded research.[1] Such issues can be examined from a range of perspectives: a sponsor, a project steering group, a researcher employed on a funded research project or a project director. In this chapter, I draw on my experience as a project director to comment on some contemporary issues concerning research sponsorship and contract research.

Sponsored Projects

Sponsorship of social and educational research takes many forms. The sponsorship of projects by the Economic and Social Research Council is one where the researcher decides on the area of study, specifies the research questions, the methodology and the approach to be taken, the time period concerned and the funding required. Such projects are subject to peer review. This is basic or fundamental research that will support the development of social science long-term rather than being of direct use to policy makers. Yet in turn, much work in the field of education can inform policy making as well as contributing to the mainstream development of social and educational enquiry. Indeed, the White Paper entitled 'Realising Our Potential' (HMSO, 1993) has suggested that fundamental research needs to be considered in terms of its link with 'wealth creation' and the 'quality of life' — terms that are now included in the mission statement of the Economic and Social Research Council and highlights the importance of fundamental research for users.

In contrast, policy makers may also commission research. Much of this work links with the notion of the customer–contractor principle that was discussed in the Rothschild Report on the *Organisation and Management of Government R and D* (HMSO, 1971). Here a fundamental distinction is drawn between basic and applied research and the way in which applied research should be commissioned. The Report stated:

This report is based upon the principle that applied R and D, that is R and D with a practical application as its objective, must be done on a contractor–customer basis. The customer says what he wants, the contractor does it (if he can) and the customer pays. Basic, fundamental or pure research . . . has no analogous customer–contractor basis. (HMSO, 1971, par. 9)

As I have indicated elsewhere (Burgess, 1993a), this customer–contractor principle can be considered in relation to educational research that is contracted by a government department, or by a local education authority or by a commercial or industrial concern. However, it is important to consider the elements involved in the customer–contractor principle and the assumptions associated with it. First, a distinction is drawn between pure and applied research. Secondly, there is a suggestion that the customer knows what is required. Thirdly, it assumes that the contractor carries out the work on behalf of the customer in order to 'answer' the questions that have been posed. But questions can be raised in relation to each of these principles. First, questions can be asked about the possibility of making distinctions between basic and applied research. In turn, we can enquire whether, as in many sponsored studies, fundamental research may lead to applied research and in turn whether applied activities may result in contributions of a fundamental kind to social theory and to social science methodology. Secondly, questions can be raised about the extent to which customers know the kind of research problems that can be posed. Indeed, customers may have a knowledge and understanding of the area in which they wish an investigation to take place, but have no notion as to how this may be developed into a series of questions linked to the social sciences and education. Finally, there is the question of methodology and the extent to which the contractor rather than the customer needs to be able to specify the methodology not only in terms of research design but also in relation to data collection, styles of data analysis and in turn the ways in which the report can be written and disseminated. Such issues take us away from the notion that contractors are mere technicians. However, when the customer–contractor principle is applied to the social sciences a further dimension is involved. In a subsequent report, Rothschild (1982) indicates that

the social science 'customer' includes all those who have a part to play in the decision making process. (Rothschild, 1982, par. 3.10)

In these circumstances, customers can commission work that will assist with policy making and decision-making — a situation that seems to have direct applicability to social and educational research. Indeed, in recent years I have worked on projects that have been commissioned by government bodies, local education authorities, industrial companies, commercial organizations and other public bodies. In all these projects, questions arise about the relationship between the customer and the contractor. But there are also other issues that have long-term implications for the social sciences. They include matters relating to the design of research projects, data collection and data analysis (see Burgess, 1993b). In addition, there are also issues concerned with dissemination and reporting (see Burgess, 1990). Such projects and the issues that surround them also raise questions about the independence of the researcher (Simons, 1984; Norris, 1990). Finally, there are also questions about funding, research careers (and in turn intellectual property rights), methodological development, ethical considerations and scholarship which will be examined in this chapter.

Funding and Planning

The sociologist C. Wright Mills writing in *The Sociological Imagination* (1970) commented on the way in which research design was often linked with funding and planning, in as far that he claimed, social scientists only felt a need to write plans when they were going to ask for funding for a specific piece of research. He continued:

> It is as a request for funds that most 'planning' is done, or at least carefully written about. However standard the practice, I think this is very bad; it is bound in some degree to be salesmanship, and, given prevailing expectations very likely to result in painstaking pretensions: the project is likely to be 'presented', rounded out in some arbitrary manner long before it ought to be: it is often a contrived thing, aimed at getting the money for ulterior purposes, however valuable, as well as for the research presented. (Mills,1970, pp. 217–18)

Here, Mills points to several dilemmas for those engaged in contract research. First, whether the research proposal is merely 'salesmanship' — an attractive proposition, carefully costed that will win the tender. Secondly, whether projects are over simplified and contrived in this context. Finally, whether such plans and proposals attempt to gain money for ulterior purposes. In response, one could argue that all research proposals are to some extent acts of 'salesmanship' in as far that they promote pieces of work the researcher may wish to conduct or in some cases has to conduct in order to remain in employment. Secondly, research proposals should not be rounded out but should demonstrate some of the possibilities and problems that might occur in the project and how these can be handled. A research proposal and indeed a research design is not a static object but a statement at a given point in time from which the researcher orientates an investigation. It is a plan about what might occur rather than what should occur. It is not a blueprint. Finally, there is the question of whether research proposals are an attempt to get funds for ulterior purposes (a statement that several commentators have made). This can be turned to the advantage of the investigator as indicated by Stenhouse (1984) when he remarked:

> When it comes to research aims, I think I have always worked with double sets of aims — one for the sponsor and one for myself! The proposal sets out the job I hope to do for the sponsor . . . the whole art of the business in funded research is to find scope for your own aims within and alongside the sponsors aims — and without costing the sponsor anything. (Stenhouse, 1984, p. 213)

While this may be a way of approaching sponsored research a question is also raised; how might this be done? In this context, I take as an illustration, research that I have conducted for Sheffield Local Education Authority.

In June 1991 the Sheffield LEA indicated that they were interested in commissioning a research project on the resourcing of Sheffield schools. In particular, the local authority was interested in four key questions which were stated as follows:

1   What principles should guide the funding of three to eighteen-year provision?
2   What is the appropriate level of funding for pupils at different stages taking into account appropriate comparisons for other LEAs?
3   What baselines should be set for class size, non contact time, management time, support time, equipment and books and non-statemented special needs support?
4   What should be the aims and funding levels of special needs and positive action? (Sheffield City Council Education Department, 1992).

The proposal continued with an outline of the timetable which it was claimed was such that the full report should be completed by Easter 1992 in order that it could be considered by schools and by the local education authority in setting the budget for that Autumn. In addition, interim findings in relation to the key questions were to be available for discussion at the end of September 1991 so that they could be used in the budgeting for 1992–3. Finally, it was signalled that the project should be commissioned by the end of June in order that work could begin before the Summer vacation.

This project was to have a steering group consisting of officers and advisers together with representatives from nursery, primary, secondary and special schools and colleges. This was the group who would be responsible for receiving the project report and liaise with the research team. They were the group who would establish the remit of the research project, choose a suitable research unit to conduct the research and receive the project reports. At this stage, there was no indication of the funding available or any details about the methodology. These gaps were subsequently filled in by an education officer in a series of telephone conversations prior to a proposal being

Table 5.1:   *Proposed Project Timetable for the Sheffield Resource Allocation Project*

September 1991	• Policy analysis, analysis of statistical data, comparison with other LEAs and Sheffield. Report on policy.
October 1991	• Main case studies in nursery, primary, secondary and further education.
November 1991	• Issue of questionnaire. Analysis of case-study data.
December 1991	• Interim report to schools and colleges (Return by 15 Dec.). • Reports of case studies.
January 1992	• Analysis of questionnaire data and report writing.
February 1992	• Final report; writing thematic report; comparisons between age phases; dissemination meetings.

written. The officer suggested that the authority would be willing to spend somewhere between £40,000 and £50,000 over a six-month period for work on resource-allocation mechanisms in Sheffield and elsewhere, the presentation of an analysis on Sheffield's spending in schools for the 3–18 age range and an analysis of Sheffield's spending by age group and by socio-geographical areas in the city. The study was to be conducted by desk research, survey investigation, and by intensive case-study work.

To assess whether a group can engage in such research activities a number of issues arise. First, does the research that is required fall within the expertise of the individual who is preparing the proposal? Secondly, does the research fit with the portfolio of expertise that the individual or group possess? Thirdly, does the research provide the investigators with an opportunity to explore a range of issues in addition to those which are required by the customer? In this instance, the research fitted with the expertise of the Centre in which I am located. We had been conducting investigations for a number of local authorities across the country (Salford, Hampshire, Coventry, Warwickshire and Solihull among others). Secondly, it fitted in the sense that we had already begun to conduct work on local management of schools and in particular had some experience of monitoring local financial management in the context of nursery schooling. Thirdly, the Centre had conducted research in a range of age phases from nursery through to further education and in addition we had worked regularly with a consultant who had direct experience of policy-focused research in the context of resource allocation. Accordingly, it seemed appropriate to offer a project proposal that could be used to conduct this study. The project specification contained in our initial research proposal indicates that we could cover all age phases represented in the authority using eight staff. In practice, only six members of staff were used and of these only four had been named in the initial proposal. The research was perceived as policy-focused and would result in statistical analysis, policy analysis and also a series of institutional accounts based on case studies. The timetable suggested is outlined in Table 5.1.

In the proposal, it was argued that the project would generate a policy analysis of resource allocation in Sheffield with comparisons to other LEAs, case studies of resource allocation within all the age phases in the city, a survey based upon an authority-wide study and a thematic report which would include recommendations. In framing the proposal I took each element contained in the specification document and suggested ways in which we would compare Sheffield with other authorities through pupil–teacher ratios, staffing analyses, incentive allowances, staff turnover and so on. Secondly, that we would study school policy and school ethos, as I argued:

> It will be essential to conduct some case studies of resource allocation in each age phase. The number of case studies to be conducted in each phase will depend on the number of schools and colleges in the Sheffield authority together with advice from the steering group members. (Burgess, 1991)

The case studies in each sector would need to provide comparative data and I indicated factors that would be covered in each case study including the deployment of staff, teacher–pupil ratios, contact ratios, teaching-group sizes, and special needs support — again the emphasis was upon areas that had been covered in the research specification with additions of my own. Overall, I stressed that comparable data needed to be collected to develop comparisons within the authority and beyond it.

By the time the authority evaluated the proposals and set up interviews three months had elapsed. I was interviewed (on behalf of our team) alongside three other teams. Although the research study brief had indicated that one team was to be used, the steering group decided to employ a team composed of staff from the universities of Sheffield, York and the Open University to conduct the survey work, while our Centre was invited to conduct the case-study work. Members of the steering group had decided to have teams that would collect different but complementary evidence with a view to links being established between the two teams (Brannen, 1992). However, the timetable had to be readjusted given that the project had been originally timed to start in the late Summer. Accordingly, we were asked to start work immediately in late September in order that reporting could occur in June 1992.

In such projects, a range of issues arise. Firstly, about the formulation and modification of the research specification. Secondly, the extent to which research careers and research teams can be developed in the time available. Thirdly, the way in which methodological development can take place within such projects. It is to some of these issues that we turn in subsequent sections. However, at this stage it is important to emphasize that winning this contract provided not only continuity of employment for some research staff but also allowed them to develop their expertise in areas in which they were already working and on which they had established research records. Nevertheless, it highlights the problem a research director has in building research teams on short-term projects and the problem researchers have in building a research career out of several short-term and seemingly loosely coupled projects.

Robert G. Burgess

Building Careers and Building Teams

A number of dilemmas surround personnel matters in funded research. These are well summed up by Wright Mills (1970) when he writes:

> Now I do not like to do empirical work if I can possibly avoid it. If one has no staff it is a great deal of trouble; if one does employ a staff, then the staff is often even more trouble. (Mills, 1970, p. 225)

Such a comment points to a problem that is often perceived by many research directors. First, what kind of staff with the appropriate skills and expertise can be effectively hired for a project? Secondly, what kinds of responsibilities does the director have to the project staff? Thirdly, to what extent can staff redefine the project? Fourthly, how can a project team be developed? Fifthly, who owns the data on such projects — the director, the fieldworkers, the team, the institution in which they work, or the research sponsor? Finally, how can comparable data be collected?

Some of these dilemmas have been discussed by a number of individuals who have worked in research teams. Porter (1984) and Brown (1994) have indicated the problems associated in contract research for itinerant researchers who can be marginal to a research project and marginal to the institutions, departments and centres in which they are located. Meanwhile, Wakeford (1985) has indicated some of the dilemmas for the directors of such projects and the extent to which project autonomy may be given to a researcher. Finally, some of the difficulties associated with the relationship between a project director and a researcher are highlighted by Bell (1977) in his discussion of work that was conducted on the Banbury re-study (Stacey, Batstone, Bell and Murcott, 1976). All these issues are present for research teams that engage in contract research. Some of these difficulties were evident in the Sheffield resource-allocation project. First, if we had won the full project I would have had difficulty in staffing it as the project had to begin immediately. The reason for this difficulty was because some of the people who were named in the original application were no longer available by the time the research came to be commissioned. In this respect, time-scales are essential for both the researcher and the research and in such circumstances a group of staff who are adequately trained for a variety of research projects need to be available. Indeed, in a visit to a government department to talk about the possibility of bidding for contract research I was frequently asked the question: 'What size is your field force?' Here, it was assumed that a relatively large group of researchers was permanently on stand-by. This in itself represents a dilemma for a research director engaged in contract research. How do you maintain a sufficiently flexible group of people who have research experience and expertise on the one hand and on the other can be deployed almost at a moment's notice? There is also a further problem of gaining staff with such expertise. Is it that social science groups in general and research groups in higher education institutions in particular have a generic set of skills that can be deployed across any project? Does expertise need to be established in particular areas? In turn, this situation also raises a number of problems for contract research staff concerning the range of their methodological training, the level of expertise required together with issues surrounding their continuity of employment and the extent to which short-team projects can contribute to a research career.

In the area in which we were awarded funding for the resource-allocation project we could build on previous experience and develop research themes. First, we had a group of researchers who had expertise in conducting case studies in a range of educational settings. Secondly, we could provide a team of researchers who had expertise in conducting case studies within particular age phases — for example Christina Hughes had conducted case studies in nursery education (Burgess, Hughes and Moxon 1989) and Christopher Pole had conducted case studies in secondary schooling (Pole, 1993). However, more was called for than those with case-study experience. We also needed expertise in resource allocation, local financial management and policy-related work. As far as local financial management was concerned Burgess and Hughes were working on another study for a local authority which was introducing local financial management into nursery schools. Secondly, as far as local financial management and resource allocation were concerned we had available the expertise of individuals who had worked in the education service and could therefore discuss these issues with the research team from the perspective of the officers and advisers of a local education authority. However, it remained important for the team to be able to translate these issues into a set of research questions that could be used in case-study investigations. Finally, all members of the team had engaged in social science research that informed policy analysis in the field of education.

The team had the necessary expertise but it was important to consolidate and build team membership so that a united and purposive research team would be developed that would share similar perspectives on the project and in turn contribute to a coherent project report (Brown, 1994; Burgess, Hockey, Hughes, Phtiaka, Pole and Sanday, 1992a). In this instance, the strategy that was used was to hold regular meetings to design and specify the research questions and in turn to discuss units of analysis and the writing process in relation to the research design and the fieldwork (see Olesen, Droes, Hatton, Chico and Schatzman 1994). Accordingly, on the basis of their literature searches, members of the team drew up sets of questions that were to be used with headteachers, governors and class teachers in schools throughout the authority in order that the case studies would deal with similar issues and include comparable data that were reliable and valid. Secondly, discussions were held about the field-work process which in turn led to themes being developed across the case studies. Whilst these were not uniform they involved sufficient similarity in order that generalizations could be developed from this multi-site case-study investigation — a style that Burgess and Pole had developed with another research team on an earlier research project (Burgess, Pole, Evans and Priestley, 1994). Thirdly, while the writing of each case study involved the person who had conducted it, the studies were also rewritten by other members of the team so that authorship genuinely belonged not with any individual but with all members of the research team.

This style of writing may give coherence to a research project but presents a dilemma for the contract researcher who may prefer individual authorship rather than collective ownership of a range of reports where individual contributions go unidentified. The potential for doing contract research involved meeting the requirements of the sponsor in terms of evidence on resource allocation, but in turn led to a number of other developments concerning the extension of our understanding of team-based research and methodological developments concerning the relationship between applied research and basic research in the context of multi-site case study (see Burgess, Connor, Galloway, Morrison and Newton 1993c; Burgess and Rudduck 1993; Burgess, Pole, Evans and Priestley, 1994).

Methodological Developments

Some methodologists, including Hammersley (1992) have suggested that social and educational researchers in general and ethnographers in particular have had little impact on policy, partly as a result of their research not being directly related to the policy-making process. Meanwhile, others have indicated the way in which ethnographic research can be shifted to make links with policy making and in that way basic and applied research can take place simultaneously (see for example Woods and Pollard, 1988; Pollard, 1984; Finch, 1985 and 1986; Burgess, 1993a). Indeed, it is often where contract research is conducted that social and educational researchers in general and ethnographers in particular are able to contribute to the policy-making process. But in turn we might ask, what is their contribution to methodological development? — an issue to which we now turn.

Many researchers have made the false assumption that standard procedures which have been used in basic research can also be utilized in sponsored and contract research, yet this is not always the case. The principle might be the same; that is to collect data that are reliable and valid. However, the means by which this is done may be different. Ethnographic research has often involved investigators working alone for periods of up to eighteen months in any research site. This is a luxury which is rarely possible in contract and sponsored research. Indeed, the Sheffield project is a useful example as the work had to be commissioned, conducted, analysed, reported and disseminated within a ten-month period. Accordingly, a different research strategy was required. Here, the principles associated with ethnography: observation and participation through the use of methods such as participant observation, unstructured interviews and documentary evidence were used but in a concentrated timespan. According to my calculations the project had been funded at a level for all costs concerning staff, travel, consumable materials and related activities that would involve a maximum of 150 days. On the basis of preliminary work, meetings, and my estimates of meetings to come I suggested to the team that the project budget in terms of days might be as follows:

	Days
Preliminary work	20
Meetings (so far)	6
Meetings to come (estimate)	14
Fieldwork (including analysis and writing)	110
Total	150

The field work involved the study of institutions associated with different age phases and the allocation of time was as follows:

	Days
1 Tertiary college	20
2 Secondary schools at 15 days	30
5 Primary schools at 10 days	50
1 Nursery school at 10 days	10
Total	110

I suggested that the time allocations should include data collection, data analysis and writing. In allocating a number of days to sites, I had attempted to take account of the complexity of the organizations that were to be studied. In order to deal with this time-scale it was important that documentary evidence was collected from all the institutions prior to the fieldwork and in turn prior to the detailed planning of that fieldwork. In this way, the documentary evidence could be used to create themes that would be taken up subsequently through interviews and observations within the institutions. Finally, many of the themes would need to be followed up through interviews conducted with headteachers, teachers and governors so that they could be used in the data analysis and writing which were all to be conducted within this time-scale.

A second issue to emerge from the case-study investigation was the use of multi-site case-study data. This is a topic that was not specified by the sponsor. Instead, it was an issue in which we were interested in exploring across a variety of projects and had already done some work in investigating in-service education and training (Burgess, Connor, Galloway, Morrison and Newton, 1993). First, we were interested to investigate ways in which multi-site case study could be conducted within one project with a research team. Secondly, we wanted to explore ways in which common sets of data could be collected. Thirdly, we wished to examine strategies for reporting multi-site case studies. Fourthly, we intended to explore ways in which generalizations could be made on the basis of multi-site case-study evidence. Finally, we wanted to develop different ways in which research report writing could be conducted in this context.

This takes us to a further area of methodological development, within this project. There was an opportunity to explore writing styles — a topic which has begun to interest a number of anthropologists and ethnographers (Atkinson, 1990; Becker, 1986). In this project, the style for analysing and writing could not be conducted in the same way as it occurs in other more traditional ethnographies, given the time available to us. Instead, a strategy had to be developed to handle the data and in turn to write about the situation studied. Accordingly, the research team devised a set of themes which were used by the individual researchers to write a first draft of the institutional case study where they had conducted the fieldwork. Among the issues that were explored was whether the project-team members would write in the first person, the extent to which verbatim quotations would be used and the extent to which conclusions and recommendations could be drawn from individual case studies. Some of these issues were resolved in team-based discussions and in turn by other members of the team taking the material that had been drafted by the case-study worker and reworking it. As a consequence, first-person accounts were not possible in this context but verbatim quotations were used and conclusions were drawn from the individual case studies. At this stage I read each of the case studies and reworked some of the data, not to bring a uniformity to them but to highlight some of the common themes that arose across the different case-study sites and which would subsequently be utilized in a thematic project report. The writing was the responsibility of the whole team and not an individual — the case studies were a team product (Burgess, Hockey, Hughes, Phtiaka, Pole and Sanday, 1992b). While this may contribute to the development of case studies, it may also raise problems for individual researchers about publication and the acknowledgment of their contribution in team-based research.

Ethical Issues: Whose Side Are We On?

Within much social and educational research there has been considerable discussion and debate about the ethical dilemmas that confront researchers in general and ethnographers in particular (see Bulmer, 1982; Burgess, 1989). In particular, ethical dilemmas are highlighted in sponsored and contract research. However, the manner in which these dilemmas arise is often different from those that occur in research over longer time periods. First, the short-time scales raise particular problems concerning anonymity and confidentiality. Often those who are receiving the reports have had some involvement in the selection of the research sites (as in the Sheffield study) or even where they have not it is possible for recognition of institutions and individuals to take place given that the research location is carefully specified. Secondly, the question 'whose side are we on?' (Becker, 1967; Gouldner, 1968) is well placed here. In particular, many contract-research projects involve the researcher in presenting draft material to those who have sponsored the investigation. In some instances, agreements are reached whereby those who have been interviewed can comment on the draft material.

The politics of the Sheffield resource-allocation project were such that an agreement had been reached whereby case studies would be returned to the schools in which they were conducted for comment. Often this meant studies being looked at by headteachers and in some cases members of senior-management teams rather than by a whole staff or by all those who had been interviewed. In the majority of cases we found that minor points of detail were picked up. There was no objection to the form case studies took, apart from in one school. Here, the headteacher questioned some of the statements we made. In one instance, we indicated that parents had been involved in painting the school — a statement which was part of a quotation we had used. However, it triggered a response from the head 'we have never had parents painting the outside windows! What some staff will say!' Secondly, it was argued that our comments that sixth-formers were used in supervisory roles in the school could not be sustained even though we had evidence to the contrary. Thirdly, it was argued that a quotation that portrayed pastoral care as 'chatting with kids in corridors' was not how things occurred in the school. Indeed, the head commented:

> It is quite outrageous and should be deleted *it is absolutely not a staff consensus* and I think it quite disgraceful that your researcher could make such an unfounded statement.

In all these instances we had evidence of the statements we had made and we also had quotations to support them. However, for the head many of the statements were just 'idiotic chit-chat at the level of the garden fence, and any researcher with some understanding would surely have simply ignored it'. Yet this is to miss the point. As far as researchers are concerned and especially all ethnographers; all comments are potential data. There is no ultimate truth and indeed the truth about a situation does not reside with one individual; especially a headteacher or a headteacher and a senior-management team. Yet the head of this particular school found difficulty in accepting this situation. He argued that some of our statements should be deleted from the report as the senior-management team could not agree with them.

This presented problems for me. As soon as a researcher operates beyond the correction of minor errors, difficulties arise. If we had taken the perspective of the head and his senior management team the report would have been different and arguments could be made that a different project had been done from the study that was commissioned. Furthermore, we would be perceived by the teachers who had been interviewed as taking sides by portraying the view of the senior-management team rather than the views that had been expressed by teachers during interviews. Accordingly, we attempted to steer a middle path by adding statements which suggested that the senior staff did not share the particular perspective that was portrayed by a particular quotation. While the head accepted the changes we had made, he still maintained that the staff views were confused. Indeed, in a letter he remarked:

> The major benefit I have derived from reading this report is the realization of how confused much staff thinking is hence the determination I have formed to provide more information this year in the hope of clarifying to them many aspects of the current management situation. The school's ability to solve its problems, improve and progress depends first and foremost on an understanding by all staff teaching and non-teaching of the situation in which the school currently finds itself. Strategies for change cannot be adequately formulated until we all understand and agree where we are now.

Such a statement indicates a misunderstanding of what a case study can do. The head thought it would portray one single view of the school and the way it operated. Indeed, it is apparent that for this headteacher the notion that a school involves members with a number of competing views and interpretations is not something that he could perceive. The result is that researchers are bound to be at odds with such headteachers who have an expectation that a case study will represent one view. Yet to represent one view would involve betraying those with whom the case-study workers have been involved. In this respect, researchers need to maintain integrity and standards of scholarship in handling such issues in contract research.

Conclusion

At this point we have come full circle to our starting point where we discussed scholarship, research and sponsorship. This chapter has focused on contract research and some of the dilemmas which arise for the research director (and in some cases the researcher) out of sponsorship. But where does such research articulate with scholarship (if at all)? At this point we might return to the work of C. Wright Mills, writing in *The Sociological Imagination* where he attempted to discuss issues pertaining to scholarly activity when he wrote:

> It is best to begin, I think, by reminding you, the beginning student, that the most admirable thinkers within the scholarly community you have chosen to join do not split their work from their lives. They seem to take both too seriously to allow such dissociation, and they want to use each for the enrichment of the other. Of course, such a split is the prevailing convention among men in general, deriving, I suppose, from the hollowness of the work which men in general

now do. But you will have recognised that as a scholar you have the exceptional opportunity of designing a way of living which will encourage the habits of good workmanship. Scholarship is a choice of how to live as well as a choice of career; whether he knows it or not, the intellectual workman forms his own self as he works towards the perfection of his craft; to realise his own potentialities, and any opportunities that come his way, he constructs a character which has as its core the qualities of the good workman. (Mills, 1970, pp. 215–16)

In this sense, if the contract researcher develops the qualities of the good worker that person will have also started to develop the attributes of the scholar in the research community. Yet that community needs to consider how to develop the career of the contract researcher who has the potential to make a significant contribution to fundamental and applied work in social research and educational studies.

Note

1   I would like to thank David Halpin and Barry Troyna for inviting me to write this paper for their seminar entitled 'Commissioned Research for Contemporary Educational Policy' in the series sponsored by the ESRC. In revising this paper for publication in this volume, I have drawn on comments I have received from the seminar participants, from CEDAR staff and from Rosemary Deem and Stan Green to whom I am most grateful.

References

ALLISON, L. (1993) 'Sorry I just teach . . .', *Daily Telegraph*, 18 March.
ATKINSON, P. (1990) *The Ethnographic Imagination*, London, Routledge.
BECKER, H.S. (1967) 'Whose side are we on?', *Social Problems*, 14, pp. 239–47.
BECKER, H.S. (1986) *Writing for Social Scientists*, Chicago, University of Chicago Press.
BELL, C. (1977) 'Reflections on the Banbury restudy', in BELL, C. and NEWBY, H. (Eds) *Doing Sociological Research*, London, Allen and Unwin.
BRANNEN, J. (Ed) (1992) *Mixing Methods: Qualitative and Qualitative Research*, Aldershot, Avebury.
BROWN, A. (1994) 'Being a researcher', in BURGESS, R.G. (Ed) *Issues in Qualitative Research*, London, JAI Press.
BULMER, M. (Ed) (1982) *Social Research Ethics*, London, Macmillan.
BURGESS, R.G. (Ed) (1989) *The Ethics of Educational Research*, London, Falmer Press.
BURGESS, R.G. (1990) 'Shooting the Messenger? A study on the Politics of Dissemination', CEDAR Conference, September.
BURGESS, R.G. (1991) 'Resourcing 3–18 year education services in Sheffield', Unpublished research proposal submitted to Sheffield LEA.
BURGESS, R.G. (1993a) 'Customers and Contractors: a research relationship?', in BURGESS, R.G. (Ed) *Educational Research and Evaluation: For Policy and Practice?* London, Falmer Press.

BURGESS, R.G. (1993b) 'Biting the hand that feeds you?', in BURGESS, R.G. (Ed) *Educational Research and Evaluation: For Policy and Practice?* London, Falmer Press.

BURGESS, R.G., CONNOR, J., GALLOWAY, S., MORRISON, M. and NEWTON, M. (1993) *Implementing In-service Education and Training*, London, Falmer Press.

BURGESS, R.G., HOCKEY, J., HUGHES, C., PHTIAKA, H., POLE, C. and SANDAY, A. (1992a) 'Case Studies: A Thematic Look at Issues and Problems', in Sheffield City Council Education Department, *Resourcing Sheffield Schools*, Sheffield, Sheffield City Council.

BURGESS, R.G., HOCKEY, J., HUGHES, C., PHITIAKA, H., POLE, C. and SANDAY, A. (1992b) *Resourcing Sheffield Schools: Part II The Case Studies*, Sheffield, Sheffield City Council.

BURGESS, R.G., HUGHES, C. and MOXON, S. (1989) *Educating the Under Fives in Salford*, CEDAR, University of Warwick.

BURGESS, R.G., POLE, C.J., EVANS, K. and PRIESTLEY, C. (1994) 'Four studies from one or one study from four? Multi-site case study research', in BRYMAN, A. and BURGESS, R.G. (Eds) *Analysing Qualitative Data*, London, Routledge.

BURGESS, R.G. and RUDDUCK, J. (Eds) (1993) *A Perspective on Educational Case Study: A Collection of Papers by Lawrence Stenhouse*, CEDAR Occasional Paper No 5, CEDAR, University of Warwick.

FINCH, J. (1985) 'Social policy and education: Problems and possibilities of using qualitative research', in BURGESS, R.G. (Ed) *Issues in Educational Research: Qualitative Methods* Lewes, Falmer Press.

FINCH, J. (1986) *Research and Policy*, Lewes, Falmer Press.

GOULDNER, A. (1968) 'The sociologist as partisan: Sociology and the welfare state', *American Sociologist*, 3, pp. 103–16.

HAMMERSLEY, M. (1992) 'Ethnography, Policy Making and Practice in Education', Paper prepared for ESRC Seminar on Methodological and Ethical issues associated with research into the 1988 Education Reform Act, University of Warwick, July 1992.

HMSO (1971) *A Framework for Government Research and Development*, London, HMSO.

HMSO (1993) *'Realising Our Potential'*, (White Paper on Science Technology and Engineering), London, HMSO.

MILLS, C.W. (1970) *The Sociological Imagination*, Harmondsworth, Penguin.

NORRIS, N. (1990) *Understanding Educational Evaluation*, London, Kogan Page.

OLESEN, V., DROES, N., HATTON, D., CHICO, N. and SCHATZMAN, L. (1994) 'Analysing together: Recollections of a team approach', in BRYMAN, A. and BURGESS, R.G. (Eds) *Analysing Qualitative Data*, London, Routledge.

POLE, C.J. (1993) *Assessing and Recording Achievement*, Milton Keynes, Open University Press.

POLLARD, A. (1984) 'Ethnography and social policy for classroom practice', in BARTON, L. and WALKER, S. (Eds) *Social Crisis and Educational Research*, London, Croom Helm.

PORTER, M. (1984) 'The modification of method in researching postgraduate education', in BURGESS, R.G. (Ed) *The Research Process in Educational Settings: Ten Case Studies*, Lewes, Falmer Press.

ROTHSCHILD LORD (1982) *An Enquiry into the Social Science Research Council*, London, HMSO.

SHEFFIELD CITY COUNCIL EDUCATION DEPARTMENT (1992) *Resourcing Sheffield Schools*, Sheffield, Sheffield City Council.

SIMONS, H. (1984) 'Principles and procedures in the conduct of an educational evaluation', in ADELMAN, C. (Ed) *The Politics and Ethics of Evaluation*, London, Croom Helm.

STACEY, M., BATSTONE, E., BELL, C. and MURCOTT, A. (1976) *Power, Persistence and Change: A Second Study of Banbury*, London, Routledge and Kegan Paul.

STENHOUSE, L. (1984) 'Library access, library use and user education in academic sixth forms: An autobiographical account', in BURGESS, R.G. (Ed) *The Research Process in Educational Settings: Ten Case Studies*, Lewes, Falmer Press.

TAYLOR, W. (1985) 'The organisation and funding of educational research in England and Wales', in NISBET, J. (Ed) *World Yearbook of Education 1985 Research Policy and Practice* London, Kogan Page.

WAKEFORD, J. (1985) 'A director's dilemma', in BURGESS, R.G. (Ed) *Field Methods in the Study of Education*, Lewes, Falmer Press.

WOODS, P., and POLLARD, A. (Eds) (1988) *Sociology and the Teacher*, London, Croom Helm.

Part 2

The Ethics of Research into Education Policy

The Constraints of Neutrality: The 1988 Education Reform Act and Feminist Research

Beverley Skeggs

'Take politics out of education:vote Conservative' — a slogan used in the Conservative election campaign — illustrates the disingenuous nature of debates on neutrality. Feminist epistemology exposes neutrality as a myth; a myth that works for the interests of particular groups and which does not just impose constraints but also imposes a particular value system with moral positions. The position which argues that neutrality is achievable ignores all the workings of power and inequalities. As Sandra Harding (1991) notes: 'this view from nowhere is generated by those who can afford the luxury of the dream from everywhere' (p. 276). John Major's comment, that the Tories were 'above issues of gender, "race" and class', (Conservative party conference, 9 October 1992) meaning they need not take cognizance of them, demonstrates the privileged and powerful position from which he speaks. Sadly, those who live structured and cultured inequalities on a daily basis cannot afford such lofty privilege. As Audre Lorde notes: 'institutionalised rejection of difference is an absolute necessity in a profit economy which needs outsiders as surplus people' (1984, p. 115). Whilst the rhetoric surrounding the ERA espouses neutrality, the government publication *Choice and Diversity: A New Framework for Schools* (HMSO, 1992) displays the non-neutral battle for hearts and minds being conducted by openly declaring that 'schools should not be, and generally are not, value-free zones'. The introduction of the Educational Reform Act (ERA) also needs to be set against the wider political attempts (such as Section 28) to dismantle and destabilize local government.

Feminist educational research has shown how the majority of schooling operates not in the interests of neutrality, rather it operates against women and for masculinity (albeit a particular form), elitism and nationalism. It also shows how certain groups are able to abuse *their* power to impose *their* values in schools and colleges. The actual reforms of the ERA make explicit the value position which generates inequalities. The ERA speaks the language of neutrality whilst holding inequality firmly in its place. It is a blatant attempt to reinforce inequalities through changes not only in the curriculum but through the moral framework of education as a whole.

In contrast, feminist research on education not only speaks from a marginalized position but also declares itself as situated knowledge (Haraway, 1988). It has nothing to hide. It is produced for a particular purpose with a specific interest: to challenge the inequality experienced by women in education. Feminist researchers such as Sandra Harding and Donna Haraway argue that all knowledge is necessarily partial and not disinterested. Duncan Graham (*Guardian*, 14 October 1992) suggests the whole ERA was introduced as a specifically partial gesture. So when feminist researchers examine the ERA they do so with a particular purpose in mind: to interrogate the rhetoric to see what it will mean in reality for the challenge or reproduction of inequalities of gender, (and hopefully, also 'race' and class).

This chapter begins by establishing the epistemological foundations to feminist inquiry.[1] It shows how feminist researchers approach research and how feminist issues on partiality have wider implications for the validity of mainstream research and educational policy. The second section examines the implications for future feminist research under the ERA. Through the organization of funding arrangements and, by ignoring the substantial body of feminist research on education, issues of inequality are being ousted from the research and educational-reform agenda. The Conservative government is able to use the mythology of the 'family' as a blatant ideological prop to disguise the inequalities it engineers. Interestingly it was hoist by its own hypocrisy recently when it tried to extend its family-ideology campaign to wider issues in the 'Back to Basics' campaign which targeted single mothers as the evil doers of the nation. The public came to realize that it was Conservative MPs that were responsible for creating many of them. The implications of 'family-values' propaganda and its impact upon educational reform is explored in the final section.

The central argument of this chapter is that the ERA is a specifically gendered (and 'raced') piece of legislation that represents an attack on all work that challenges inequalities. It is part of what Whitty (1990) identifies as a short-term measure designed to ensure that the pervasive collectivist welfare ideology of the post-war era is restrained. By setting an educational agenda, through a National Curriculum, which either ignores gender explicitly, or mystifies gendered power relations in the vacuous term 'the family', the inequalities that are reproduced through schooling are likely to continue, if not become worse. Feminist research is therefore essential to monitor and counter the effects of this blatant piece of social and moral engineering. Because feminist research takes power as a central organizing principle of social relations, it is able to make apparent the underlying interests that inform educational reform. Feminist research on the family is particularly helpful in pointing out the contradictions between government rhetoric and women's everyday reality. The chapter begins with a discussion of the practices of feminist research. I do this, because so many of the debates seem unfamiliar to educational theorists.

Doing Feminist Research

Feminist researchers are not a homogeneous group; they inhabit as many positions as do male researchers. Most subject disciplines have feminist researchers (see Spender, 1980). It is also difficult to define the haphazard development of feminist research since 1970, when Golde edited the first feminist methodology text, *Women in the Field*. The history of feminist research lies as much in practitioner and activist research (such as teachers and rape crisis centres) as in its interdisciplinary form in academia. It also operates at many levels: policy, ethnography, action, pragmatism, etc. There are also differences between the feminist theory that informs feminist methodology and that which informs practice. For the purposes of this chapter, I adopt Guba's (1990) model of three fundamental research questions that inform the constitution of any research project. These interrogate each level of the research process, demonstrating how knowledge is produced:

1 What is there that can be known — what is knowable? This is the *ontological* question; it deals with the assumptions one is willing to make about the nature of reality.
2 What is knowledge and what is the relationship of the knower to the known? This is the *epistemological* question. The assumption that one makes about how knowledge is produced depends on how one conceives of reality (ontology).
3 How do we find things out? This is the *methodological* question. How this is answered depends on what decisions have been made about ontology and epistemology.

The Ontological Question

In response to the ontological question, feminist research begins from the premise that the nature of reality in western society is unequal and hierarchical, in which women have less access to positions of economic security and power. Believing that social order is organized on the basis of inequality, the knowledge to which women have access is considered to be different to that of men (obviously also circumscribed by class and 'race'). Ontology also asks what is there that can be known? Because women and men have differential *access* to economic and discursive positions, the gendered knowledge produced is likely to be dissimilar.[2] Rattansi (1992) argues that we have different discursive resources that we draw on to make discursive configurations — the way ideas and arguments are given shape. Hence our social location, our situatedness in the world will influence how we speak, see, hear and know. My own feminist research suggests that women have access to a great deal of information about masculinity, all of which assumes positions of responsibility such as for the emotional management of relationships and men and as a great deal of cultural output is about male anxiety (film, literature, art, etc.), women learn a great deal about men. Men, however, have restricted access to knowledge about women and, as recent surveys have shown, they have especially limited knowledge about women's bodies and sexuality.[3] The students I studied were able to use their knowledge of masculinity to undermine its legitimation and power; they were also able to occupy masculine subject positions (such as objectification). It is less likely that men will have a similar amount of knowledge about women or a desire to occupy female subject positions, because there is less social value attached to femininity. Therefore, I argue, women and men have differential access to, and desires for, different gendered knowledge.

This is over-layered, and mediated, through other access positions to discourse, such as 'race' and class. This is not an empirical argument, such as that suggested by Stanley and Wise (1983) who argue that the similarities in women's experience enable research to be feminist. This would deny all the power relations and differences between women. Nor would this argument support a spurious dichotomy between experience versus method (Hammersley, 1992), which ignores how both experience and method are a product of discursive positioning. Rather, it suggests that any feminist ontology needs to take into account the access to, and discursive positions available to, different groups, which are likely to lead to the production of different knowledge. This applies just as much to the researcher as to those being researched. We need to know what partiality, what standpoint and which discursive positions the researcher occupies, to understand what values, interests and power they are likely to represent. When we interrogate something like the ERA we need to know not only why it was produced, in whose interests, whose knowledge is being produced and how power occurs in this process, but also what are the interests of the researcher. It is only then we can understand the contextual validity of the research.

The awareness of access to different discursive positioning, suggests that we can only ever produce partial knowledge. This has led Donna Haraway (1988) to argue for a feminist objectivity. This challenges previous feminist thinking, which dismissed objectivity as the mechanism by which men are able to ignore the gendered production of their work. Haraway, however, argues that objectivity has always been about a particular and specific embodiment. It is about limited location and situated knowledge.

Only partial perspective promises objective vision (1988, p. 583). Therefore, there can never be an unmediated account. Unlocatable knowledge, Haraway argues, is irresponsible knowledge. Irresponsible necessitates being called to account. Phillips (1990) argues that what is crucial for the objectivity of any inquiry is the critical spirit in which it has been carried out:

'Objectivity' is the label that is used for inquiries which are prized because of the great care and responsiveness to criticism with which they have been carried out. Inquiries are stamped as subjective when they have not been sufficiently opened to the light of reason and criticism. (Phillips, 1990, p. 34)

This is what we need to do with the ERA — we need to ask of any research on it: in which partiality is it located? And we also need to ask, if it has been subject to rigorous inquiry. Knowing, the aim of all research, is a political process, so all knowledge is intrinsically political (Ramazanoglu, 1992).

The Epistemological Question

This can be developed in relation to epistemology. A feminist epistemology (the nature and grounds of knowledge) depends on how we conceive of reality (ontology) and how we study it (methodology). A feminist ontology would argue that knowledge is always partial and always produced for particular interest. The marginality of women and their lack of access to formal institutional knowledge production means that their interests and voices are less likely to be heard and are always measured against the universalisms promoted by those who speak from positions of power. A feminist epistemology would suggest that the distribution of knowledge is one means by which a particular form of masculinity becomes institutionalized. Feminist epistemology also considers what kind of things can be known, who can be a knower and how beliefs are legitimated as knowledge. So in relation to the ERA feminist research asks: What are the outcomes of legislation that presumes to know about education? What does it know and why? Why does it not know about the knowledge which has been excluded? How has this come about? It also asks what the relationship of the knower is to the known. Many male researchers are normalized in the process of research; they are able to leave their gender, and its accompanying institutionalized power positions, unquestioned. For instance, the majority of research on classroom interaction, or on power relations in the classroom ignores sexuality as a ubiquitous organizing principle. Warren (1988) points out that, even when sexuality is mentioned by male social scientists, they frequently refer to the pervasiveness and power of sexual urges, rather than to the institutionalized power to which feminists refer. Moreover, Kelly (1992) notes how heterosexuality is so 'normal' that it is not noticed by most researchers. Yet, the researcher inhabits the same power relations of gender, 'race' and class inside, as well as outside, the research.

Mies (1983) suggests the importance of studying crisis or ruptures in the pattern of normality, so that the pathology of the normal may be perceived. Stanley and Wise (1983) argue that maleness, heterosexuality and whiteness (I'd add middle-classness) all work by being states of *unawareness* in which the key power of the privileged groups lies in not noticing their privilege. Gender operates as a vehicle that 'naturalizes' power asymmetries; yet gender is also a category that women have to live and confront on a daily basis (Riley,

1987). Some feminist researchers have stressed the role of empathy (Stanley and Wise, 1983). This, however, can ignore other inequalities, such as 'race' and gender, that make empathy impossible. It may be more useful to learn from cultural theory which suggests that responses to researchers may be structured through points of resistance. We need to know what, and how, points of resistance operate between the researcher and the researched to understand how the knowledge of the research was conducted with, through and against power relations.

Early feminist research argued that the power relations between the researcher and the researched should be non-hierarchical. This is now dismissed as naive by those who point to the need for an acknowledgment of power and difference between women. All agree, however, that research should not be produced which could lead to oppression of the researched. Oakley (1981) suggests that researchers should productively use their power by giving any useful knowledge that they have to the researched. Feminist researchers recognize their responsibility to those being researched. They operate an ethical code in which the surveillant, objectifying aspects of research are put under scrutiny (see Walkerdine, 1986). Bhavnani (1994) suggests that the crucial question for all (feminist) researchers to ask is 'does the analysis reinscribe the researched into powerlessness, pathologized, without agency?'

The desire not to reproduce inequality in the process of research has led many feminist theorists to suggest that men cannot do feminist research because of the wider social relations that they occupy which give them the power to look at women.[4] Vision is always a question of the power to see (Haraway, 1988). The male gaze is institutionalized through the media, arts, film, literature, etc. and it gives men the legitimacy to look publicly at women. Valerie Walkerdine (1984) suggests that the power of the researcher to objectify and scrutinize the 'subject' of research is a process similar to that of the male gaze.[5] This process becomes even more complex if one takes into account the work of Lacan (1977), reworked through a feminist theory, to suggest that the category 'woman' is itself the product of male fantasy (Walkerdine, 1989).[6]

The Methodological Question

I shall now turn to the methodological question of how we find things out. Again it is very difficult to construct a sense of homogeneous feminist response. In fact I've argued elsewhere that research can be feminist if it draws on feminist theory; centres on gender (and its relation to heterosexuality, 'race' and class); exposes power relationships in the structuring of difference and inequalities; and if the research can be transformative (Skeggs, 1994). This does not mean there is a feminist methodology. It is the underlying ontology and epistemology that define research as feminist. The methods we use are not gendered; it is the use to which we put them that is. It is similar to capital, which also is not gendered, but through struggles between groups with differential amounts of power becomes so. So, whilst quantitative methods have been seen to be historically in the province of men, and have been used against powerless groups, this does not mean that they have to remain associated with masculinity; different methods become gendered in the process of their use (see Kelly *et al.*, 1992).

Dickens *et al.* (1983) argue:

> Demands that feminists produce a unique methodology act to circumscribe the impact of feminism . . . We feel it is time to abandon what amounts to a defensive strategy. It has to be recognised that feminist research is not a specific, narrow methodology, but research informed at every stage by an acknowledged political commitment. (Dickens, 1983, p. 2)

The methods used are simply the means to carry out research that will lead to the transformation of the inequalities that women experience. These inequalities are not just related to gender; white feminist theory is becoming increasingly aware of the interrelationships between gender, 'race', class and sexuality. Denise Riley (1987), for instance, has suggested that because of the complex cultural connections between the different structural and discursive features in women's lives, the category 'woman' is no longer appropriate to describe the homogeneous nature of women's experience. Women are never just women. The noun 'womanhood' is only meaningful — indeed only exists — with reference to a fusion of adjectives which symbolize particular historical trajectories, material circumstances and cultural experiences (Brah, 1992).

However, Riley (1987) argues that the category 'women' should still be used to organize political struggle. Feminist research can respond in a similar way, using the category 'woman' to interrogate differences between women (Hooks, 1984). For instance, Gorelick (1991) argues that we must trace how the processes of racism, imperialism, class and national, religious and sexual oppression are connected to each other and determine, in very different patterns, the lives of all and each of us. If we only concentrate on differences between genders, the complementary system of heterosexuality is reproduced (Roman and Apple, 1990). Gender is an essential tool to help us understand other variables (Gelsthorpe, 1992).

Rather than centring just on the 'experience' of women, feminist research now centres on power.[7] Opposition to male power (be it structural, institutional, discursive or interactional) is one of the central organizing principles that, feminists argue, unites all women, of whatever difference. Feminist research is not research about women, but research for women, to be used in transforming sexist society. An assumption of feminist research is that knowledge must be elicited and analysed in a way that can be used by women to alter oppressive and exploitative conditions in their society (Cook and Fonow, 1986). This is why it is unlikely that many men will be interested in pursuing feminist research; they would have to pursue research for the benefit of women. It would mean that they would have to oppose the power they benefit from, and often reproduce unconsciously, on a day-to-day basis. This is also why it would be impossible to study rape, domestic violence and pornography, etc., from a perspective that claims 'neutrality'. Female researchers (not always feminist) are positioned in gendered power relations that, on a daily basis, reproduce their gendered inequality. Sexual harassment is not absent from the research process (see Warren, 1988; Skeggs, 1992).

Fine and Gordon (1991) also suggest that feminist research would involve the study of *what is not* by disrupting prevailing notions of what is inevitable, what is seen to be natural and what is considered impossible. They argue that we need to document what is not measured by studying the damage of *not* changing social conditions — such as not providing decent sex education, not providing HIV/AIDS awareness campaigns, not pursuing research that takes gender, 'race', sexuality and class into account. By illustrating what is not yet imaginable, through the construction of new representations and frameworks (such as sex education that deals with female desire), Fine and Gordon maintain that research can be productive in challenging inequalities rather than reproductive. Thus, feminist research sets its own agenda. However, this is becoming increasingly difficult as the next section will demonstrate.

The Possibilities for Feminist Research in the ERA Climate

This section examines how the future of feminist research is precarious. Lack of research funding defines gender as inconsequential, as an issue not worthy of consideration. This is consolidated by the ignorance of policy makers and other researchers who (choose?) to ignore gender, enabling a hegemonic educational agenda to remain in place. This sets firm limits on the range of educational knowledge available.

Feminist research (like antiracist,, antielitist, and lesbian and gay research) usually confronts the status quo. One thing the British Conservative government has taught us is that it does not appreciate this sort of research; it is at odds with the attempt to promote social order through the mythic creation of a 'family'. Rarely is research directly censored, an exception being when Margaret Thatcher intervened directly to stop the ESRC's study on sexual behaviour. Rather, funding is made more difficult for research projects that do not fit the political agenda. It is the ability to set the agenda that demonstrates the operation of government power. Fortunately, because the research-funding bodies are so diverse and bureaucratic, it is possible to evade direct control. However, the fear of being dismantled, or of prosecution (under Section 28), has established a culture of self-surveillance, in which high-risk projects that do not fit the political agenda are deemed to be too hazardous. Thankfully also, the political agenda is confused and contradictory; some of the important work on sex education has been funded through the DHS rather than the DES/DFE. Educational funding bodies increasingly suggest that only designated policy research will be funded.

LEAs are suffering from the concerted attacks on local government. This has had an impact not only on direct funding of research projects, but also on the GRIST funding it once allocated. The transfer of development and training budgets to schools, through LMS and opting-out, means that research which challenges the status quo is less likely to be funded, not necessarily because it is seen to be threatening, but because other priorities have been established. 'Professional' development is one means whereby the research agenda can be set. The increasing survivalist mentality of teachers suggests that any research that does not fit into their attempts to deal with the National Curriculum may be seen as less important. Secondments and the funding of teacher research are also decreasing. Many teachers now self-fund their research as an investment in their future careers. Investments are less likely to be made in areas that are designated controversial and may restrict promotional opportunities. For instance, research that mentions sexuality is increasingly unlikely to appear on the agenda (Kelly, 1992).

The ESRC still funds research that does not fit neatly with government rhetoric, but the numbers of funded, full-time research students in education are rapidly decreasing. One paradox in the decrease in funding for feminist, educational, doctoral research and the promotion of market forces may be that those who can afford to pay for themselves will continue to pursue research that cannot be controlled. However, internal university research scholarships are harder to come by, and university pump-priming funds are unlikely to be given unless the research can be shown to be likely to generate further national funding.

The opportunity for women to become researchers, especially working-class women (black and white) has, as Deem (1981) noted, been dependent upon, not only educational openings, but also the provision of child-care facilities. Failure to fund, and direct cuts on, pre-school education has increased the responsibilities of women who want to pursue or continue with study, but, interestingly, has not decreased their involvement in education: over four-fifths of the increase in part-time student numbers between 1980–1 and 1988–9 has been women (*Social Trends,* 21, 1991). This, David (1991) argues, signifies the increasingly complex and 'public' nature of women's social lives; women are now taking on responsibility for education as well as mothering and paid employment. However, cuts in adult education and the shifting of research funding from adult to school education suggest a lack of concern with 'non-traditional' students, likely to last as long as numbers can be found elsewhere (Johnson, 1992). However, the effect of these funding restrictions on type of output is not known. It is somewhat ironic that the majority of feminist research in education was published well after the 1979 election. The resilience of feminist researchers and the pervasiveness of feminism cannot be underestimated.

Even when research is carried out which shows how gendered inequality structures classroom life, policy makers are often able to ignore it. This is clearly evident in the lack of action in schools, colleges and universities to deal with the problem of sexual harassment experienced mainly by girls, but also by women teachers. Evidence for this has been well documented by: Halson (1989); Beynon (1989); Cunnison (1989); Cowie and Lees (1981); Holly (1989); Jones (1985); Kelly (1989); Lees (1986); Mahoney (1989); Ramazanoglu (1987); Skeggs (1991a); Walkerdine (1981); Wolpe (1988); Willis (1977). The history of feminist research suggests that not only is it ignored by policy makers but, sadly, often by other researchers. Even when research sets out specific policy directives, those with power can decide whether or not to implement them. Or, even when funding criteria specifically promote equal opportunities, as happened with the TVEI, in practice this has to be set against other school policies, and the general individualism and competitiveness of schooling that besets such initiatives.

None of this should surprise us when we note the absence of gender from the directives of policy makers, and how low gender is on the teacher unions' agenda. The implementation and design of the National Curriculum ignored issues of gender, 'race', class and sexuality; Duncan Graham claimed they were 'too delicate' (Arnot, 1992). It also failed to take into account the recommendations of the EOC (1989). Working groups have not, to date, taken a stand on the promotion of antisexism or antiracism. Miles and Middleton (1990) document the lack of anything other than lip-service to equal opportunity in the ERA. In fact, they suggest that it is likely to reinforce inequality through its hidden curriculum on gender and place in jeopardy the small number of equal-opportunity initiatives that have been undertaken. They cite the use of sexist language in the working of the Act as an example of the priority accorded to gender. Burton and Weiner (1990) argue that the subject content and pedagogy of the National Curriculum have regressed to styles that reassert male-centred forms of knowledge. The demise of cross-curricular themes, the only area where issues of gender were likely to appear in a critical fashion, suggests the setting of an education agenda undisturbed by issues of inequality. Yet feminist educational research over the last twenty years has shown us that gender (femininity and masculinity) is an ubiquitous and damaging feature of classroom life.

So, we see the multitude of different ways in which gender is made invisible or irrelevant to schooling. It can be included in schooling as a token gesture, written into policy documents but with no support, resources, evaluation or monitoring. It can be part of a more general policy adoption (as in the TVEI case) but, then, its effects have to be set against the rest of the internal discourses of the school. If these internal discourses remain unchallenged they will continue to reproduce inequalities as 'normal'. Gender can be lodged off the educational agenda by rewriting it through other more powerfully promoted discourse, such as the family, as will now be discussed.

Setting the Agenda

The Centre for Contemporary Cultural Studies notes:

> The family is not . . . a merely dependent institution, with no deter-
> minacy of its own. It is not merely transformed by capitalism and
> by the development of schooling; it, or its salient relations, also con-
> tribute to the complex determinations on schooling in absolutely central
> ways. Indeed, it has systematically shaped the very conception of
> 'education' itself. (CCCS, 1980, p. 25)

It is this which the government needs to understand when it attempts to include 'family values' on the educational agenda. The family is not simply an ideological term which can be filled with political values. It is a lived social relationship, with institutional and structural forms. It may operate as a social metaphor in the world of film and television but, feminist research suggests, it is unlikely that its metaphoric nature can be transferred successfully to the education system.

The initial impact of the Thatcher government was on economic and family policy rather than education and local government. Nor did the first Thatcher government use explicitly antifeminist statements (Kelly, 1992), (as the Moral Right in the United States was able to do through the Reagan government, Dworkin (1983)).[8] Rather, as David (1991) has shown, by elevating the 'family' as central to social stability and moral rectitude, a different set of values was established to replace the small public (and educational) space that feminist arguments had won. The nostalgic idealization of motherhood in the 'family values' propaganda is not dissimilar to the remythification of the colonial past (Mercer, 1988). This idealization is now being used in the 'Back to Basics' campaign. It is an attempt to create a discursive shift from gender to a supposedly ungendered family; from inequality to social stability. The focus on the family is also an attempt by the government to relinquish responsibility for social problems as Peter Lilley (Social Security Secretary) noted at the Conservative party conference, asserting that it was no longer possible to argue that unemployment, poor housing or poverty caused social problems, he pointed to the collapse of the traditional family (see *The Guardian,* 8 October 1993, p. 7 for full report).

The emphasis on 'parent power' in the educational reforms is, however, specifically about gender. As David (1991) notes, a sexual division of labour emerges between the different responsibilities that parents are seen to have: fathers are to make organizational and economic decisions, mothers are to become increasingly involved in educational provision. As David notes:

> Women as mothers will, in all likelihood, be expected to care for, and
> be involved in the regular and daily schooling of their children, whilst

at the same time now involved in extra-curricular activities as parents, such as school governors, and also in paid forms of employment, including as teachers. They may also be involved, whilst bringing up children, in the education process itself, on the assumption that education can bring about improvement not only in their own lives, but also those of their children. (David, 1991, p. 445)

Moreover, the ideological emphasis on 'parent power' is based on a model of a family that is indeed rare in England: the heterosexual couple with children represents only one quarter of all families. The majority of households are headed by single women. Thus when the government speaks of the family and 'parent power' its message may conflict with the everyday experience of most 'families'. The educational reforms have not taken into account the reality of women's lives and so their rhetoric may have little impact. In fact, the media ridiculing of the 'Back to Basics' campaign may suggest that rhetoric can never work when it is so distanced from reality. This gap between rhetoric and women's lives has led some feminists (Segal, 1983) to argue that this is why the tide of feminist consciousness has not been stopped.

The promotion of a 'rights' discourse in the ERA is another way of moving issues of inequality off the educational agenda. 'Rights' encode the power to 'choose' as democratic, thereby deflecting attention away from the question of who has access to 'choose'. Also, as 'rights' are given to parents and families, they are withheld from women as a social group, and from lesbians and gay men. When governors are given 'rights' over sex education they are taken away from teachers and children, or given back when the government realizes that it may have made a mistake. When parents are given 'rights', mothers are given more work and responsibility (David, 1992). In the giving and taking of 'rights', the State retains the right to intervene.

Rachel Thompson (1992) notes how young people's identities, and ultimately their lives, have become expendable in relation to the public discourse on the family. She documents a battle being fought between moral paternalism ('family' values) and public-health pragmatism in relation to sex and HIV/AIDS education. Thus circular 11/87 points out that: 'the benefits of stable marriage and the responsibility of parenthood are appreciated' (p. 4). While Section 28 (Local Government Act 1988) lays down that: (1) A local authority should not — (b) promote the teaching in any maintained school of the acceptability of homosexuality as a pretended family relationship. This exists alongside Circular 11/87 which speaks of the 'objective and balanced manner' required to discuss sex education (p. 4).

A sex-education programme that takes into account issues of gender, race, class and sexuality is a potential challenge to the government's promotion of the ideal family (Lenskyj, 1990). A sex-education programme that does *not* take account of these issues is likely to lead to an increase in HIV/AIDS, and the promotion of inequality.[9] The research by Holland, Ramazanoglu and Scott (1990) suggests that whilst the responsibility for condom use is given to young women, they do not have the social power to do anything about it, for fear of being labelled and condemned. Traditional sex education, which promotes girls as receptors of uncontrollable male urges, reproduces the socio-biological argument that men cannot be held responsible for the sexual violence that they commit (Wolpe, 1987; see also Aggleton, Homans and Warwick, 1989). Szirom's (1988) research concludes that boys only consider their own satisfaction to be important in sex-education lessons. The silencing of female sexuality operates to deny women autonomy over their own bodies and lives (Measor, 1989; Kelly, 1992). Fine (1988) defines this as the authorized suppression of a discourse of female sexual desire. More disturbing, this has meant that sexual abuse is being left undetected, because children do not have the language to articulate their experiences. The silencing of lesbian and gay sexuality denies the realities and complexities of young people's lives (Kelly, 1992). Worse, one in five of lesbian and gay pupils interviewed by Trenchard and Warren (1987) had attempted suicide. The failure to challenge the power relations underpinning heterosexism, and the male dominance within it, means that girls are continually undermined by what Holly (1989) defines as a 'predatory heterosexual environment'. Kelly (1992) argues:

> So long as sexuality is not regarded as a basic equal opportunities issue, the only or dominant form of sexuality which is affirmed in schools is a macho male heterosexuality. The majority of students are not only excluded in this process, but are potential targets for abuse from those boys, young and adult men who choose to use this potential source of power over others. (Kelly, 1992, p. 32)

Yet another contradiction emerges in the distance between Conservative-party rhetoric and everyday reality. The public forum contains increasing amounts of sexually explicit materials: Madonna, for instance, incessantly demands a woman's right to the expression of her sexuality; young women's magazines can openly talk about the clitoris. Yet schools are silenced on the same issues.

It is not only the New Right, in its contradictory struggles, who have attempted to wipe challenges to family life off the political agenda (Durham, 1990), seeing feminism as an 'ideological extravagance', 'deeply inimical to the family' (Centre for Policy Studies, in Campbell, 1987). The ERA was introduced at a time when concerted media campaigns had attempted to trivialize antisexist and antiracist campaigns. The liberal backlash to left-wing educational initiatives, conducted in the name of a challenge to 'political correctness' is part of the general discursive condition produced by those threatened by any challenge to themselves and the status quo.

This discursive condition is also apparent in theory. Some versions of post-modernism dismiss the concern with inequality as unfashionable (see Skeggs, 1991b). Fortunately, few educationalists fell for the marketing of

postmodernism's seductively easy analysis. However, there has been a movement away from the principles of social democracy that informed feminist
educational theory and practice (Kelly, 1992). It is now realized that social
democratic principles only reinforce individualism and the sexual divisions
within and between the public and private domains. These strands have im-
pacted in different ways to delegitimate the study of power and inequality.
The lack of a coherent oppositional response to the ERA may be a product of
this process (Arnot, 1992).

This article is part of an attempt to scrutinize how power and inequality
appear on an education and public agenda. It has been shown that even when
faced with public discreditation (through political campaigns), decreasing funding for research, a wilful ignorance of feminist research from formulations
of government policy, and an attempt to occupy the educational agenda with
family values that both silence and reproduce inequality, feminist research
continues. It is tenacious. It is creative in finding funding: the DHS and local
government have been sources for health-education research. Private sponsorship is also possible: the Wellcome Foundation funded the sexuality research
censored by Thatcher.

We should not forget the knowledge that previous feminist research
on education has provided, such as: the interrelationships between gender,
race, class, sexuality and nation; the gendering of classroom interaction; the
sexualizing of schooling; the legitimation of the use of school space by boys
to the detriment of girls; the mastery of reason; the problems with critical
pedagogy; the sexist teaching materials that can be used; the gendering of
school knowledge; the access to school subjects; the gendering of resources;
the domestication of working-class girls' schooling; the 'trial by maleness'
that boys have to endure to prove themselves and the way in which schools
produce gendered, governable subjects.[10] Nor should we forget the feminist
theory that has informed methodology and wider social issues, such as the
construction of rationality and the discursive production of knowledge.

The key issues for educational research in the future are to investigate
how all educational reforms impact upon class, gender and 'race'. This will
involve monitoring the effects of appraisal and merit payments on a predominantly female workforce and examining the effects of opting out. The absence
or presence of equal-opportunity policies and sex education will be of central
importance here. How governors are trained is also central to equal opportunity issues (see Deem, 1989). Monitoring of the use and meaning of parental
'rights' (for as David (1991) has noted, 'parent' has become the public term for
'mother') is needed. Evaluation of the professional development that teachers
receive; provision, admission and selection to grant-maintained schools (EOC,
1989) is also a gendered issue, as is membership of assessment and testing and
curriculum working groups. All these educational reforms need to be kept
under scrutiny.

Whether any Conservative moral stronghold can be built into the education system remains to be seen. At this moment, the government's values for

education seem to lag behind even the media representations of gender, 'race' and sexuality, not to mention reality. The feminist consciousness that is now being documented amongst school and college students (see Frazer, 1989; McRobbie, 1991; Skeggs, 1991a) is in advance of the teachers, and certainly way ahead of the educational planners. This is not to deny the important inroads that teachers have made through antisexist and antiracist work. For this we should be grateful. Rather, it suggests that educational reforms which promote values of inequality and divisiveness may not be as successful as was first anticipated. The hegemonic battle continues.

Notes

1   I wish to thank with gratitude and appreciation Val Atkinson, University of York and Erica Stratta, Worcester College of Higher Education for their sharp commentary.

2   Harstock, N. (1983) argues that because of the different material positioning of women, they occupy a particular standpoint. Standpoint theory is hotly debated in feminist theory (see Harding, 1991 and Alcoff and Potter, 1993).

3   See recent surveys in *Cosmopolitan*, *Company*, *She* and *Marie Claire*. Whilst these do not comply with the standards of social science research, they are useful indicators of general discursive knowledge.

4   Kremer (1990) argues that it is unlikely that men could do feminist research because they are usually outside of the generation of theoretical ideas that informed particular responses to methodology. Hammersley (1992) writes about feminist research having not done it nor been involved in the generation of any feminist ideas on methodology. In so doing he makes many mistakes (see *Sociology*, vol. 26. no. 2).

5   Fernando (1992) argues that black people have also been divested of subjecthood, as objects of white scrutiny and classification. So the process of objectification needs to be carefully set against sexism and racism.

6   Lacan (1977) argues that, under patriarchy, men (obviously only those who have power are able to put their ideas into distribution and circulation) create as their object not women as they really are, but fantasies of what men both desire and fear in the other. Walkerdine (1989) argues that women, then, become the repositories of such fantasies. Gorelick (1991) maintains that women are likely to feel a different relationship to the researched, if they are female, because 'the woman' is subject to finding herself mirrored in them.

7   The concept 'experience' divides many feminist theorists. Some, classified as empiricists, believe that women's experience is the basis of all feminist knowledge. But as Harding (1991) points out, it cannot be that women's experiences in themselves or the things that women say provide reliable grounds for knowledge claims about social relations. After all, experience is shaped by social relations and access to particular ways of experiencing.

8   Although the New Right in the mid-1980s identified feminist as a threat to social order, see R. Tingle (1986).

9   Juhasz (1990) shows how in the representation of HIV/AIDS in mainstream TV documentaries, that the threat that women currently pose is not just viral transmission but the very gains of the feminist movement.

10 Riddell (1990) already suggests that as the National Curriculum becomes more complicated it resembles the option choice system.

References

AGGLETON, P., HOMANS, H. and WARWICK, I. (1989) 'Health education, sexuality and AIDS', in. WALKER, S. and BARTON, L. (Eds) *Politics and the Process of Schooling*, Milton Keynes, Open University Press.

ALCOFF, L. and POTTER, E. (1993) (Eds) *Feminist Epistemologies*, London, Routledge.

ARNOT, M. (1992) 'Feminism, education and the New Right', in ARNOT, M. and BARTON, L. (Eds) *Voicing Concerns: Sociological Perspectives on Contemporary Education Reforms*, Wallingford, Triangle.

BEYNON, J. (1989) 'A school for men: An ethnographic case study of routine violence in schooling', in WALKER, S. and BARTON, L. (Eds) *Politics and the Process of Schooling*, Milton Keynes, Open University Press.

BHAVNANI, K.K. (1994) 'Tracing the contours: Feminist research and feminist objectitivy', in AFSHAR, H. (Ed) *Feminist Understandings of Race and Gender*, London, Macmillan.

BRAH, A. (1992) 'Difference, diversity and differentiation', in DONALD, J. and RATTANSI, A. (Eds) *'Race', Culture and Difference*, London, Sage.

BURTON, L. and WEINER, G. (1990) 'Social justice and the National Curriculum', *Research Papers in Education*, 5. pp. 203–27.

CAMPBELL, B. (1987) *The Iron Ladies*, London, Virago.

CCCS (1980) *Unpopular Education*, London, Hutchinson.

COOK, J.A. and FONOW, M.M. (1986) 'Knowledge and women's interests: Issues of epistemology and methodology in feminist sociological research', *Sociological Inquiry* 56, pp. 2–29.

COWIE, C. and LEES, S. (1981) 'Slags or drags', *Feminist Review*, 9, Autumn, pp. 17–33.

CUNNISON, S. (1989) 'Gender joking in the staffroom', in ACKER, S. (Ed) *Teachers, Gender and Careers*, London, Falmer Press.

DAVID, M. (1983) 'Sex, education and social policy: A new moral economy', in WALKER, S. and BARTON, L. (Eds) *Gender, Class and Education*, Lewes, Falmer Press.

DAVID, M. (1991) 'A gender agenda: Women and the family in the new ERA?', *British Journal of Sociology of Education* 12, 4, pp. 433–46.

DAVID, M. (1992) 'Parents and the state: How has social research informed education reforms', in ARNOT, M. and BARTON, L. (Eds) *Voicing Concerns: Sociological Perspectives on Contemporary Education Reforms*, Wallingford, Triangle.

DEEM, R. (1981) 'State policy and ideology in the education of women 1944–1980', *British Journal of Sociology of Education* 12, 2, pp. 131–44.

DEEM, R. (1989) 'The new school governing bodies — are gender and race on the agenda?', *Gender and Education*, 1, 3, pp. 247–60.

DICKENS, L. *et al.* (1983) 'Is feminist methodology a red herring?', Letter to the editor of *Network* (Newsletter of the British Sociological Association), 26, 2 May.

DURHAM, M. (1990) *Sex and Politics: The Family and Morality in the Thatcher Years*, London, Macmillan.

DWORKIN, A. (1983) *Right Wing Women*, London, The Women's Press.

EOC (1989) *Gender Issues: The Implications for Schools of the Education Reform Act 1988*, Manchester, EOC.

FERNANDO, S. (1992) 'Blackened images', *Ten8* 2, 3, pp. 140–5.

FINE, M. (1988) 'Sexuality, schooling and adolescent females: The missing discourse of desire', *Harvard Educational Review*, 58, 1, pp. 29–53.

FINE, M. and GORDON, S.M. (1991) 'Effacing the center and the margins', *Feminism and Psychology* 1, 1, pp. 19–25.

FRAZER, E. (1989) 'Feminist talk and talking about feminism: Teenage girls' discourses of gender', *Oxford Review of Education*, 15, 3, pp. 281–90.

GELSTHORPE, L. (1992) 'Response to Martyn Hammersley's paper on feminist methodology', *Sociology*, 26, 2, pp. 213–19.

GOLDE, P. (1970/1986) *Women in the Field: Anthropological Experiences*, Berkeley, University of California Press.

GORELICK, S. (1991) 'Contradictions of feminist methodology', *Gender & Society* 5, 4, pp. 459–77.

GRAHAM, D. (1992) *The Guardian*, 14 October.

GUBA, E.G. (1990) 'Subjectivity and objectivity', in EISNER, E.W. and PESHKIN, A. (Eds) *Qualitative Inquiry in Education: The Continuing Debate*, Columbia University, New York, Teachers College Press.

HALSON, J. (1989) 'The sexual harassment of young women', in HOLLY, L. (Ed) *Girls and Sexuality: Teaching and Learning*, Milton Keynes, Open University Press.

HAMMERSLEY, M. (1992) 'On feminist methodology', *Sociology* 26, 2, pp. 187–207.

HARAWAY, D. (1988) 'Situated knowledges: The science question in feminism and the privilege of partial perspective', *Feminist Studies*, 14, 3, pp. 575–99.

HARDING, S. (1991) *Whose Science, Whose Knowledge*, Buckinghamshire, Open University Press.

HARSTOCK, N. (1983) 'The feminist standpoint: Developing the ground for a specifically feminist historical materialism', in HARDING, S. and HINTIKKA, M. (Eds) *Discovering Reality: Feminist Perspectives on Epistemology, Metaphysics, Methodology and Philosophy of Science*, Dordrecht. Reidel Publishing Co.

HMSO (1992) *Choice and Diversity: A New Framework for Schools*, London, HMSO.

HOLLAND, J., RAMAZANOGLU, C. and SOCTT, S. (1990) 'From panic stations to power relations: Sociological perspectives and problems', *Sociology* 24, 3, pp. 499–518.

HOLLY, L. (1989) (Ed) *Girls and Sexuality: Teaching and Learning*, Milton Keynes, Open University Press.

HOOKS, B. (1984) *Feminist Theory: From Margin to Center*, Boston, South End Press.

JOHNSON, A. (1992) 'Changing research focus', Paper presented to ERG (Educational Research Group) University of York, 16 June 1992.

JONES, C. (1985) 'Sexual tyranny in mixed schools', in WEINER, G. (Ed) *Just a Bunch of Girls*, Milton Keynes. Open University Press.

JUHASZ, A. (1990) 'The contained threat: Women in mainstream aids documentary', *Journal of Sex Education*. 27, 1. pp. 25–46.

KELLY, L. (1989) 'Our issues, our analysis: Two decades of work on sexual violence', in JONES, C. and MAHONY, P. (Eds) *Learning our Lines: Sexuality and Social Control in Education*, London, The Women's Press.

KELLY, L. (1992) 'Not in front of the children: Responsibility to right-wing agendas on sexuality and education', in ARNOT, M. and BARTON, L. (Eds) *Voicing Concerns: Sociological Perspectives on Contemporary Educational Reforms*, Wallingford, Triangle.

KELLY, L., REGAN, L. and BURTON, S. (1992) 'Defending the indefensible? Quantitative methods and feminist research', in HINDS, H. PHOENIX, A. and STACEY, J. (Eds) *Working Out: New Directions for Women's Studies*, London, Falmer Press.

KREMER, B. (1990) 'Learning to say No: Keeping Feminist Research for Ourselves', *Women's Studies International Forum*, 13, 5, pp. 463–7.

LACAN, J. (1977) *Ecrits: a selection*, London, Tavistock Books.

LEES, S. (1986) *Losing Out: Sexuality and Adolescent Girls*, London, Hutchinson.

LENSKYJ, H. (1990) 'Beyond plumbing and prevention: Feminist approaches to sex education', *Gender and Education*, 2, pp. 217–30.

LUKES, S. (1975) *Power: a Radical View* London, Macmillan.

LORDE, A. (1984) *Sister Outsider*, New York, Crossing Press.

MAHONEY, P. (1989) 'Sexual violence in mixed schools', in JONES, C. and MAHONEY, P. (Eds) *Learning our Lines: Sexuality and Social Control in Education*, London, Women's Press.

McRobbie, A. (1991) *Feminism and Youth Culture: From Jackie to Just Seventeen*, London, Macmillan.

Measor, L. (1989) 'Are you coming to see some dirty films today? Sex education and adolescent sexuality', in Holly, L. (Ed) *Girls & Sexuality: Teaching and Learning*, Milton Keynes, Open University Press.

Mies, M. (1983) 'Towards a methodology of feminist research', in Bowles, G., Duelli, N. and Klein, R. (Eds) *Theories of Women's Studies*, London, RKP.

Mercer, K. (1988) 'Recording narratives of race and nation', *Black Film, British Cinema*, London, ICA document 7.

Miles, S. and Middleton, C. (1990) 'Girls' education in the balance: The ERA and inequality', in Flude, M. and Hammer, M. (Eds) *The Education Reform Act 1988: Its Origins and Implications*, London, Falmer Press.

Oakley, A. (1981) 'Interviewing women: A contradiction in terms', in Roberts, H. (Ed) *Doing Feminist Research*, London, RKP.

Phillips, D.C. (1990) 'Subjectivity and objectivity: An objective inquiry', in Eisner, E.W. and Peshkin, A. (Eds) *Qualitative Inquiry in Education: The Continuing Debate*, Columbia University, New York, Teachers College Press.

Ramazanoglu, C. (1987) 'Sex and violence in academic life or you can't keep a good woman down', in Hanmer, J. and Maynard, M. (Eds) *Women, Violence and Social Control*, London, Macmillan.

Ramazanoglu, C. (1992) 'On feminist methodology: Male reason versus female empowerment', *Sociology*, 26, 2, pp. 207–13.

Rattansi, A. (1992) 'Changing the subject? Racism, culture and education', in Donald, J. and Rattansi, A. (Eds) *'Race', Culture and Difference*, London, Sage.

Riley, D. (1987) 'Does sex have a history? Women and feminism', *New Formations*, 1, pp. 35–47.

Roman, L.G. and Apple, M.W. (1990) 'Is natualism a move away from positivism? Materialist and feminist approaches to subjectivity in ethnographic research', in Eisner, E.W. and Peshkin, A. (Eds) *Qualitative Inquiry in Education: The Continuing Debate*, Columbia University, New York, Teachers College Press.

Segal, L. (1983) 'The heat in the kitchen', in Hall, S. and Jacques, M. (Eds) *The Politics of Thatcherism*, London. Lawrence and Wishart.

Skeggs, B. (1991a) 'Challenging masculinity and using sexuality', *British Journal of Sociology*, 12, 2, pp. 127–39.

Skeggs B. (1991b) 'Postmodernism: What is all the fuss about?', *British Journal of Sociology of Education* 12, 2, pp. 255–67.

Skeggs, B. (1992) 'Confessions of a feminist researcher', *Sociology Review* 2, 1, pp. 14–18.

Skeggs, B. (1994) 'Producing feminist ethnography', in Maynard, M. and Purvis, J. (Eds) *Researching Women's Lives*, London, Falmer Press.

Spender, D. (1980) *Man-Made Studies*, London, Pergamen Press.

Stanley, L. and Wise, S. (1983) *Breaking Out: Feminist Consciousness and Feminist Research*, Routledge and Kegan Paul.

Szirom, P. (1988) *Teaching Gender? Sex Education and Sexual Stereotypes*, London, Allen and Unwin.

Thompson, T. (1992) 'Unholly alliances: The politics of sex education', Paper presented to Activating Theory Conference, University of York, October.

Tingle, R. (1986) *How Public Funds are used to Promote Homosetuality Among Children and Young People*, London, Pickwick.

Trenchard, L. and Warren, H. (1987) *Something to Tell You*, London, Gay Teenage Group.

Walkerdine, V. (1981) 'Sex, power and pedagogies', *Screen Education* 38, Spring, pp. 14–26.

WALKERDINE, V. (1986) 'Video replay: Families, films and fantasies', in BURGIN, V., DONALD, J. and KAPLAN, C. (Eds) *Formations of Fantasy*, London, Methuen.

WALKERDINE, V. (1989) 'Femininity as performance', *Oxford Review of Education*, 15, 3, pp. 267–79.

WARREN, C.A.B. (1988) *Gender Issues in Field Research*, London, Sage.

WHITTY, G. (1990) 'The new right and the National Curriculum: State control or market forces?', in FLUDE, M. and HAMMER, M. (Eds) *The Education Reform Act 1988: Its Origins and Implications*, London, Falmer Press.

WILLIS, P. (1977) *Learning to Labour; How Working Class Kids Get Working Class Jobs*, Farnborough, Saxon House.

WOLPE, A.M. (1987) 'Sex and schools: Back to the future', *Feminist Review* 28, pp. 37–49.

WOLPE, A.M. (1988) *Within School Walls: The Role Of Discipline, Sexuality and the Curriculum*, London, Routledge.

Chapter 7

Political Commitment in the Study of the City Technology College, Kingshurst

Geoffrey Walford

The Research Context

This chapter considers the relationship between political commitment and research objectivity in a study of a City Technology College conducted between 1987 and 1990.[1] The results of the research have been published in book form (Walford and Miller, 1991) and in a series of articles (e.g., Walford, 1991a and b).

The announcement that the first of the new City Technology Colleges was to be in Solihull was made in February 1987. It led my colleague Henry Miller and me to contemplate conducting research on it, for Solihull is only a few miles from Aston University where we worked, and I had just published an article on an unsuccessful attempt to reintroduce selective education within the borough (Walford and Jones, 1986). We felt well placed to undertake an investigation of the nature and effects of the college.

The study that we eventually conducted used a mixture of qualitative and quantitative research methods. We saw the project as one of describing and analysing a school situation which was of interest in its own right because of its unusual nature. We wished to know what a CTC would be like — how it might differ from other schools, what the curriculum and teaching would be like, what the backgrounds of teachers and pupils would be, and how pupils' experiences in a CTC would differ from those of pupils in other schools. In order to gather information on these topics a 'compressed' ethnographic study was conducted over one term (Walford, 1991c). We also wished to examine the CTC's effect on other nearby schools, so we interviewed local politicians, LEA administrators, the heads and some teachers from neighbouring schools, industrialists, parents and pupils. Overall, our aim was to give an account of the practical effects of government policy at the micro-level. In many ways it was an example of the simple 'nosiness' of the sociologist about how organizations structure themselves, and how these different structures affect the lives of those within them. We expected that there would be an interesting story to tell about the CTC, which many would wish to read.

A Political Motivation

While our interest in undertaking the research might, in part, be explained in terms of the 'nosiness' of the sociologist about organizations and the effects of policy, we did not approach the research with a neutral stance about the CTC concept. Our initial interests in the CTC were linked to my continuing research on private schools (Walford, 1987, 1988; Robson and Walford, 1988) and privatization (Walford, 1990). In fact, we were extremely hostile to the CTC concept and saw it as the first stage of a wider privatization process. We were also firmly against the idea of selection of children for particular schools, especially where the schools involved were designed to be better funded and resourced than nearby schools. We feared such selection would have severe detrimental effects on those children rejected and on other nearby schools. Thus, when we embarked upon this policy evaluation we already had our own ideas about that policy and we wished to expose what we thought the problems were.

Our research was, to a large part, politically motivated. We believed the topic to be worth our research time and effort because of its political importance. The CTCs were surrounded by politics, and represented the first stage of the increased diversity of schools that was the centrepiece of future Conservative education policy. We wished to gain information about the CTC because we hoped that this would influence future political events. Our objective was not to try to influence those involved in the college itself, nor was it to try to influence conservative policy makers at a high level (we had long since given up any ideas that they might be open to logical argument!). However, one of our primary objectives was to present research information and analysis which might have some small influence on the way the national electorate voted in the next General Election.

This centrality of the topic to the Conservative Party education programme not only led us to tackle the research, but also structured the research timetable. To a large extent we 'cut the cloth' to fit the time available within a political context. Thus, following the pattern of previous Conservative governments, it was reasonable to expect that there would be another election during in 1991. We hoped that the results of our research might have some small impact on the result of this election. We hoped to be able to show that the CTC programme had severe problems and was acting to the detriment of many children. We recognized that, if we wanted to make any impact on the result of the election that we expected in 1991, we would have to work very fast on the research. We would also need to present our results in such a way that they would be picked-up by the press and might be of use in the Labour Party's armoury.

Partisanship and Neutrality in Research

On reading the preceding paragraphs many of those on the political Right (and not only those on the Right) would, no doubt, argue that such political motivation automatically invalidates any results of the research. How can partisanship on such a scale be compatible with social science research? Should not social science be neutral and objective in its stance?

My belief is that such partisanship *is* compatible with social science research. Indeed, I take it as axiomatic that the motivation for conducting all research is linked to subjective political evaluations of what is important and unimportant. At the same time I believe that it is still possible (and desirable) to fight for some form of neutrality and objectivity in the way in which research studies are conducted.

This idea is far from new. Weber's idea of value neutrality, for example, has a very similar emphasis. As Hammersley (1992) points out:

> For Weber, the phenomena investigated by the social scientist are
> *defined* in terms of practical values. There is no question of those phe-
> nomena being value free in some absolute sense. At the same time,
> he argues that once defined these phenomena should be investigated
> in a way that (as far as possible) suspends practical value judgements
> in the attempt to discover the truth about them. (Hammersley, 1992,
> p. 104)

In looking at these potential dilemmas, I find an early discussion by Alison Kelly (1978) particularly useful. Kelly's article considers the question of what constitutes feminist research. She argues that feminist research cannot be defined simply as research which supports the aims of feminism as that would imply that the results of research are known in advance. This is unacceptable as the essence of research is that it sets out to explore the unknown. But she agrees with Myrdal (1969) that:

> There is an inescapable *a priori* element in all scientific work. Ques-
> tions have to be asked before answers can be given. The questions are
> all expressions of our interest in the world: they are at bottom
> valuations. (Myrdal, 1969, p. 9)

The motivations of the researchers are thus an important element in whether or not a particular piece of research should be regarded as feminist. In part, it is feminist if the reason for doing the research is feminist. But Kelly feels that this alone is an inadequate criterion, and goes on to reformulate the question 'What is feminist research?' in terms of 'At what points does feminism enter the research process?'

Kelly's model of social research is based largely on her own quantitative, international comparative studies of girls' and boys' achievement in school science. But there is no particular reason why her basic framework of understanding cannot equally well be applied to more qualitative social research, and to all forms of overtly committed research.

In her analysis, Kelly divides the research process into three rather crude stages:

- choosing the research topic and formulating hypotheses;
- carrying out the research and obtaining the results; and
- interpreting the results.

She argues that a feminist commitment enters the research in the first and the third stages, but that researchers should seek to avoid any political or social commitment during the second stage. In particular, she rejects the idea that objectivity and rationality are masculine traits, and that there is a 'masculine bias' embedded in traditional social science methodology. She sees feminist research (and by implication all committed research) as being a catholic activity, embracing a wide range of methodologies, and accepting the results that are produced once the questions have been formulated and the appropriate methods selected. Commitment can enter the process again at the stage of interpretation, after the results have been produced, but not to the extent that unfavourable results are suppressed.

I recognize that this view of feminism has been strongly contested. Stanley and Wise (1983, p. 22), for example, reject Kelly's three-fold division of the research process and her view that particular research methods should not be identified with specific commitments (see also Stanley, 1990), but I hope to show in this chapter that the three-fold classification does have some utility. Its strength is that it forces the researcher to face his or her own subjectivity and commitment, to make these clear and open, and to try to ensure that the 'middle stage' of the research is as free from them as possible. Good research should include a 'search for subjectivity' (Peshkin, 1991, p. 285) which will enable the degree of objectivity of the 'middle stage' to be enhanced. This 'objectivity' is not an absolute, but is part of a process or, as Phillips (1990) argues:

> 'Objectivity' seems to be a label that we apply to inquiries that meet certain procedural standards, but objectivity does not *guarantee* that the results of inquiries have any certainty. (Phillips, 1990, p. 23)

The book, *City Technology College* (Walford and Miller, 1991), covers a variety of different interlinked topics concerned with the college and its relationships with other nearby schools. It thus may be seen as a series of research questions and research results and analyses. In the next two sections I wish to show how Kelly's framework can be applied to some examples from this research.

Quantitative Data

The first example from the study is largely quantitative, and the research process can thus be discussed fairly straightforwardly in terms of Kelly's three-fold scheme. It relates to the closure of one of the secondary schools in the catchment area of the CTC which was announced about a month after the CTC opened. When we first started the research we had not anticipated that such a scheduled closure would occur so quickly, but it led to an immediate and obvious research question: Could the establishment of the City Technology College, Kingshurst be identified as the reason for the closure of a nearby local authority school, Simon Digby School?

To most local teachers, parents and politicians the answer to such a question was unambiguously 'yes' — it seemed almost too obvious to question. The whole catchment area of the CTC, which extended into East Birmingham and North Solihull, had rapidly declining secondary school rolls. Over the years, several schools in the area had been closed to adjust the accommodation available to the decreasing numbers of pupils. One of the schools to close was the old 11–16 Kingshurst Comprehensive School, the buildings of which formed the basis of the new CTC.

In spite of this, and other, recent school closures and the continuing falling rolls in the region, the government's wish to get agreement for at least one CTC before the 1987 General Election meant that it gave substantial financial backing to establish Kingshurst CTC in North Solihull. When, about a month later, Solihull LEA announced that it was entering into a period of consultation over the closure of Simon Digby School it seemed obvious that the reopening of the Kingshurst site had caused an alternative school to be closed instead. It seemed that a clear case of careful planning had been overturned by the introduction of an expensive CTC, and that here was good ammunition for arguing against CTCs. The research question we asked was selected because we thought that we already knew the answer and believed that the answer would show some of the problems of the overall policy.

However, when we actually examined the data (Walford and Miller, 1991, pp. 135–8), we found that the situation was not so simple. The analysis showed (much to our dismay) that it was highly likely that Simon Digby School would have closed whether or not the CTC had been established. In the data collection and analysis stage of the research we attempted to be as objective as we could. We collected all the data to which we had access and interpreted the data in a way which we felt any other fair researcher would agree with. The unfortunate part, from our politically committed viewpoint, was that it did not show what we hoped — it actually weakened the arguments being used by local Labour politicians and trade-unionists.

In spite of this finding, we decided that we had to include these results in the book. Kelly's 'middle stage' of research, in practice, implies the duty to publish results which do not agree with personal commitments. However, Kelly argues that commitment can again enter at the third stage of research

— interpreting the results. In this example of the closure of Simon Digby School our own commitment shows through in the interpretation that we give to the findings. For example, we discuss the variety of possible definitions of space in secondary schools, and argue for the advantages of a generous definition. Further, we consider the wider question of Simon Digby's attempt to become grant-maintained. We argue that the particular conjunction of historic events at that time made it likely that Simon Digby would be forced to close whether or not a CTC was in the area, but that the changed circumstances of just a year or two later would have made the presence of the CTC a significant factor in whether Simon Digby would have closed.

The Ethnographic Record

It is relatively easy to apply Kelly's understanding of how commitment enters research to quantitative examples such as the one above. With ethnographic work, however, the 'three stages' of research are less well defined — they overlap, and the process has a more cyclical nature. The 'middle stage' of striving for objectivity occurs repeatedly. Yet, I would wish to argue that it is useful to again separate out particular aspects of the process and to attempt to conduct that 'middle' stage of the research in as objective a way as possible. I would not wish to deny in any way the fact that subjectivity is embodied within ethnographic work, but I would argue that good ethnography should have an element within the research method where objectivity is sought — even if never achieved.

Four of the chapters in *City Technology College* are derived from my short period of observation and interviewing within the CTC Kingshurst. The formal interviews were mainly conducted towards the end of my stay. The initial period was spent simply trying to understand what being in the CTC was like for staff and pupils. In the usual ethnographic fashion I tried to follow selected staff and pupils through their day. I took very few notes in the classrooms, but recollected at length using a tape recorder at the end of each day. I tried to describe what I had seen in each of the lessons, noting anything which struck me as being routine, unusual, or of special interest. I also noted my conversations with staff and students, and my feelings about how the research was going. Description, hunches, problems and even tentative hypotheses were all jumbled onto the innumerable tapes.

I present below extracts from the tape I made resulting from my first day at the CTC. I have selected this particular tape because I believe it indicates the assumptions that I had about what the CTC would be like before starting the research, and the way in which those assumptions were quickly challenged. This tape should thus be analysed in the search for subjectivity, such that the processes of gathering data on the various topics covered can aspire to be more objective. Looking back on the tape now, I am surprised by the number of topics which occurred in this first tape which became topics which I investigated further. I have indicated in another article (Walford, 1991c) that I was closely 'managed' during the first days of my stay, so it is even more surprising that so many areas of interest should have occurred so quickly. All of these comments come from the first 3/4 hour of tape.

2 October 1989

1 Second of October; Good Morning America. One of those days when you just don't know why on earth you're here. You're still tired because you're away from home again, and you wonder what on earth you are letting yourself in for. You know it's going to be a real strain of a day.

2 Second of October. It's now about six o'clock in the evening, and I'm in the Nelson Building bar drinking a well-deserved gin and tonic . . .

3 It is strange how 'normal' the school is in some senses . . .

4 And there was a lot of wasted time. I mean, most of the kids were totally unoccupied most of the time. They were occupied for just that five or ten minutes in which they were involved in the videoing. The rest of the time they were sitting round doing nothing. Looking, smiling, laughing, as appropriate, but not doing anything constructive at all. And when we replayed the videos there were a few comments about how you might do it better, but it did seem a total waste of time, really. It seemed that the video had been used, ok, to make an end product, and that was good, I suppose, because it made them take it seriously, but I didn't see the point of the video, really.

5 One of the interesting things is that the atmosphere is rather nice. When things went wrong the kids certainly didn't laugh, it was that they wanted things to go well. I noticed one girl in another lesson who stooped down and picked up something that had been dropped on the floor — a piece of equipment, because she thought that was appropriate. Just putting it on a desk out of the way so that it wouldn't get damaged.

6 The kids are *very* working class kids. Very working class. The Brum accents, the friendly Brummies, the 'chummy Brummie' as one of the girls said her 'selling' speech about her friend. They seem very lively and chirpy, but you also wonder what they are going to be like in a few years time. At the moment they are 11, 12, some 'coming on 13' as they made it known. And they are very controllable at the moment, and very nice too, but then most kids are at that age. I just wonder — at another point I was in the registering period for the afternoon, and one boy had come in white trousers, no tie, a rather strange shirt, and he got told off for that — totally non-school uniform basically — but I just wondered how it was going to last, you know, in the next few years.

7 In the lessons there was a lot of talk. Friendly talk, casual talk, very nice talk, very relaxed atmosphere, but I wasn't actually sure that much was happening in that English lesson at all.

8 Assembly was *very* formal. Children lined up outside the entrance to the hall, and filed in to their seats. Staff either sat or stood round the outside. Valerie Bragg was at the back, standing as the kids came in, and left it to the coordinator for Post-16, who was standing at the front. It was very quiet, some music was being played on the piano. When everyone was in, the children were asked to stand — they had been all sitting on seats — and Valerie Bragg walked from the back, down the central aisle, to the front . . .

9 Sat through a two hours biology lesson with him, on flowers and sexual reproduction, which was *long* and fairly tedious. Basically what they did was, in those two hours, look at a diagram first of a flower, explaining what the flower was all about, then looked at a real flower, dismembered it, stuck bits into their books and labelled them, wrote a section — paragraph on each part. Then, moving from there, they watched a video for about twenty minutes, I suppose, in a group, and then clustered round a microscope which had a camera on it which allowed you to see what you would see. There was quite a lot of technology used there, nice to have the camera there and so on . . . but I wasn't clear that the technology was really very vital . . . the kids didn't have any real practical work at all with microscopes — all they did was see what he had done on the one microscope with the camera on it . . . He finished about twenty minutes early, and allowed them to start what was really homework, and we dragged on to four o'clock . . . It wasn't a very exciting lesson.

10 In the lesson where they were 'selling' their friends they said what they liked and disliked. Actually all they liked, in fact. And what their favourite subjects were. The favourite subjects were English and drama often, and a couple of the girls, and I think a boy, made a very special point of saying that they didn't like science at all — which is fascinating.

11 It's interesting the idea of being a CTC. It isn't really in some senses, because there's lots of other things going on. For example, the little girl who showed me round at first was playing a lot of instruments, in the orchestra and so on. And there's also lots of other things going on — sport is important, and drama is important as well.

12 I've remembered the library. It really is very poorly equipped, which means that there are hardly any books in it at all — so few in fact that the books are placed on the shelves face forward to make it look as if there are more books . . . It is actually interesting that there isn't *that* much equipment around. There are the computers, of course, but not really that many computers even.

I would emphasize that these notes were simply talked into a tape-recorder. They record my first impressions, some of which I now feel were unfair. They clearly show my own subjectivity of response to a new situation. Most obviously, the first extract (1), which was made while I was still in bed and worrying about the day ahead, and the second extract (2), which was made in the bar where I debriefed, were typical of the rather self-pitying (but very therapeutic) personal responses that I recorded about my feelings. But many of the other extracts show my subjectivity in other ways. Extracts (4), (7) and (9) seem to imply that I have an idea of teaching and learning which stresses children being 'on task' for as much of the time as possible. Extracts (4) and (9) also show a scepticism about the possible overuse or misuse of sophisticated technology in teaching. The doubts expressed in extract (6) seem to indicate a rather prejudiced view about accents, working-class children and schooling.

Reviewing these notes that I made about that first day, it is clear to me that they were *my* notes. No other researcher would have talked these notes into a tape-recorder. They would have selected a different range of topics, and discussed them in diverse ways. They would have perceived the English and biology lessons in their own unique ways, and remembered a different range of activities that occurred during the day. Yet, I believe it is still possible to use Kelly's three-fold conceptualization of the research process in the analysis of these notes and in the research work that followed.

Social Class

Extract (6) shows that my unstated assumption was that the CTC would select many more middle-class children than it did. I knew that the catchment area was officially supposed to be as 'inner-city' as possible, but I hardly knew the actual area at all before I went there. On the first day of my research period I was clearly still influenced by the middle-class associations of the 'Solihull' location, and the belief that the CTC was likely to select a disproportionate number of middle-class children. My unstated hypothesis was that a disproportionate number of middle-class children would benefit. As the extract shows, this initial hypothesis began to be questioned on the very first day, but it rapidly reformulated itself into a more general one which asked about the social-class backgrounds *and* other characteristics of the selected children. The hypothesis was widened, in part, because I recognized that social class alone was unlikely to provide any ammunition which could be used against the CTC policy. Thus, when pupils were later interviewed and answered questionnaires, there was an extended section which tried to examine the whole process of choice of the CTC and selection by the CTC. The 'hypothesis' was thus committed to trying to find weakness and unfairness in the selection procedure, but in the actual data-collection processes the aim was to be as objective as possible.

Quantitative data were eventually collected on the social-class distribution of the children selected by the college and these were compared with the social-class composition of the area. The samples of children who completed the questionnaire and who were interviewed were selected to be as representative as possible of the pupil populations. The questions were asked in such a way as to give the children a chance to say what they believed to be the case. Clarifications of any possible ambiguities were asked for. Thus, for example, it would have been to my political advantage to have allowed children's description of their father's work as 'manager' to stand uncontested, but the search for objectivity led me to question further and to try to assign children to particular class locations as fairly as possible.

Children were also given time to talk about the selection process, and the analysis was conducted in such a way that all comments were considered and classified. Uncertainties were sometimes classified twice. There is, of course, still subjectivity in the allocation of answers and comments to particular categories and in the choice and definition of categories. But the aim was that any 'reasonable person' would have come to an analysis as close as possible to the one conducted.

The third stage of research, the interpretation, allows subjectivity to enter once again. It became clear that, overall, the CTC was selecting very few children from social class I and II. It would have been possible to have presented the data in a way that suggested that the CTC was that selecting children who were reasonably representative of the social-class distribution of the catchment area. This information is made available in the book, and indeed we make it clear that the middle-class had not made significant inroads to the CTC as some commentators (e.g., Morrell, 1989; Simon, 1988 and Walford, 1990) had suggested. However, the book also notes that there were differences between the social-class distributions of the first and second intakes — there were more social-class I and II in the second intake — and implies that there may be a trend towards more middle-classness that should be watched. The presentation of the social-class distributions in two separate tables was designed to make a political point which researchers with other commitments would have avoided.

Technology

Extracts (4), (9), (11) and (12) refer in different ways to technology and facilities. They indicate I had held a whole host of unarticulated assumptions about the CTC's technological nature and abundance of facilities which were rapidly challenged. The lack of books in the library simply shocked me. That so many of the children seemed to enthuse over what I saw as 'non-technological' areas such as drama and music, and some actively disliked science, struck me as decidedly odd. These initial impressions and challenges to my assumptions led to more formulated hypotheses about the extent to which the CTC could really be seen to emphasize technology, and also to question once more the selection process.

This initial surprise led to a more thorough examination of the nature of the curriculum than might otherwise have been the case. It led to a range of tentative research questions, and I began to look in a systematic way at the use of technology in the teaching I observed. In the book, a table is given (table 4.1) of the periods allocated to each subject area, and this is discussed in some detail. It would be a dull and uninteresting table if it were not for the fact that it illustrates just how little technology appeared on the formal curriculum at that time. The data were collected and analysed in as objective a way as possible, yet the discussion emphasizes the lack of technology, and goes on to discuss the ways in which the curriculum is both familiar and unfamiliar. The discussion is an expression of a subjective commitment to show that the CTC policy was not working in the way the government might wish.

This commitment also shows itself in the desire to explore in more depth the importance of technological interest and aptitude in the selection process. It was stated in the initial CTC booklet (DES, 1986) that, 'A prime consideration in the selection of pupils will be whether they are likely to benefit from what the CTC offers', yet even on this first day it seemed that some of the children actively disliked the scientific aspects, which I saw as being central to most views of what a CTC was supposed to offer. A research question developed which asked 'How important was the pupils' interest in technology in their decision to apply?' In order to answer it a specific question was included in the questionnaires and interview schedules used with the representative samples of children. The result was that few of the children saw the technological aspects of the CTC as being of prime importance in their own decision to apply for the CTC. By using systematic techniques, the research method tried to encompass objectivity, yet the decision to publish this information in a separate paper (Walford, 1991b) once again shows subjectivity and commitment. The information about the role of technology in the choice of the CTC was included within a paper that discussed the importance of children themselves in the decision-making process. It made points which might be usable in any attack of the government's increased commitment to parental choice, and also argued that the CTC idea did not seem to be a particularly efficient or effective way of dealing with perceived problems in technological education. This paper was published before the book — just in case a General Election was called earlier than expected.

Conclusion

In this chapter I hope to have shown that the ideas of commitment and objectivity are not incompatible. I have given several examples from the work on the City Technology College, Kingshurst where I believe Kelly's three 'stages' of research model is helpful in examining where commitment and the search for objectivity should come in research. Without objectivity as a goal social research becomes indistinguishable from journalism or political polemic. I believe such a development would be highly undesirable and that academics have the responsibility to ensure that they seek objectivity within a framework of commitment.

Note

1   My sincere thanks go to the principal, staff and students of the City Technology College, Kingshurst, for allowing me to enter their world and to experience their kindness and hospitality. Although this project could not have been completed without their generous help, the responsibility for the contents of this chapter is mine alone. The study was funded by the Social Innovation Research Group at Aston Business School, and through a consultancy to an ESRC-funded research project on City Technology Colleges directed by professors Tony Edwards and Geoff Whitty (grant no. C00232462). I am also most grateful to my co-author Henry Miller for his continued help and comradeship.

References

DEPARTMENT OF EDUCATION AND SCIENCE (1986) *City Technology Colleges. A new choice of school*, London, HMSO.

HAMMERSLEY, M. (1992) *What's Wrong with Ethnography?* London, Routledge.

KELLY, A. (1978) 'Feminism and research', *Women's Studies International Quarterly*, 1, pp. 225–32.

MORRELL, F. (1989) *Children of the Future*, London, Hogarth Press.

MYRDAL, G. (1969) *Objectivity in Social Research*, London, Duckworth.

PESHKIN, A. (1991) Appendix: 'In search of subjectivity — one's own', in PESHKIN, A. *The Color of Strangers. The Color of Friends*, Chicago, Chicago University Press.

PHILLIPS, D.C. (1990) 'Subjectivity and objectivity: An objective inquiry', in ELLIOT, J., EISNER, E.W. and PESHKIN, A. (Eds) *Qualitative Inquiry in Education: The continuing debate*, New York, Teachers College Press.

ROBSON, M.H. and WALFORD, G. (1988) 'UK tax policy and independent schools', *British Tax Review*, 2, pp. 38–54.

SIMON, B. (1988) *Bending the Rules*, London, Lawrence and Wishart.

STANLEY, L. (1990) (Ed) *Feminist Praxis*, London, Routledge.

STANLEY, L. and WISE, S. (1983) *Breaking Out: Feminist consciousness and feminist research*, London, Routledge and Kegan Paul.

WALFORD, G. and JONES, S. (1986) 'The Solihull adventure: An attempt to reintroduce selective schooling', *Journal of Education Policy*, 1, 3, pp. 239–53.

WALFORD, G. (1986) *Life in Public Schools*, London, Methuen.

WALFORD, G. (1987) 'How dependent is the independent sector?', *Oxford Review of Education*, 13, 3, pp. 275–96.

WALFORD, G. (1988) 'The Scottish Assisted Places Scheme; A comparative study of the origins, nature and practice of the APS in Scotland, England and Wales', *Journal of Education Policy*, 3, 2, pp. 137–53.

WALFORD, G. (1990) *Privatization and Privilege in Education*, London, Routledge.

WALFORD, G. (1991a) 'City Technology Colleges: A private magnetism?', in WALFORD, G. (Ed) *Private Schooling: Tradition, Change and Diversity*, London, Paul Chapman.

WALFORD, G. (1991b) 'Choice of school at the first City Technology College', *Educational Studies*, 17, 1, pp. 65–75.

WALFORD, G. (1991c) 'Researching the City Technology College, Kingshurst', in WALFORD, G. (Ed) *Doing Educational Research*, London, Routledge.

WALFORD, G. and MILLER, H. (1991) *City Technology College*, Milton Keynes, Open University Press.

Chapter 8

Researching Inside the State: Issues in the Interpretation of Elite Interviews

Stephen J. Ball

Introduction

This chapter is a reflection upon, and a second order analysis of, aspects of the interpretational work done for my study *Politics and Policy Making in Education* (1990). That study, which was an attempt to describe and analyse changes in the processes of policy making in English education, focused upon the origins and construction of the 1988 Education Reform Act. The Act provided a 'case' for the policy-making analysis. The primary data for the study were a set of forty-nine interviews with key 'policy makers'. The research was in part about events and processes, but it was also about meanings, discourses and practical ideologies, about position and shifting patterns of influence, about 'the will to truth'. Here my concern is not with the conduct of the research (see Ball, 1994). Rather, I want to explore some of the interpretational and theoretical difficulties involved in working with data of this sort.[1] In particular, I want to examine the relationship between theory and data. Most analysts leave the interpretational relationships between data and analysis heavily implicit. And I was somewhat chastened by a remark in a paper by Gewirtz and Ozga on this issue. They said 'constraints on space and the fact that the work is still in progress (not to mention the difficulty of the task) inhibit us from offering here an exposition of the developing relationship between the informing theoretical perspective, its associated propositions, and the empirical data' (Gewirtz and Ozga, 1990, p. 41). They may have been wise to have avoided the issue.

Beginnings

Let me rehearse briefly the intellectual beginnings of this study. These provided the interpretational resources and constraints brought to the data. There are three influences of particular importance.

1. In both the conception and conduct of the research I drew upon my experiences with ethnographic research methods. My predilection was to

attempt to engage with the field of study in some way and to explore, develop and test concepts and theory in direct relation to first order data. However, I realized from the start that this would mean having to grapple with questions about agency and the ideological category of the individual. The purposes and intentions of political actors are important but they do not provide a sufficient basis for the interpretation of policies and policy making. And the interpretation of primary, qualitative data is not necessary limited to a conceptualization of intentions.

2. Althusser's work on the theory of the state provided the basic conceptual structure for the organization and analysis of my research material (Althusser, 1969). But Raymond Williams on competing interests in, and definitions of, what it means to be educated (Williams, 1961) and Saunders (1986) on the State as a constellation of sites whose determination by the economy is both general and varied, rather than specific and identical were also of major importance. In particular, I came to see education policy as caught between two partially discrete crises of legitimation; one economic (a crisis of capital accumulation) and one political (a crisis of order and authority). Different aspects of policy, sometimes different aspects of the same policy seemed to articulate aspects of these crises. Thus, while I do not see the State as a committee acting in the interests of the bourgeoisie, I do accept that the problem of capital accumulation and the maintenance of its conditions provides the major problem, constraint and interest effect in the working of the State. Nonetheless, a set of conceptual, interpretational and analytical subproblems are thrown up when attempting to work inside the State; the degree of relative autonomy of the State from the economy; the extent to which the State (always or sometimes) acts in its own interest; the differentiated nature of capital and the economy and the different interests that are thus articulated and represented 'in' and acting 'upon' the State; the contradictory problems thus generated for the State and the contradictory or incoherent responses constructed and elicited. Theoretically, given the above, we should not always expect to find policy coherence and should not be surprised to see struggle within the State over the definition and purpose of policy solutions. In simple terms, I was keen to attempt to capture and try to account for patterns, contradictions and incoherences and above all to portray and explore the complexity in policy making and in policies.

3. An interest in the work of Foucault and particularly his notion of discourse led me to attend to the infrastructure of power/knowledge which 'speaks' policy. Discourses embody and produce relations of power through the promotion of certain subjectivities and meaning systems over others. But, importantly 'discursive reality is not determined by any one discursive system because discourses depend on active subjects for this realisation and these subjects are always positioned inter-discursively' (Yeatman, 1990, p. 164). In a variety of ways policy seems to provide a paradigm of discourse.

In relation to these interpretational resources, my primary methodological point then is that, as data, the actors' 'voices' elicited in the fieldwork for the study can be understood and interpreted in at least three different ways — the data is polyvocal.

First, as 'real stories'; as accounts of what happened, who said what, whose voices were important. What is of interest here are descriptions of events, the account of character and key figures, moments and debates 'inside' policy. This is the 'how' of policy, the practicalities.

Second, as discourse; as ways of talking about and conceptualizing policy, the discourses which speak policy and speak the actors (rather than the reverse). The assertions, judgments, axioms and interpretations of actors are central here. The reiteration of basic principles in and between interviews is important. This, in a sense, is the 'why' of policy; the 'types of knowledge' which provide justification and explanation for certain policy solutions and exclude others.

Third, as interest representation (but not in any simple pluralist sense). This is data as indicative of structural and relational constraints and influences which play in and upon policy making. In particular, the ways in which policy making within the State is related to the 'needs' of capital and civil society or the technical problems of the State itself. This is the 'because' of policy.

Thus, any one 'slice of data' can be 'heard' via one or more mode of epistemological vocality and different modes let us say different things about policy. Accordingly, no one interpretational mode or set of theoretical tools or interpretational stance is adequate or exhaustive of the analytical possibilities of policy analysis. The same data can be subjected to very different types and levels of interpretation. By engaging with 'direct evidence' in this way we are also confronted directly with complexity, unable to gloss over contradictions, and must face up to incoherence.

Interpretation

Let me try to make sense of this with some examples which illustrate my engagement with data. I will make some comments on a series of extracts from interview materials which relate to both methodological and theoretical issues of interpretation. I begin with Alan Ainsworth, Chairman of the FEU (Further Education Unit).

SB: Presumably one of the problems in obtaining the new impetus, the new role and the money required, is as you said earlier on, that Kenneth Baker doesn't exactly pop down and put his head round the corner and see what . . .

AA: Well, it's not only that. I think . . . It's difficult to know precisely whether Elizabeth House has given way . . . for instance . . . non-advanced further education . . . It says it hasn't, it acts as though it has, it's almost as though FE1 and FE2 and FE3, it's almost as though they, as units, are expendable. They behave

> as though they were potentially expendable. I am utterly appalled by the lack of coherence between the sections, they're almost competing with one another. It's absolutely ridiculous in the way in which the thing is done. One is just not certain. One day you get a signal that says they are really interested and involved, after all. Then the next day you get something that suggests they're not. The whole of the positioning in regard to FE in particular, is that they've certainly lost the high ground, they've given the high ground away. And that other thing that goes with that is in one sense I'm not bothered about whether the FEU is part of the DES. The FEU is essentially there to support the further education system and we have to support it in the sense that with the limited means at our disposal, we can't do all that much. But it's a fact that in 1989–90 we'll be getting something like twice the amount of money from the Training Commission and NCVQ than we will be from the DES. (Ainsworth interview, 9.9.88)

Analytically this extract provides some very interesting issues, but my reading of this piece of interview text was also related to several other interviews. It cannot be understood/interpreted alone (see Boyson below). It appears to speak both to the educational culture and preoccupations of the DES, with the academic rather than the vocational curriculum, and the concomitant marginalization of vocational interests in the DES. But also in more general terms, it points up the way in which receptivity to interest articulation is distributed unevenly across the State. The DES appears strongly predisposed not to give great credence to the instrumental voices of capital. But the threat of Department of Employment/Manpower Services Commission takeover of or merger with the DES in the mid-1980s had produced a response of sorts. Nevertheless, we only have to look at current curriculum policy in and around the DFE to see the persistence of the academic culture and the receptivity there to the voices of cultural restoration. The micro-political and ideological struggles within the State, over policy emphasis and crucially over funding, and the incoherences within the State that produce and arise from these struggles are also indicated in the interview. Substantively, the extract above makes the uncertain status of FE in the DES very clear.

In part the conduct of the research traded upon these kinds of personal and revelatory accounts. They illustrate the closed and internecine nature of policy making within the British State and the problems involved in researching policy making. The insertion of DTI and DoE into areas of FE funding and policy and the speaker himself 'as a business man inside the State' are indicative of a shift in the legitimated interests represented in, and acting upon, policy. As Dale (1992) puts it: 'Modes of interest representation lay down which "voices" are considered legitimate in policy formation' (p. 212). Alan Ainsworth is (or was) personnel director of Players Cigarettes:

AA: I've been in personnel management ever since in the CGB, ICI, and for the last 18 years with Imperial Tobacco. I got involved in education . . . for about 10 years I did WEA lecturing . . . principally on current affairs, because I liked doing it. I did . . . I got involved with the local CBI as a representative . . . one of their representatives on the East Midlands Regional Examining Board. I then got invited by the CBI to join a panel of the old Schools Council . . . which was essentially a consultative . . . I'm not talking about the Schools Council, this particular body that I was on was a consultative body, involving full time members of the Schools Council, which I wasn't a full time member of . . . but it also involved industry, educationalists and the TUC . . . and we talked essentially about . . . essentially liaison between industry and education . . . in the broadest sense . . . When that body was dissolved, I was asked to chair the schools liaison panel of the CBI . . . which I've been doing since about 1980 now. And during that spell I got invited to join the SCDC, during its first three years. That first three years ended last May/June, at which point I was invited by Baker to chair the FEU, which I now do . . . so I'm still on the CBI . . . still chair the CBI Schools Panel . . . I'm a member of the CBI Education Training Committee, and I chair the FEU, so I've got a fairly broad bag of exposure to, as it were, the system. (Ainsworth interview, 9.9.88)

When he speaks within the State he speaks for, stands for industry and capital, he is discursively and symbolically positioned in this way as an ideological subject, he can be 'heard' in these terms. Structural interests and discourse are intertwined here. While in the most straightforward sense Alan Ainsworth does not see himself this way, he is clearly articulated by 'a perspective' — a set of concerns and a language rooted in the interests of his employers and colleagues; although he is clearly education-friendly. (The same point would apply to other different sorts of discursive actors). As Milliband points out: '. . . even though the will to think in "national" terms may well be strong, businessmen involved in government and administration are not very likely, all the same, to find much merit in policies which appear to run counter to what they conceive to be the interests of business' (1982, pp. 54–5). Or, to put it another way, in Bourdieu's language of habitus: 'types of behaviour can be directed towards certain ends without being consciously directed to these ends or determined by them'. Business people are increasingly well represented in the sub-government of education although it would appear that in some instances they are there to be 'seen' rather than 'heard'. But it is necessary to appreciate their presence not simply as symbolic or even solely in terms of interest articulation; the values and perspectives they bring can alter the culture and assumptive world within which policy making is set. Policy is, in a sense, an assertion of voice, or a cannibalization of multiple voices. Policy influence is a struggle to be heard in an arena where only certain voices have legitimacy at any point in time.

Let me add now a brief extract from an interview with Philip Merridale, Chief Education Officer of Hampshire.

> PM: . . . so Carlisle who was still trying, I think, to operate within the system and by consensus was perceived to be too soft . . . and disappeared . . . and you can never tell. This is the sort of thing, where somebody like myself who at that time would be in and out of what are described as the corridors of power. You might be in the corridor, but you haven't opened the door of the sanctum . . . so when you go to see somebody who isn't there, nobody tells you why he isn't there . . . you have to form your own conclusions . . . but you'll remember that Carlisle was replaced by Keith Joseph. And Keith Joseph was your sort of zero budgeting philosopher . . . his view was that you shouldn't accept anything until you have dissected right the way through the whole proposition that was being put to you . . . back to first principles . . . and he . . . of course spent quite a considerable period of his early time at the DES engaged in philosophic exploration, seeking to find out what was wrong with the education service . . . and what was wrong with the way we administered the education service. Sadly, I think that when . . . I had the longest period of close collaboration, at the highest level of government, with Keith Joseph, because I was by that time the Chairman of the Council of Local Education Authorities, the Chairman of the ACC Education Committee and the leader of the employers negotiating body, the Burnham Committee, so I was, as it were, the commander in chief of the armies . . . of the Philistines. (Merridale interview, 17.2.88)

Both these interview texts speak to and about policy in a number of ways. They can be read in different ways. They must be understood in terms of the claims, implicit and explicit, being made by the speaker and the way the speakers position themselves within the policy process. There are strong realist stories here but these are not simple guileless descriptions of events or processes, they are also sophisticated interpretations of events. The researcher's task is to interpret the interpretations. They contain both first and second-order accounting. They are complex, difficult and demanding. And Merridale's extract highlights a particular challenge for the policy analyst. The focus on the role of particular actors like Keith Joseph, in terms of modes of decision-making and policy debate and policy ownership, points up the issue of the *personalization* of policy (McPherson and Raab, 1988, p. 65). There are clearly attractions but also enormous dangers involved in reducing policy making to the skills, beliefs or personality of individual actors. Nonetheless, sometimes we need to understand the role and contribution of key individuals. Dale (1989, p. 89) reflecting upon the phenomenon of Thatcherism, makes the point that 'a crucial factor in uniting various strands into a coherent philosophy and policy is Mrs Thatcher's own personal political stand'. CCCS (1981, p. 14) make the point that 'it is important not to lose a sense of authorship or agency, or of the rush and muddle of decision-making "at the top". Both are correctives to the tendency to ascribe perfect knowledge and conspiratorial intent to politicians or to "the State" ' (p. 14). But they are also very concerned that a concentration on the individual 'is deeply problematic, theoretically and politically' (p. 14). My point is that we need to analyse and understand rather than assume the role of individuals in policy formation — neither ignoring nor taking for granted 'the individual'. Thus, we can accept Keith Joseph as having made a very personal political and philosophical input into educational policy, but there is more to this than personality or personal commitment. The appointment of Keith Joseph as Secretary of State in place of Mark Carlisle signalled two important things. First, that education was to be brought into the policy mainstream. Joseph was a political heavy-weight in the party and personally close to Mrs Thatcher. Second, education was to be brought within the orbit of radical Thatcherite policy making. Joseph was a key party intellectual, often credited with converting Mrs Thatcher to neo-liberal economics (Kavanagh, 1990). Young (1990, p. 43) comments that, 'The Thatcher–Joseph connection became one of the most formative political relationships of modern times.' A 'wet' Carlisle was thus replaced by the ultra 'dry' Joseph. Knight (1990, p. 145) comments that: 'To the educational radical-right, Carlisle's *making savings and improving the efficiency* approach (though government inspired) lacked conviction and appeared as a sop to the demands for a *social market economy*'. And while Joseph is often portrayed, as by Philip Merridale, as being open and his susceptible to convincing argument, his political convictions were clearly to the fore in his engagement with the 'educational establishment'. Rather than seeing Joseph in terms of great reforms we need to concentrate upon his reworking of the landscape of educational policy and his dismantling of the existing context of influence within which education policy formation was set. In particular, the teachers' industrial action resulted in a thorough displacement and demoralization of the teacher unions and the marginalizing of LEA negotiating bodies. The Schools Council was dismantled ('. . . it wasn't making any contribution on the big issues of policy, simply another producers' lobby' (Interview with KJ). This disposed in advance of a great deal of potential opposition to reforms to come. And in all this the position of the Secretary of State in relation to policy was significantly changed (with new powers accruing directly) and so concomitantly was the role of the DES officials and the HMI. ('If we had a more rigorous HMI that would be a comfort . . . I don't want to damn them out of hand, but I think they followed the fashions' (KJ). In addition, Joseph provided legitimation within the apparatus of the Conservative Party for the radical-right think tanks (CPS, IEA, Freedom Association, Social Affairs Unit, Adam Smith Institute). The possibilities which lay before his successor, Kenneth Baker, were therefore very different from those faced by previous incoming secretaries. Arguably, Joseph contributed in a major way to the shifting of the discourse within which policy was set. As he put it in interview: 'I think what I can claim to have achieved is to have shifted the emphasis from quantity to quality, and that I think is now accepted across the House. . . .' He succeeded in putting a whole new agenda into the politics of education, an agenda which is still being worked through by Conservative Secretaries of State; (e.g., 'I'm very very uncertain about whether teacher training colleges are any damn use' (KJ)).

Interestingly, the interview conducted with Keith Joseph was decidedly thin as regards realist descriptions of the policy process but his style of response in interview was certainly amenable to discursive analysis and an understanding of the play of power/knowledge upon the possibilities of policy. Keith Joseph adumbrated some of the assumptive landscape over which policy ranged and the ideological touchstones which informed 'policy talk' and 'policy thought'; only certain sorts of things were sayable about policy. Here again, we can cease to treat the respondent as author of the interview text. 'Instead of constituting the language that creates the world, the speaking subject is constituted by its place within a linguistic system' (Taylor, 1986, pp. 13–14). As noted already Keith Joseph is a key speaker of the New Right. His position in the party and in government provided a basis for a 'true discourse' of 'respect and terror' (Foucault, 1971).

Let me try to broaden the perspective by looking at another 'character' in the changing Conservative politics of education of the 1970s and 1980s — Rhodes Boyson — the man Dale (1989, p. 77) calls 'the chief propagandist' of Thatcherism.

SB: Well this says . . . 'although a more sympathetic Minister was a necessary beginning to the promulgation of the right's ideology in the Party [they mean Margaret Thatcher as Minister of Education] . . . the promulgation of the right's ideology in the Party had to take place in a number of arenas. One important arena was the Conservative Political Centre which publishes discussion documents for use both nationally and locally. Rhodes Boyson was active here, and active as a link between the Black Papers, the NCES on the one hand and the Conservative party activists on the other, publishing *Battle Lines for Education* (1973) and *Parental Choice* (1975)'. Would you see yourself as that . . .?

RB: Yes, you do . . . you look at it afterwards and you can see what you've done. I mean you don't actually assess everything. It's like somebody running the mile. You don't feel your pulse as you run the mile, but afterwards you can say I remember him . . . I thought at that time I'd have to catch up or drop behind. You're doing it . . . it's like asking a footballer how he scored his goal . . . but he looked afterwards and thinks . . . that's a damn good move I made there. In so far as that I . . . bridged the economic and the political right, and probably nobody else in the Party did. So the one's who agreed with me on economics would have taken the education for granted, and those who agreed with me on education, would have accepted my views on economics. That was the factor . . . most people were either . . . In the Tory party there's a lot of people who understand economics, there's not many people who understand education. The fact that the economists in the Party knew I understood economics and knew my stuff, they would accept, looking back, I mean there's a lot of truth in what you've just said . . . that they would accept my educational ones, as having merit, almost like in scholarship, because they'd read the other.

SB: Were you influenced by the new right economist Hayek?

RB: Yes, I'm a member of the Mont Pelerin, I have been heavily influenced by Hayek, not by Popper but Hayek, who's a personal friend of mine. When I read his *Laws of the Constitution* . . . and the rest of his books, it's actually what I believe. That he actually verbalised my belief . . . and gave it, shall we say . . . not more credibility, but he raised it to a higher level. What I knew by instincts, since I'm basically an instinctive player, and then I go away and think about what I've done . . . he actually put down, so that he took me further . . . and I realised why I felt that way . . . I mean I don't agree with all of Hayek, but I mean Hayek has been fantastically influential . . . more than anybody else. Well there are two people who are influential, Lord Harris of Highcross . . . the Director of the Institute of Economic Affairs . . . because he has such an exciting mind, and we're such close friends. I met him in '68 and Hayek, and his writing, I mean those are the two most . . . have influenced . . . firstly Brian Cox had been influential on me, because I respect him so much as an individual, so does my wife, that he . . . has an integrity of view, but for the overall scene, Harris and even more so Hayek . . . because he's not . . . unlike some economists, just a plain economist. I mean he is a philosopher . . . you go back to political economy with him, and the natural sciences and the rest . . . he has a roundness . . .

SB: Right, right . . . again the link between the economic and the political you mentioned, it's very interesting in as much as . . . you had your relationships with the Institute of Economic Affairs . . .

> RB: Yes, I was probably the only person who walked through all
> these groups. (Boyson interview, 29.2.88)

This extract indicates the difficulties involved when respondents are required to reminisce and comment on their personal role in influence networks. As a career politician Rhodes Boyson is unlikely to deny the kind of role I suggest for him and yet he is clearly hazy about the period and the events to which I am referring. We tend to neglect problems of memory and accuracy when evaluating interview data. But he does go on to indicate the relationships between social networks and political networks in and around the 'context of influence' in relation to policy. He is also indicating the development of a discursive climate and the building of a discursive formation within arenas of policy, based upon Hayekian neo-liberal economics. Here, people are both actors and discourses. They stand for particular ideas and perspectives. They are in a sense sites of articulation. Their personal and discursive credibility are mutually reinforcing. Both Boyson and Joseph, it turned out from interviews, are members of the Mont Pelerin society.

I moved on in the interview, perhaps too precipitately — but time was pressing for Rhodes Boyson was waiting in his rooms on the Northern Ireland Office for a division bell to ring — to pick up the issue referred to above by Alan Ainsworth: the role of vocational education within conservative education (or DES) policy. Here I was looking for another view of DES/DoE relations and influence and the impact of the MSC on DES credibility (triangulation and corroboration). The response again illustrates the role played in this kind of data by respondents' 'claims'. However, it also provides a sidelight on the relationships between the departmental culture of the DES, legitimate interest representation and education policy.

> SB: One omission in a sense . . . particularly if you look at the things,
> the Hillgate Group, the CPS . . . are talking about, which is
> interesting in relation to say some of the interests of Keith
> Joseph . . . is vocational education.
>
> RB: Yes, Yes.
>
> SB: There doesn't seem much said about the role of vocational education. It seems much more straight down the line liberal
> curriculum . . . position . . . would that be accurate?
>
> RB: Yes, I think so, I mean . . . the academic . . . the old school
> master, who went from school . . . to university, and then back
> to school, knew and still knows very little about life outside
> there, particularly now national service has ended. But he does
> know the liberal curriculum, and . . . I mean, the teaching profession has very little enthusiasm for vocational education, and
> still hasn't. That's why the TVEI had to be done from outside.
> I was involved in bringing that in, with the Department of

Employment . . . as the Minister of Education responsible when it came in.

SB: Oh . . . [Unintentionally here I seem to convey my scepticism about RB's strong claims about involvement and advocacy of vocational education and he appears to respond by toning these down].

RB: So I mean I accepted it, because . . . I accepted it because the less able child will only work if there's going to be a carrot at the end which will get him a job. But the . . . my colleagues, who are less earthy than I am, since my first experience . . . secondary modern schools, are the actual after the liberal curriculum . . . very strongly . . . they are basically . . . you could almost say classical liberals.

SB: Right, but one thing people often say about . . . particularly TVEI, that there was a lot of resistance from DES officials, because this was seen to be a . . . [Here the interviewee searches for a diplomatic word and interestingly the interviewer provides his own, and thus gives strong confirmation of the point being made].

RB: A takeover.

SB: Yes.

RB: Well I mean, DES could have done it, but the DES had no intention of doing it. And the pace was made elsewhere, so then it had to run after it for a bit, otherwise it was going to lose the whole of its schools . . . (Boyson interview, 29.2.88)

The antiquated and 'Conservative' language use tells us something about the assumptive framework within which education policy is 'talked' about. And again we glimpse the struggles for influence and control taking place inside the State and education policy making.

Very little of this sort of material appeared in the book, but it played a very important role in the development of my understanding and eventually my attempts to explain education policy. There is a difference between data as *evidence* and data as *background*. Background, as general commentary upon policy making provides insight into the discourses and constraints which informed and affected policy makers. Evidence, as more specific description gives indication of the when, where and who of policy formation. Both are important.

Conclusion

How does all this relate to other attempts at analysing contemporary education policy? As part of his formulation of levels of abstraction Dale (1992) differentiates between the politics of education, educational politics and educational practice, arguing that these levels are 'differently constituted' and 'that different forms of analysis would have different effects upon them' (p. 211). The relationship between education and economy in this explication of 'levels' is 'shaped by the response to problems and possibilities "delivered" by the world economy and the country's place within it contained in the "modes of regulation" prevailing within the country, and the historic bloc that dominates it' (p. 211) [And presumably the problems of the State itself]. Dale's brief references to 'modes of interest representation' which 'lay down which "voices" are considered legitimate in policy formation' (p. 212) might be another way of formulating some of what I understand as discourse. Using Dale's system *Politics and Policy Making* operates across the levels of national politics and the politics of education. Policy plays across all of these levels and is mediated, interpreted and has effects across all these levels. It is a 'continual process in which the locii of power are constantly shifting as the various resources implicit and explicit in texts are recontextualised and employed in the struggle to maintain or change views of schooling' (Bowe, Ball and Gold, 1992). Interviews with policy makers can clearly illuminate the ways in which 'possibilities' are framed and articulated in relation to specific areas of policy. This is what elsewhere Dale (1989, p. 35) calls 'selectiveness'; he argues that: 'Policy options are selected on the basis of solutions available, and often it seems, questions are framed with available answers in mind. What appear as the available answers will result from the particular combination of bureaucracy/technology dominant in a state apparatus at a given time.' But the problem always remains that by focusing on the figures which move across the policy landscape we may neglect the geomorphology of the landscape itself and changes in its terrain and substructure. On the other hand, a preoccupation with dominant modes of political rationality and global economic forces may lead to a misleading neglect of transformative activities and the possibility of surprise. It is the interplay between figure and landscape that is important theoretically and empirically.

However, the contemporary sociology of education is theoretically conservative and circumspect. Indeed the field is in danger of becoming a backwater cut off from theoretical developments and experiments in other sociological specialisms. Many writers appear content with recycling off-the-peg theory and have abandoned attempts at theoretical development. There is a tendency towards what Dale (1992, p. 207) calls 'evocation' rather than 'explanation', what he refers to also as the 'naming' (or 'renaming') of theoretical spaces and 'theoretical painting by numbers'. And hostility often stands instead of critical analysis. Policy research in particular points up the inadequacy of this kind of continual reshuffling and redeployment of theory. In urging the need for more attention to theoretical development I am not advocating 'ad hocery'. But there is a place for more theoretical risk-taking and a need for the playfulness that Wright Mills (1959) sees as crucial to the sociological imagination: 'The sociological imagination can also be cultivated; certainly it seldom occurs without a great deal of often routine work. Yet there is an unexpected quality about it, perhaps because its essence is the combination of ideas that no one expected were combinable . . . There is a playfulness of mind at the back of such combining as well as a truly fierce drive to make sense of the world, which the technician as such usually lacks' (1959, pp. 232–3). As part of a move to more adventurousness we need to give more attention to the problems and processes of interpretation (the relation between data–explanation–theory) as I have attempted to do, here, albeit with some difficulty. 'Building theory, by its very nature, implies interpreting data, for the data must be conceptualized and the concepts related to form a theoretical rendition of reality (a reality that cannot actually be known, but is always interpreted)' (Strauss and Corbin, 1990, p. 22). But also we need to pursue thorough empirical study of the policy process; but not simply 'bits and pieces' of policy which are treated in isolation from politics and economics and other policy arenas. Yet, accounts of research continue, with odd exceptions, to separate out conduct or method from the substance of analysis. Interpretation, the link between data and theory remains obscure. This not only raises questions about the validity claims that analysts make for their work but also bears upon the kind of apprenticeships we offer to noviciate researchers.

Note

1   This is a much shortened version of a paper presented at the ESRC seminar series at the University of Warwick. I have found it necessary, in order to meet the word limit for this collection, to curtail exposition and discussion of some of the issues identified. I am grateful to Trinidad Ball, Mary Darmanin and Tony Knight for their helpful comments on the earlier drafts.

References

ALTHUSSER, L. (1969) *For Marx*, London, Allen Lane.
BALL, S.J. (1990) *Politics and Policy Making In Education*, London, Routledge.
BOURDIEU, P. (1990) *The Logic of Practice*, Cambridge, Polity Press.
BOWE, R., BALL, S.J. and GOLD, A. (1992) *Reforming Education and Changing Schools*, London, Routledge.
CCCS (1981) *Unpopular Education*, London, Hutchinson.
DALE, R. (1989) *The State and Education Policy*, Milton Keynes, Open University Press.
DALE, R. (1992) 'Recovering from a Pyrrhic Victory? Quality, relevance and impact in the sociology of education', in ARNOT, M. and BARTON, L. (Eds) *Voicing Concerns*, Wallingford, Triangle.
FOUCAULT, M. (1971) *L'Ordre du Discours*, Paris, Gallimard.
GEWIRTZ, S. and OZGA, J. (1990) 'Partnership, pluralism and education policy: A reassessment', *Journal of Education Policy*, 5, 1, pp. 35–46.
KAVANAGH, D. (1990) *Thatcherism and British Politics. The End of Consensus?*, Oxford, Oxford University Press.
KNIGHT, C. (1990) *The Making of Tory Education Policy in Post War Britain*, London, Falmer Press.

McPherson, A. and Raab, C. (1988) *Governing Education*, Edinburgh, University of Edinburgh Press.

Milliband, R. (1982) *The State in Capitalist Society*, Oxford, Oxford University Press.

Mills, C.W. (1959) *The Sociological Imagination*, Harmondsworth, Penguin.

Offe, C. (1984) *Contradictions of the Welfare State*, London, Heinemann.

Ryan, M. (1989) *Politics and Culture*, London, Macmillan.

Saunders, P. (1986) *Social Theory and the Urban Question*, London, Hutchinson.

Scheurich, J. (1992) 'A Postmodernist Review of Interviewing: Dominance, Resistance and Chaos', Paper presented at the Annual Meeting of the American Educational Research Association, San Francisco.

Strauss, A. and Corbin, J. (1990) *Basics of Qualitative Research: Grounded Theory Procedures and Techniques*, Newbury Park, CA, Sage.

Taylor, M.C. (1986) 'Introduction', in Taylor, M.C. (Ed) *Deconstruction in Context: Literature and Philosophy*, Chicago, University of Chicago Press.

Williams, R. (1961) *The Long Revolution*, London, Chatto and Windus.

Woods, P. (1986) *Inside Schools*, London, Routledge and Kegan Paul.

Yeatman, A. (1990) *Bureaucrats, Technocrats, Femocrats: Essays on the Contemporary Australian State*, Sydney, Allen and Unwin.

Young, H. (1990) *One of Us*, London, Pan Books.

Chapter 9

Sex, Lies and Audiotape: Interviewing the Education Policy Elite

Jenny Ozga and Sharon Gewirtz

Introduction

This chapter looks at some of the ethical issues raised in the course of our research into elites in education policy making. We want to begin with a general discussion about the relationship between values and research in education policy studies in which we identify the ethical concerns of a critical theory approach to education policy research. We consider some of the practical constraints which may inhibit the thorough application of such an approach, before moving on to discuss ethical issues in relation to our own study. In particular, we discuss the values and theory underpinning our research and some of the consequent ethical dilemmas we confronted in the collection of data.

So where do the 'sex' and 'lies' come in? Well, if the attention-getting title of our chapter is translated into more conventional usage, we will be concerned with problems and issues which arise in the gathering of life-history interview evidence from polished and experienced policy practitioners in the context of a strong theoretical framework. Hence the 'lies'. The 'sex' refers to our acknowledgment as the research progressed that the fact that we were both women eased our access to our almost exclusively male interviewees and that our non-threatening and sympathetic self-presentation was also a useful research tactic. This area of concern — the relationship of researcher and researched — is not unique to our project, and in our discussion we will draw on the experience of others, particularly where feminist scholarship has highlighted the issue of power relations in the research process. At the same time, however, we will attempt to identify the particular problems and issues which arise from researching powerful — or once powerful — individuals for the purpose of exploring the education policy-making process.

But first we wish to identify and discuss a key area of interest to us, and one which tends to be neglected in the education policy field, that is the relationship between the ethical and value perspectives of the researcher, the focus and design of the research, and the theoretical approach adopted.

The Ethics of Education policy Research

We are concerned that on the whole researchers of education policy have tended neither to be explicit nor reflexive about the values or theories which inform or inhere in their work. Firstly, we believe that what we do when we set out to understand education policy must, of its nature, be 'theorized' as we are seeking to make statements about how things connect, about how things come to happen as they do and, simply put, theories are statements about such matters. However, theories are not all of the same size, weight, complexity or quality. Theories may seek to explain only individual cases, or they may point to patterns of phenomena. Whatever their quality, their purpose is to help us sort out our world, make sense of it, provide a guide to action and predict what may happen next. We construct theories routinely by thinking about information we routinely collect. Thus there is no question of divorcing 'theorizing' from data collection. Rather our argument is that we need to look at our research activity in a self-conscious, theorized way, interrogating our theoretical 'hunches' and their associated sensitizing concepts while looking at policy at the macro, meso or micro levels, or all three.

But in addition to this we need to be reflexive about the relationship between value positions and theory, the embeddedness of theory in values. As Dunleavy and O'Leary (1987, pp. 337–8) point out in their discussion of state theory, value positions form the broad background against which theoretical positions are developed or selected, and these in turn impact upon the selection of evidence. Cox's well-known elaboration of the differences between problem-solving and critical theory is important here. Cox (1980) emphasizes the need for reflexivity in theoretical development and for appraisal and reappraisal of perspectives in which the problematic becomes one of 'creating an alternative world'.

Critical theory in relation to education policy is not implicated in the solution of problems — or at least not in the solution of problems defined by administrators and policy makers. Working within a critical frame places requirements on the researcher to pursue ethical-research principles and to assess research activity in relation to what might be broadly termed social-justice concerns (Gewirtz, 1993). Does the research imply consent to the maintenance, justification and legitimation of regulatory institutions? What is its potential contribution to freedom from arbitrary, coercive power? Does it support the development of human capacity, respect for human dignity and worth, a more equitable distribution of economic and social goods and an expansion of economic opportunity to meet need? This might indicate that critical theorists have rather inflated expectations of the outcomes of policy research. We maintain that research *can* make a contribution to the goals embedded in these questions in three ways. First, it can draw attention to, and challenge, the assumptions informing policy and it can expose the effects of policy on the ground, in particular where policies increase inequality and impact unfairly on particular groups. Second, research can set out to explain how injustices and inequalities are produced, reproduced and sustained. Third, as Harvey (1990) and Troyna (1994) remind us, research can provide a basis for the development of strategies of social transformation. It could be suggested that research in education policy which does not accept any of these obligations is unethical in its lack of recognition of the intrusive power of the State and the repressive character of much state action, including action in the sphere of education policy.

The antithesis of critical theory is problem-solving theory which 'takes the world as it finds it, with the prevailing social and power relationships and the institutions into which they are organized, as the given framework for action.' (Cox, 1980). It approximates to C. Wright Mills' 'bureaucratic ethos'. 'Research for bureaucratic ends', Mills (1959, p. 117) writes, 'serves to make authority more effective and more efficient by providing information of use to authoritative planners'.

We do not underestimate the barriers to pursuing a critical theory or social-justice orientation to education policy research, or for that matter to policy research in general. The funding of research can operate in a number of ways to shape our work. Who funds us, the duration of grants and the particular foci of funded research may all have an impact on the theory and values which underpin our work. Where institutions of the State are the clients of research it is not surprising that a bureaucratic or problem-solving approach is adopted. It goes without saying that the Department for Education, for example, is neither interested in the exposure of the unjust consequences of its policies nor in theories of the State. It would thus be most inappropriate to say the least to apply a social justice or critical theory approach in work for such a client. Even where the client is a local authority hostile to the government, it is unlikely that the theoretical stance will be anything but problem-solving. Local authorities cannot afford to channel scarce resources into exposing unequal power relationships or the inequities of central state-induced changes. Their concerns are somewhat more immediate — how best to cope with these changes.

The influence of 'independent' funding bodies on the research they fund is less clear-cut. Seasoned fund-seekers are likely to sculpt their research proposals according to the perceived preferences of funders and to employ a neutral, apolitical language. Self-censorship may also operate at later stages of the research process, that is beyond the framing of proposals — in the selection and analysis of data and in the writing up. For, once the research agenda is set, there is pressure to conform to that agenda, at least in the preparation of interim and final reports for funding bodies. There is no formal reason why a dual strategy cannot be adopted — that is, write up in one way for the funders and in another for publication. However, academics need funding to continue their work, to survive in the academic world. Therefore there is pressure on researchers to channel their energies into satisfying their funders in order to maximize their chances of being successful in future research grant applications. What they write for their funders can also be reproduced as publications, for publications also mean money for university departments. In these circumstances it is very tempting to put any social justice agenda on the back burner.

Other disincentives to a critical-theory approach are the time-scale and foci of research funding. Projects are normally funded for short periods ranging from one to three years. Furthermore, grants tend to be allocated for researching specific areas of policy, for instance, local management of schools, assessment, the National Curriculum or aspects of it, city technology colleges and grant-maintained schools. Thus funding patterns tend to encourage research which is restricted latitudinally and longitudinally. There is a danger that this may produce analytical distortions, what might be called a 'snapshot effect', the essential characteristics of which are a preoccupation with detail and a loss of perspective. We can become so engrossed in a tiny area of study over a short period that we lose a sense of how the aspect we are exploring interacts with other aspects of policy and how it relates to broader trends which might only become apparent over a longer period of time. The funding-induced fragmentation of policy studies also mitigates against a class-centred theoretical approach since the class effects of policy may be the product of whole 'packages' of reforms working together rather than disparate elements of it.

It is not only particular sources and the mechanics of funding which can encourage a problem-solving theoretical approach. The relationship between researcher and researched can produce a similar effect. Those whom we research often have expectations of the outcome of our studies which may not match our own theoretical or value concerns. In some cases, the expectations of the researched, while different from our own, are not incompatible with ours, as researchers. But often the two sets of expectations conflict. We might be tempted to meet the expectations of those we research for two reasons. First, there is the ethical consideration that we should be reciprocating, that those whom we are researching are putting time, effort and perhaps some degree of emotional labour into our research and that we should therefore produce work which they feel is of some value. Second, we might be motivated by a concern to retain access. If we want to continue our research then we might be tempted to present our data in non-threatening ways. This form of self-censorship may be particularly attractive where we are researching institutions or people hostile to a critical theory perspective and it produces ethical dilemmas. The researcher needs to assess the value of retaining access where doing so may result in the permanent exclusion of critical perspectives and the possible legitimation of unjust social policies.

Issues of confidentiality may restrict the scope of education policy research. The 'Radcliffe Principles' inhibit serving and former ministers and public servants from disclosing particular kinds of information. The restricted categories include information likely to:

- be destructive of the confidential relationships between Ministers, or between Ministers and their advisers, and between either Ministers or advisers and outside bodies and private persons — the period of sensitivity under this heading is taken to be 15 years;
- reveal opinions or attitudes of identifiable individuals;
- reveal personal assessments or criticism of identifiable individuals within government. (HMSO, 1976, vol. 6386, paras. 46–56)

There have been some recent spectacular departures from this code of conduct (see for example, Clarke, 1993) but the existence of the principles, together with the thirty-year rule, is a probable disincentive to policy researchers. It is also likely that researchers are reluctant to make use of particular research methodologies when attempting to study policy, knowing that there will be problems with, for example, the unstructured interview or life-history methodology.

The Elites Project

We now want to place our own research within the ethical terrain mapped out above and to consider some of the specific ethical issues which we confronted in the elites project. The project was concerned to explore the nature of 'partnership' in post-war policy making. The period from 1944 onwards (lasting perhaps until the early 1970s) is often described by analysts of education policy as the apotheosis of partnership (see, for example, Kogan, 1975). As the policy-making climate became more confrontational in the 1970s and 1980s, contrasts are drawn with the earlier post-war period and differences underlined. The result, in the presentation of post-war policy making, is an increased emphasis on a broad consensus about aims which are seen to be achieved by negotiation and consultation through recognized channels (McNay and Ozga, 1985; Ranson and Tomlinson, 1986). A strong incentive for our project was the desire to explore the extent to which there really had been a 'consensus' about the scope of education, and we admit to a degree of scepticism about the concept of partnership and about the rate of change in policy direction and retention.

The project exists on a number of levels. It is at one and the same time an historical story of post-war education policy in England, an engagement in debate on theoretical perspectives on education policy (and a challenge to some conventional explanations of the period) and an attempt to make use of life-history methodology in a (relatively) novel way. The project is also part of a larger attempt to uncover and discuss some of the fundamental issues in education policy: questions about what it is for, what it can achieve and how it is structured — that is questions about its source, scope and pattern — which must be addressed, we believe, if any worthwhile research activity is to take place. However, this is not the place to rehearse these issues, and readers with an interest in them are referred to Ozga (1987), Gewirtz and Ozga (1990) and (1994), Ozga (1990) and Dale and Ozga (1991). We want here to draw attention to the relationship between the project's theoretical and empirical focus, its methodology and our values as researchers.

We started from an established and developed theoretical position underpinned by a particular set of ethical concerns. That position and those concerns shaped our selection of the research topic, our methodology and our interpretation of evidence. As historians and marxists, we believed that insufficient attention was being paid to the deep structures of English education, and to the sedimented patterns of differentiation which so characterize English provision. And we felt that insufficient attention was being paid to analysis of the role of the State in education, to the contradictory demands upon it and to the economic and political constraints which helped determine the pattern of provision. It seemed to us that there was overmuch attention paid to (relatively superficial) change, to education politics and to politicians, and to the surface noise and activity in the policy-making arena. We believed that we could draw on the work of some historians of education (notably Simon, 1965, 1974a, 1974b and 1988; and Johnson 1989) to develop both a rather different account and a rather different set of explanations. That account would recognize the continuity of central control, despite stylistic changes, and see in its different manifestations evidence of direct or indirect rule (Lawn and Ozga, 1986). As Johnson puts it, if differentiation is seen as 'the hallmark of English education' not only in organizational form but in determining curriculum categories, then there is considerable interest in tracing the long-term preoccupation of policy makers with maintaining the principle through the constant definition and redefinition of hierarchies of educational structure and context:

> Within state schooling the elementary–secondary division has been reinterpreted, first in the grammar secondary-modern split, then in the distinction between direct grant and other former grammar schools and the comprehensives, and even within the comprehensive system itself. There has been a constant tendency to revert to bipartite or tripartite division across very different formal structures. (Johnson, 1989, pp. 98–9)

Our main focus of enquiry in the 'Elites Project' was on permanent officials in both central and local government of education. Our interest in continuities led us to this choice, and we wished to explore the nature of the State administration within the State apparatus, following Poulantzas' arguments on the critical role of bureaucratic organization in maintaining the dominant ideology (Poulantzas, 1976). Those ideas also led to an interest in the class nature and composition of the state bureaucracy and to an exploration of the ways in which it contributed to the production and use of knowledge as a means of reproducing unequal power relations.

In adopting our state-centred approach to post-war education policy making we were bringing with us a desire to give proper attention to the intrusive power of the State and the repressive character of much state action. Such action includes use of arbitrary, coercive power to reduce opportunity for the development and expression of human capacity, and the failure to respect human dignity and worth, or to secure consent in the maintenance, justification and legitimization of regulatory institutions (including schools). We were allied therefore to a critical theory perspective and concerned to contribute to at least two of the three tasks of critical theory outlined in the preceding section — that of exposing the assumptions informing policy and its oppressive effects and that of explaining how injustices and inequalities are produced, reproduced and sustained. We are less confident about the extent to which we were contributing to the third task, providing a basis for the development of strategies of social transformation, although clearly social transformation must be predicated on an accurate understanding of the operation of power in society.

Thus our values informed our theoretical approach which led to our focus on officials. This in turn had implications for our methodology. We were faced with the necessity of researching these officials in a way which allowed us to establish their backgrounds, their shared assumptions, their formative experiences and their conceptions of themselves. We were also obliged, because of our commitment to reflexivity, to ensure that we were open to the consequences of such an approach in terms of revision or alteration of our theoretical perspective, and this gave a further incentive to the use of life-history methodology in the collection of material.

The life-history method we employed was not based on attempted comprehensive coverage, but on Bertaux's notion of 'representativeness' (Bertaux, 1981). We identified suitable informants by mapping administrative careers and identifying 'stables' of administrators who were clustered around particular directors of education. Publications, official correspondence and archives gave us information about those who were active and influential. Once started on the process, it took on a momentum of its own, as all our interviewees talked about one another, introduced us to former colleagues and told us about significant others. (The interconnectedness of the people we studied was at one and the same time an aid to the research process and a finding of the study. We are aware that it may have enhanced the impression of community and social solidarity.)

Our interest in the repressive nature of much State action and in the reproduction of unequal power relations does not sit comfortably with the pursuit of a close research relationship with individuals who had identified closely with state power and authority in what was widely perceived as the extension of State responsibility for the welfare of its citizens. The resultant compromise, dissembling and difficulty is discussed below.

But before turning to the problems associated with the life-history method applied to researching the powerful, we wish briefly to discuss in relation to our own project the issues of funding and confidentiality which we have identified as potential barriers to the pursuit of a critical theory approach to policy research. The 'Elites Project' proposal for funding was quite explicit about the theoretical concerns of the project but that was possible because we secured our funding from the Open University's Research Committee. The Open University had supported the preparation of teaching material which introduced explicit theoretical perspectives (including marxism) to the study of education policy, and this, perhaps, helped in securing support for the research. We also avoided the potential problems of the 'snapshot effect' likely to emanate from a limited period of funding and a narrow focus of enquiry. Because we were researching the past we were able to retain a sense of perspective. Also our research focus was not a narrow policy but the people who made and implemented policy. We were able to be selective about the issues we considered and we pinpointed those which illuminated particular policy-making strategies. The critical case of the development plans, for instance, was used to demonstrate how 'partnership' in practice was very different from orthodox notions of 'partnership'. In particular we examined how the bureaucratic processes associated with the design, submission and approval of development plans functioned to frustrate attempts by some local education authorities to establish local systems of secondary schooling according to comprehensive principles (Gewirtz and Ozga, 1990).

On the issue of confidentiality, the Radcliffe Principles, summarized above, did not act as a disincentive to us. We were inviting our respondents to talk about events which took place more than fifteen years previously and were therefore not subject to the restriction on information likely to be 'destructive to confidential relationships'. And our analysis was not dependent on personal indiscretions about other actors in the period under investigation; we were interested in the respondents themselves, in their backgrounds, their assumptions and values, their connections and in the political culture in which they operated. We do not believe that those rules of confidentiality, to which our respondents were still subject, threatened our objectives. At the same time, we were free from the pressure of retaining future access, as the focus of the enquiry was historical.

We now want to move on to some of the ethical issues raised by the relationship between researcher and researched within the context of a life-history methodology when the researchers are marxists and feminists and the researched are an elite, almost exclusively male, fraction of the State bureaucracy. This is where the 'sex' and 'lies' come in.

There are ethical issues common to all life-history work, and some that were given an additional dimension by the nature of the project and of the group under discussion. Life-history work is ambiguous and the position of the researcher ambivalent. It is intrusive, seeking as it does a full account, with no filtering out of the personal and private. Its strength lies in that recognition of the need to connect and record the full life, and not to treat one part as separate from the whole. Its intrusiveness has been justified on the grounds that it gives a voice to and records the experience of those who have been hidden from history or from sociological enquiry — much life-history work records the experience of the dispossessed and the disadvantaged. There are exceptions to this general rule however (e.g., Ferraroti, 1990), and there is a case for the incorporation of life-history approaches into all forms of enquiry as a means of furthering the interrogation of the structure–agency relationship.

We were not traditional life or oral historians, recording accounts and presenting them without commentary or mediation. There is an ethical issue, then, at the very heart of any life history research which is used as a basis for interpretation or analysis by the researcher. The ethical issues we confronted are not confined to this project, and include the basic difficulty of avoiding the exploitation of any research 'subject', and of respecting their presentation of self and the understanding of the situation that it expresses. Although these concerns are more commonly expressed by feminist researchers research-ing women (for example, Oakley, 1981; and Finch, 1984) or by researchers like Mac an Ghaill (1988) working with black youth, it would be wrong to assume that the male-elite group members in this study were not vulnerable to exploitation or misrepresentation. Indeed, our particular view of their role and function as a state bureaucracy made them particularly vulnerable to the selective interpretation of the researchers. We looked for evidence of a closed, elitist conspiracy and we found it. (Just as those who look for policy communities find them.)

Indeed, the more we disentangle the research process and the research relationship, the more complex and messy it becomes. There was, of course, the issue of access, and our presentation of our intentions and interests to our potential 'subjects'. We did not declare our theoretical orientation, nor de-scribe our project as an investigation of the elite fraction of a state bureaucracy with special reference to its class composition and interests. Instead, we said we wished to explore the nature of partnership, paying proper attention to the role of officials. This was true, but also flattering, and played to the group's prejudices (they despised politicians). We were greatly helped in our access to the group by the fact that one of us had worked closely with a former deputy permanent secretary, who introduced us to his former colleagues, reassuring them that we were 'quite harmless'. That individual was well aware of the ways in which one of us saw the world, which is some extenuation of the presentation of the project — he believed that Marxism was a disease of youth and would wear off.

There were other factors which assisted access. We were dealing with the past, and that made an important difference, as we have explained elsewhere (Gewirtz and Ozga, 1994). Recent history was also on our side, as there was a widespread feeling of disillusionment among our informants, consequent on policy change and the increased influence of politicians. The fact that they were retired was helpful: these were people who were not necessarily reconciled to inactivity; they welcomed the opportunity to revisit their active past, and to comment on the shortcomings of their successors. It is undoubtedly the case that we exploited their intelligence and sharpness: these individuals believed themselves to be skilled in assessing individual character and competence, and they enjoyed the opportunity to display this skill in commenting on one another. As a group they were incurious about our motives and intentions, and felt that they were contributing to the recording of a remarkable period of public service.

These, then, are some of the ethical issues raised by access. We now turn to the matter of location of the interviews. We did the early interviews together, but as the project progressed, one of us (SG) did more of them. Most interviews were recorded in the informants' homes. There was little alternative, as few of them had access to neutral office space, and they much preferred us to come to them. At the time we felt that this arrangement was appropriate in that it gave them control of the event; however there are issues raised by this that might merit consideration. Although our reception varied, almost all our informants offered us hospitality and made us welcome in their homes. Some confined us to a fairly formal and barren space, which provided little information about their personality or interests. (Typically, these individuals were also the least likely to offer self-conscious personal accounts, but concentrated on the formal and factual. There was, in effect, a correlation between the sterility of their observations and the sterility of their surroundings.) The point we are making here though is that we were guests, and treated with courtesy. We were introduced to other family members, and offered (and partook of) their hospitality. We broke bread with them. The resultant breaking down of researcher–subject boundaries is a feature of life-history work, and not necessarily problematic. However, there is a particular ethical issue here, in relation to our presentation of ourselves and our project: we presented ourselves as unthreatening and rather innocent, and compounded the problem by engaging in a social relationship. We do not know the extent to which this is a shared problem in researching education policy; we feel we cannot be the only researchers who have presented themselves in this way, or given a diluted version of their intentions in order to gain access. We are also not the only researchers to feel caught by the help and trust offered to us. MacPherson and Raab (1988) (who were much more explicit about what they were doing and who separated the political from the personal) indicate some unease:

> Our approach has a number of implications. First and foremost, people have helped and trusted us, and this has influenced all of our decisions about the presentation of evidence . . . In a sense our research was tapping the trust which binds members of the policy

community together across dispersed structural locations and even across lines of conflict on particular issues. We, in turn, were trusted and vouched for . . . If trust and help took us into the policy community, were we also 'taken in' in other ways? Was it gullibility that rendered us harmless? (MacPherson and Raab, 1988, p. 62)

Perhaps each 'side' colluded in the self-conscious self-presentation of the other. We offered an unthreatening, interested and sympathetic version of ourselves; they offered us their smooth and polished self-presentation, which incorporated gentlemanly hospitality and courtesy. We each had a purpose in view, and there was even a degree of gentle mockery of us (as innocent enquirers) and of themselves (as harmless old codgers whose day was done). We feel, perhaps, less uncomfortable than we should about the relationship that developed with our informants because of the degree of sophistication they exhibited. Not many were so vain or self-important that we led them into indiscretion or self-glorification. The interaction was complex, however, and its subtleties extend beyond the kind of textual analysis that focuses on events or themes. It encouraged much more, and could be characterized as the self-conscious presentation of 'the public servant', a sort of composite of all the virtues of humane, service-oriented, Fabian-influenced bureaucracy. The social characteristics, the self-deprecation, the humour, and the affected confusion were allied to strong beliefs, clearly articulated, an assumption of superiority, and impatience. Our informants also shared the capacity not merely to present in this manner, but to tell their stories fluently and in a deliberate, considered way, which gave us considerable unease, methodologically. Yet it is one of the things which supports our argument about the significance and power of this bureaucracy. Our concern about the accuracy of these accounts led us to concentrate in the original seminar on the methodological issues raised in assessing such evidence.

We did not feel under any obligation to challenge the narratives of our informants, to interrupt the flow and push for clarification of particular issues. We did not see that it was part of our task to fracture the polished surface presented to us. This was not because we were compromised by our self-presentation as innocent and eager listeners, but because the polished nature of the account was an object of study and required to be recorded and absorbed as presented. Of course, we used other methods to 'check' what was said, drawing on our shared experience as historians — we do not wish to give the impression that we simply accepted the official version. We used recognized secondary sources to guide us towards primary sources. We knew where to look for relevant documentary evidence — the Public Records Office archives, the Alexander collection in Leeds, Lady Shena Simon's collection in Manchester, and other public and private collections of educational papers. (For a good review of such material see Gosden, 1981.) We made use of such sources and the accounts of others as a basis for comparison and cross-checking of informants' accounts as well as to help us 'map' the period. The memoranda and correspondence prepared by Ministry officials held at the Public Record Office and released under the thirty-year rule were especially helpful. These papers were confidential, for internal consumption, and represented the main form of communication within the Ministry and with local authority officers. They were very detailed and contained lengthy expositions of departmental positions, as well as uninhibited comment on developments and individuals. Methodologically, then, we were combining the relatively straightforward with rather more complex and potentially contradictory approaches.

If these are the ethical issues connected to the second part of our title, 'lies', then those connected with 'sex' now require discussion. The central issue here was again one of self-presentation, connected with our informants' perceptions of women. It is more properly described as a gender issue. Feminist researchers, for example, Finch (1984) have discussed the extent to which researchers control and direct their 'subjects'. Such researchers moved from expression of their sense of the inappropriateness of the forms and methods of research in exchanges between women to a more general critique of the apparently accepted power relations which are encapsulated in much social science research — in data collection and analysis. Our gender did have an impact on the research and on the relationship with our informants. As noted above, it assisted us in gaining access, as we were perceived as unthreatening and relatively unimportant because of our gender. However, there were other effects, which provide an ironic commentary on the feminist critique of power relations, with which we were familiar and which we endorsed. We were viewed as women in very stereotypical ways, and thus fell 'naturally' into the role of attentive listener. We were assumed to be receptive and sympathetic, and colluded with that version of ourselves because it was productive for the project.

We were thus compromised on two grounds, as marxists and as feminists. We did not make our perspective on the project clear to our informants, and we allowed ourselves to be patronized by them. We reflected back to them their own prejudice that power and authority were the province of men. Indeed, it is interesting that our one woman informant, Gwenneth Rickus, Chief Education Officer for Brent between 1971–84, suggested that we should be cautious of the way in which the male directors of education presented themselves which she felt exaggerated their role. She made the following point in relation to the respective power of directors and councillors:

> I often got the impression that Chief Education Officers felt they told their committees what to do. But I wasn't convinced that it was necessarily like that but it was part of them putting forward the male view of their position, that in fact they might well have been more obviously challenged than they said but they weren't going to admit it when they were talking outside the authority. (Personal interview, n.d.)

In our defence, we would argue that it was not our concern to attempt to persuade our informants of the importance of our theoretical perspective, nor to attempt to challenge the sexism of senior public servants. Had we attempted either, we would have lost access. Nor are we unique in our compromises: many researchers simplify or moderate their explanations of their intentions, and select a presentation of self which will reassure the audience and assist in the enquiry. These are compromises that we all make if we are at all self-conscious about our presence in the research.

Conclusion

Here we come full circle, and return to our introductory discussion of the aims of the project, its theoretical underpinning and its methodology. The ethical issues clustered around 'sex and lies' cannot be viewed separately from theoretical and methodological issues. They are the product of an uneasy relationship between theory and method. We would also suggest that these issues have become increasingly significant to us because of the growing importance that we would place on recognition of the researcher's effect on the research process. We have described a model which is not at all connected with conventional procedures of detachment and non-involvement. We do not wish to deny the disturbing and contaminating presence of the researcher, as such accounts do, whether they be 'positivistic' or 'naturalistic'. As Stanley and Wise (1993) put it:

> Our experiences suggest that 'hygienic research' is a reconstructed logic, a mythology which presents an oversimplistic account of research. It is also extremely misleading, in that it emphasizes the 'objective' presence of the researcher and suggests that she can be 'there' without having any greater involvement than simple presence. In contrast, we emphasize that all research involves, as its basis, an interaction, a relationship between researcher and researched . . . Because the basis of all research is a relationship, this necessarily involves the presence of the researcher *as a person*. Personhood cannot be left behind, cannot be left out of the research process. (Stanley and Wise, 1993, p. 161)

Our research is an unusual mixture — or collision? — between theory-driven enquiry and a methodology which both requires and sustains involvement, personal disclosure, exchange, trust and the building of relationships. Both the theoretical underpinning and the methodology left us vulnerable to ethical dilemmas. We consider such vulnerability to be shared, but not much discussed in education policy studies, where enquiry (even ethnographic study) is neither strongly theory-driven nor much concerned with the researcher's relationship to the research. Perhaps this is because education policy studies are constituted at the level of 'common sense' as political rather than personal. Perhaps it is simply that the difficulty of access to people who 'make' policy precludes anything other than conventional enquiry.

References

BERTAUX, D. (1981) (Ed) *Biography and Society: The Life History Approach in the Social Sciences*, Beverley Hills, Sage.

CLARK, A. (1993) *Diaries*, London, Weidenfeld and Nicholson.

COX, R. (1980) 'Social forces, states and world orders', *Millenium: Journal of International Studies*, 10, 2, pp. 126–55.

DALE, R. and OZGA, J. (1991) *Understanding Education Policy: Principles and Perspectives* (E333 Module 1), Walton Hall, Open University Press.

DUNLEAVY, P. and O'LEARY, B. (1987) *Theories of the State*, Basingstoke, MacMillan.

FERRAROTI, F. (1990) *Time, Memory and Society*, New York, Greenwood Press.

FINCH, J. (1984) ' "It's great to have someone to talk to": The ethics and politics of interviewing women', in BELL, C. and ROBERTS, H. (Eds) *Social Researching: Policies, Problems, Practice*, London, Routledge and Kegan Paul.

GEWIRTZ, S. (1993) 'Recent education policy research and the neglect of social justice issues', Paper presented to CES Research Seminar, King's College London, March 1993.

GEWIRTZ, S. and OZGA, J. (1990) 'Partnership, pluralism and education policy: A reassessment', *Journal of Education Policy*, 15, 1, pp. 37–48.

GEWIRTZ, S. and OZGA, J. (1994) 'Interviewing the education policy elite', in Walford, G. (Ed) *Researching the Powerful in Education* London, University of London.

GOSDEN, P. (1981) 'Twentieth century archives of education as sources for the study of education policy and administration', *Archives*, 15, 66.

HARVEY, L. (1990) *Critical Social Research*, London, Allen and Unwin.

HMSO (1976) *Report of the Committee of Privy Councillors on Ministerial Memoirs* (Radcliffe Report) London, HMSO.

JOHNSON, R. (1989) 'Thatcherism and English education', *History of Education*, 18, 2, pp. 91–121.

KOGAN M. (1975) *Educational Policy Making*, London, Allen and Unwin.

LAWN, M. and OZGA, J. (1986) 'Unequal partners: Teachers under indirect rule', *British Journal of the Sociology of Education*, 7, 2, pp. 225–38.

MAC AN GHAILL, M. (1988) *Young, Gifted and Black*, Milton Keynes, Open University Press.

McNAY, I. and OZGA, J. (Eds) (1985) *Policy Making in Education: The Breakdown of Consensus*, Oxford, Pergamon/Open University Press.

McPHERSON, A. and RAAB, C. (1988) *Governing Education: A Sociology of Policy Since 1945*, Edinburgh, Edinburgh University Press.

MILLS, C.W. (1959) *The Sociological Imagination*, New York, Oxford University Press.

OAKLEY, A. (1981) 'Interviewing women: A contradiction in terms', in ROBERTS, H. (Ed) *Doing Feminist Research*, London, Routledge and Kegan Paul.

OZGA, J. (1987) 'Studying Education through the lives of the policy-makers: An attempt to close the macro–micro gap', in BARTON, L. and WALKER, S. (Eds) *Changing Policies, Changing Teachers: New Directions in Schooling*, Lewes, Falmer Press.

OZGA, J. (1990) 'Policy research and policy theory: A comment on Fitz and Halpin', *Journal of Education Policy*, 5, 4, pp. 359–62.

PLUMMER, K. (1983) *Documents of Life*, London, Allen and Unwin.

POULANTZAS, N. (1976) 'The capitalist state', *New Left Review*, 95, pp. 63–83.

RANSON, S. and TOMLINSON, J. (1986) *The Changing Government of Education*, London, Allen and Unwin.

SIMON, B. (1965) *Education and the Labour Movement 1870–1920*, London, Lawrence and Wishart.

SIMON, B. (1974a) *The Two Nations and the Education Structure 1780–1870*, London, Lawrence and Wishart.

SIMON, B. (1974b) *The Politics of Educational Reform 1820–1940*, London, Lawrence and Wishart.

SIMON, B. (1988) *Bending the Rules*, London, Lawrence and Wishart.

STANLEY, L. and WISE, S. (1993) *Breaking Out Again*, London, Routledge.

TROYNA, B. (1994) Critical social research and education policy, *British Journal of Educational Studies*, 42, 1, pp. 70–84.

Part 3

Methodological Perspectives on Research into Education Policy

Chapter 10

Ethnography, Policy Making and Practice in Education

Martyn Hammersley

In this chapter I want to look at the question of what the relationship should be between ethnographic research, on the one hand, and educational policy-making and practice, on the other.[1] This is an issue that acquires particular significance against the background of the Education Reform Act and associated recent legislation. I believe that this legislation highlights some serious problems with current conceptualizations of the research–practice relationship. It certainly throws substantial doubt on the well-foundedness of any optimism researchers may have had about the influence of their work on national policy making in education. It is not just that educational research played little or no role in shaping the Act, but even more that in many respects the legislation goes in opposite directions to those indicated by its findings (Smith and Smith, 1992; Gipps, 1993). And, in the case of ethnography, the conflict runs even deeper. The very presuppositions on which recent government policy has been based (for example about the possibility and significance of quantitative measurement of educational outcomes) are at odds with the methodological orientation of ethnographers. Distrust of input and output measures like test scores and examination results, and an emphasis on the importance of educational *processes*, are characteristic of that orientation. For these reasons, ethnographers have long been at the forefront in criticizing reliance on quantitative measures, on the grounds that these presuppose simplistic conceptions of human social behaviour and of how it can be understood.[2]

Of course, most ethnographic research has not been directed towards shaping national policy. To the extent that it has been concerned with influencing educational policy and practice, it has mainly been addressed to those on the ground: to teachers, above all, but also to local authority advisers, governors, etc. And it may be argued that this is where the greatest scope for ethnographic influence lies. However, recent national policy has restructured the conditions in which teachers and others work in such a way as to reduce that scope substantially; not least by increasing administrative pressures. And the changes in initial teacher training and in-service education of teachers also seem likely further to limit the influence of educational researchers and teacher educators.[3]

However, I want to suggest that recent legislation has simply worsened a problem that was already there, and that developments *within* the field of research have also exacerbated it. I have in mind here the various challenges to what we might call the enlightenment thinking that has shaped social and educational research. In exploring this problem, I will look at the recent history of ethnography, particularly in the context of the sociology of education; and then go on to examine two sources of doubt about the contribution that research can make to practice. First, though, it might be useful to outline some contrasting models of the research–practice relationship.

Some Models of the Research-practice Relationship

We can usefully conceptualize variation in the relationship between research, on the one hand, and social, educational and political practice, on the other, in terms of three ideal-typical models. The first of these, long influential in the academic world but now under pressure, is what I will call the 'disciplinary model'. Here the goal of research is to contribute to knowledge in a particular discipline, perhaps with abstract theoretical knowledge being given priority. While such work may ultimately make a contribution to practice, this contribution is not intended to be very immediate or specific. It is a matter of general-purpose knowledge or of modifying assumptions about the social world that underly a wide range of forms of practical activity. Indeed, the knowledge produced is valued as much for its own sake as for any instrumental value it has.

A second model, also institutionalized in many fields, is what is sometimes called the 'engineering or policy research model'.[4] This conceptualizes the process of research as follows: a practitioner or group of practitioners has a problem, the solution to which requires information or understanding that they do not have. The researcher is called in to provide that knowledge or understanding. The sort of information required can vary widely. It may be descriptive information about a target population, as in market research. It may be explanatory, concerned with why some unforeseen problem with policy implementation arose. Equally, it may require an evaluation of whether a policy achieved its targets, or of whether it has done so in the most cost-effective way. Again, it could be prescriptive, concerned with the whole task of finding an effective and efficient means of achieving a goal. However, the parameters of the inquiry process are set narrowly: the aim is to solve a problem, and both the problem and what constitutes a solution are defined by the sponsors. Furthermore, the audience for the report (which may be oral and even secret rather than written and public) is closely defined. And there will also usually be a time schedule that the researcher must meet if the work is to be of any use. Research of this kind fits neatly into the Rothschild mould (Rothschild, 1971), and is becoming increasingly common in the field of education under the influence of recent government policy.

Finally, there is what I will call the 'critical model'. Here, research may relate to a particular policy problem, but this is likely to be a perennial issue rather than a problem facing a particular group of practitioners at a particular point in time. In addition, there is likely to be reliance on a distinctive and comprehensive political perspective that gives coherence to the work. Not only is the problem for investigation selected by the researcher, it may be conceptualized in ways that relevant practitioners do not appreciate (in both senses of that word). Nor will the audience usually be closely specified or restricted. The aim, if you like, is to contribute to discussion in the public sphere, and thereby to 'enlighten' various sorts of practitioners. Here the researcher's role is that of social critic.[5]

These three models give us a sense of the range of sorts of relationship that may hold between research and practice, they are not intended to be exhaustive. In the next section I want to look at orientations towards politics and educational practice on the part of researchers in the sociology of education.

A Historical Sketch of the Relationship Between Research, Politics and Practice in the Sociology of Education

We can usefully start with the political arithmetic tradition which dominated research in the sociology of education in the 1950s and early 1960s.[6] Work of this kind was structured by three central concerns. One was to contribute to the discipline of sociology. A.H. Halsey, a central figure, belonged to what he himself has called 'the first group of career sociologists in Britain' (Halsey, 1982, p. 150). And the work of political arithmeticians was explicitly tied to general theoretical developments in that field and to research in other substantive areas besides education. They saw themselves as contributing to a discipline that was still struggling to establish a secure place for itself within universities, and one which had a crucial role to play in the modern world.[7] A second goal was to influence policy makers, both at national and at local government levels. The political arithmeticians were not simply concerned to understand modern society, they wanted to shape it; and they were probably more successful in this respect in the field of education than most subsequent sociologists and educational researchers have been. Furthermore, this interest in shaping policy and practice was related to a third concern, a commitment to democratic socialism.[8] In their review of the history and character of the political arithmetic tradition, Halsey *et al.* (1980) emphasize this practical political commitment:

> These writers were concerned to describe accurately and in detail the social conditions of their society, particularly of the more disadvantaged sections, but their interest in these matters was never a disinterested academic one. Description of social conditions was a preliminary

to political reform. They exposed the inequalities of society in order to change them. The tradition thus has a double intent: on the one hand it engages in the primary sociological task of describing and documenting the 'state of society'; on the other hand it addresses itself to central social and political issues. It has never, therefore, been a 'value free' academic discipline, if such were in any event possible. Instead, it has been an attempt to marry a value-laden choice of issue with objective methods of data collection. (Halsey *et al.*, 1980, p. 1)

What is distinctive about the orientation of the political arithmeticians is the way in which theoretical and practical goals are combined, representing a kind of amalgam of the three models I identified in the previous section. None of the three concerns is felt to be in conflict with the others. Each is fully compatible with, perhaps even conducive to the pursuit of, the others. This view was possible because these researchers saw modern societies as evolving towards social democracy under the driving force of technological development.[9] From this point of view there is a happy coincidence between the ideal of social democracy and the needs of economic development. Thus, in the course of their discussion of secondary schools and the supply of labour, Floud and Halsey comment: 'freedom of vocational choice and movement are both the citizen's right and the conditions of a fluid and economically distributed labour supply, which is, in turn, a prerequisite of the high level of economic prosperity on which the Welfare State depends (Floud and Halsey, 1956, p. 63).

Furthermore, in the context of modern, technological society, the political arithmeticians of the 1950s and 1960s saw sociology as playing a key role in facilitating the process of social and economic development. It provided a map of the path ahead based on theoretical understanding of the past and of developments in other societies. In addition, empirical sociological research showed where the priorities for further progress lay; for example pointing out that the selective education system was not providing equality of opportunity and not maximizing economic exploitation of the available pool of talent, this indicating the need for a shift to a comprehensive system of education. And, given that progress towards democratic socialism was not only possible but was in the interests of all, it could reasonably be assumed that at least some politicians and policy makers were predisposed to take account of the knowledge produced by sociologists, and that their actions on the basis of this knowledge would facilitate social progress. I am not suggesting that the political arithmeticians believed that progress was inevitable or that their advice would necessarily be heeded, simply that they assumed that conditions were open to benign influence.

I will refer to the orientation of the political arithmeticians in short-hand terms as the enlightenment conception of the relationship between research and practice.[10] This involves the assumption that cognitive and political progress are built into the process of historical change, albeit perhaps as potentialities rather than inevitabilities, and that they are closely related to one another. Above all, what we have here is a substantial optimism about the ability of researchers to produce the knowledge that is required by policy makers and practitioners, and about the capacity of that knowledge to generate desirable change.

In the late 1960s and early 1970s the political arithmetic tradition came under increasing criticism, and there emerged a 'new sociology of education'.[11] In part, this reflected theoretical changes in sociology; in particular the growing influence of western marxism, of symbolic interactionism, and of phenomenology. There was also a shift in methodological terms. Political arithmetic was predominantly quantitative in orientation, reflecting a commitment to a view of science as essentially concerned with measurement and statistical analysis, and probably also a judgment about what sorts of evidence were most likely to influence policy makers. The 1960s and 1970s saw increasing criticism of quantitative method, and more and more use of ethnographic techniques within sociology and elsewhere. Also significant was a shift in target audience, from national and local educational policy makers to teachers.[12] With the expansion of higher education, and especially of preservice education of teachers, there was now a large market for publications on education that would be directly relevant to teachers. Most of the political arithmetic research was not addressed to them, and was not of immediate relevance because it did not focus at school level. Here there was a fortunate meshing of some of the recent changes in sociology with the new demands made on the sociology of education: an ethnographic focus on micro-level processes within schools and classrooms was one of the results.

Much of the work in the new sociology of education also involved a political shift away from the social democratic ideas typical of the previous generation to more radical views, often combining Marxism (especially the young Marx) with anarchist ideas. Here the new sociologists reflected the political spirit of the 1960s. Gone was the previous sense of slow evolution in a leftwards direction. There was still optimism about the prospects for change, but this was to be radical change forced by rebellion from below, not a mere continuation of what had gone before managed by those already in power. Associated with this was a modification in attitude towards the nature of education. Whereas the political arithmeticians had been concerned with the unequal distribution of opportunities for education, many of the new sociologists challenged what counted as education in contemporary society. Thus, much of what the previous generation had believed should and would be inherited by a socialist society, for example acceptance of the value of science and of professional expertise, was now questioned. These began to be seen above all as devices by which dominant groups maintain their power.

The 'new sociology' was not a single coherent movement, and we can identify three different strands of ethnographic work associated with it. One was the development of what has come to be called critical ethnography, initiated in the work of Keddie (1971), Sharp and Green (1975), and Willis

(1977), and to be found more recently in the writings of feminists and antiracists.[13] Second, there was the emergence of new qualitative forms of curriculum evaluation and the development of the teacher-action research movement (Stenhouse, 1975; Hamilton *et al.*, 1977; Simons, 1987; Elliott, 1991a).[14] Finally, there was a stream of interactionist ethnography, exemplified in the work of Delamont, Woods, Hargreaves, Ball, Pollard, Burgess and others' (see, for example, the articles in Hargreaves and Woods, 1984 and Hammersley and Woods, 1984). These divisions were never watertight, but they represent important differences in tendency that display a fragmentation of the old sociology's enlightenment commitment.

As its name implies, critical ethnography adopted something like what I referred to earlier as the critical model. Work in this tradition emphasized the connection with politics, albeit with a change of political ideals from political arithmetic. At the same time it maintained a link with the discipline of sociology, through elements within that discipline which shared its political orientation.[15] However, by contrast with the old sociology of education, the relationship to educational policy making and practice came to be a problem for the critical tradition. Its political orientation held out little hope of influencing civil servants or governments (even Labour ones). Instead, as I have noted, the primary audience came to be teachers or at least student teachers.[16] But the question inevitably arose of the degree to which teachers were in a position to act on the knowledge provided by the new sociologists so as to bring about social or even educational transformation. Early work in this tradition was criticized for its neglect of the constraints under which teachers work (Whitty, 1977). And there was a resulting swing to analyses that, as a result of the influence of Althusser (1971) and Bowles and Gintis (1976), left little theoretical space for teachers to resist the system (Arnot and Whitty, 1982). Moreover, while such deterministic positions were quickly abandoned, the problem of the relationship between sociological critique and political practice was not solved (as indeed it has not been within Marxism generally).[17]

Work in the field of curriculum development and evaluation took at least two forms, these varying in their orientation to the three concerns that were central to political arithmetic. The democratic evaluation movement, exemplified in the work of MacDonald and his co-workers, presented the role of the evaluator as that of a neutral broker among the various interest groups whose views were to be represented (Simons, 1987). As Elliott has argued, this claim to neutrality is somewhat misleading; the democratic evaluator is better seen as a social critic operating on the basis of a liberal conception of how the common good is to be determined. Indeed, Elliott describes democratic evaluation as a vision of a possible future, in which educational-policy decisions are made through a process of discussion involving those at the grass-roots not just those at the top (Elliott, 1992). In this sense, the work of the democratic evaluators, like that of the critical ethnographers, reflects a primary commitment to politics, in this case seeking to establish democratic

procedures of accountability in relation to both policy makers and practitioners. Some versions of teacher-action research also place considerable emphasis
on a political orientation, and one very similar to that of critical ethnographers
(for example Carr and Kemmis, 1986). However, other strands of this tradition have put greater stress on the link with educational practice, on enabling
teachers to become reflective practitioners and to use research techniques to
resolve their practical problems (for example Nixon, 1981; and Hustler *et al.*,
1986). Here the link between research and practice is closest in some respects
to the engineering model. Finally, none of these approaches placed much
emphasis on the goal of contributing to disciplinary knowledge.

By contrast, the interactionist tradition gave primacy to the relationship
between ethnographic research and the sociology of education as a discipline:
to the construction of a body of knowledge about teacher and pupil perspectives, patterns of classroom interaction etc. The other two concerns, politics
and the link with policy making and educational practice, remained largely in
the background. In short, this work has been close to the disciplinary model.
And, not surprisingly, interactionist ethnography has been criticized for its
theoretical weaknesses from a political point of view (for example, Sharp,
1982), and for its distance from, and alleged arrogance towards teachers (for
instance, McNamara, 1980; see also Hammersley, 1981). While there have
been attempts by interactionists to create syntheses with critical ethnography
(for example Hargreaves, 1980) and to draw in some elements from the action
research tradition (Woods, 1986, chapter 1; Woods and Pollard, 1988, Introduction), these have not resulted in a new position balancing the three concerns, but rather in fragmentation of the tradition.

In each of these forms of ethnographic research emerging from the new
sociology of education, then, only one or two of the three concerns that
structured the old sociology of education have been given emphasis. This is
not to say that enlightenment faith in the contribution of knowledge to the
achievement of the good society has disappeared. It continues to lie behind
much thinking and writing about the role of social and educational research.
For example, Pollard (1984, p. 179) has argued that '[. . .] the developments
which are necessary to reinvigorate the contribution of ethnography to our
social scientific understanding are very close to those which are necessary to
make it a more effective source of informed policy'. And he goes on to claim
that for both purposes 'it is the quality of the work which is of paramount
importance' (pp. 182–3). Despite the fact that Pollard is writing about a
different approach to research (ethnography) which is seeking to influence
a different sort of policy maker (teachers in the classroom), he retains the
enlightenment optimism of the political arithmeticians regarding the prospect
of producing sound knowledge and the capacity of that knowledge to shape
practice in desirable directions. Finch (1986) shows more awareness of the
problematic relationship between research and policy making, but she too
retains faith in the capacity of research, especially qualitative work, simultaneously to pursue its own goals and to enlighten policy makers and produce

progressive policy. However, it is becoming increasingly difficult to defend this enlightenment optimism. One reason for this is that it relies on a theory claiming to provide a meta-narrative about change in society, towards the achievement of rational political ideals, brought about through the dissemination of research-based knowledge; and such theories are under increasing challenge. Support for the technological functionalism on which the political arithmeticians relied collapsed in the 1960s and 1970s, along with that for other sorts of sociological functionalism. And the main alternative, Hegelian Marxism, underwent a similar decline in the 1980s, as a result of the criticisms of structuralists and post-structuralists. In the remainder of this chapter I want to look at two more specific aspects of the challenge to the enlightenment paradigm which relate directly to the pursuit of educational research.

Two Challenges to the Enlightenment Paradigm

Two currently influential lines of argument imply severe limits on the contribution that social and educational research can make to practice. The first concerns the nature of policy making and practice itself; the second relates to the character of the knowledge produced by research.

Recent work dealing with the influence of social research on policy making suggests that high expectations about this influence are ill-founded. It has been argued that such expectations assume a linear rational model of the decision-making process that is empirically inaccurate (Weiss and Bucuvalas, 1980).[18] However, the argument has been extended beyond this. It is not just that, as a matter of fact, the government, the DfE etc. do not make policy in the way implied by this model, the point is that there are good reasons for policy makers not to do so. For instance, it may be that no rational solution to the problems they face is possible within the time-scale imposed and the resources available, or perhaps the problem cannot be clearly enough defined for them to decide what would be the most appropriate direction in which to look for a solution. As a result of such difficulties, as Lindblom and Cohen (1979, p. 10) point out, whereas researchers tend to assume that problems should be solved by policy makers gathering and analysing information, with research findings being the major input, in fact much problem-solving 'is and ought to be accomplished through various forms of social interaction that substitute action for thought, understanding and analysis'. As examples they cite delegation, negotiation, voting, and the market mechanism (not to mention reading the entrails of fowls and trials by water and fire!). They emphasize that public policy making is a political process, not a matter of intellectual problem-solving (see Gregory, 1989); and that even where a rational knowledge-based solution is sought, research information is usually only a small part of the knowledge used, practical experience and skilled judgment being much more important.

This latter point resonates with a shift that has taken place in conceptualizations of the process of teaching. There has been increased emphasis on the role of practical judgment and skill on the part of teachers, resurrecting the old saw that teaching is an art not a science.[19] Where from the point of view of a crude positivism the traditional practices of teachers are based on folk knowledge that must be eliminated in favour of sound, scientifically validated techniques, from this perspective they are seen as more or less skillful and principled adjustments to circumstance that it may not be possible to better.[20] This position does not imply a blanket validation of the practices of teachers, simply that evaluation of them must take place in context, and has to draw on practical wisdom not just on theory. This clearly has important implications for the role of the educational researcher.

There is much to be said for these ideas about the character of policy making and practice. At the very least they throw doubt on the idea that educational research can provide a knowledge-base that will enable the policy maker or teacher to solve his or her problems simply by following prescriptions. But, more generally, they represent a useful counterbalance to over-rationalistic interpretations of educational policy making and practice. There is a conflict here not just with the enlightenment paradigm built into the old sociology of education, but even with the assumptions about the relationship between research, politics and practice embodied in the new sociology of education. For example, the critical model also places great emphasis on the value of theory in guiding practice. Indeed, research in this tradition is premissed on the idea that through social transformation the gap between theory and practice can be overcome.[21] And while the democratic evaluation movement gives little emphasis to the role of theory, it does assume that policy is, or ought to be, made through public discussion. A similar problem arises with teacher-action research: here there may be an excessive optimism about the contribution that a research orientation can make to teaching; a misguided attempt to reconstruct practice on the model of intellectual work (Hammersley, 1993b).

The second problem for the enlightenment paradigm arises from the growing influence of epistemological scepticism and relativism. That influence is to be found all across the humanities and the social sciences today, but was present even in the symbolic interactionism and social phenomenology that shaped the new sociology of education. When Herbert Blumer talks of different groups occupying different worlds (Blumer, 1966, p. 540) and Berger and Luckmann declare that reality is socially constructed (Berger and Luckmann, 1967), it does not take much of a leap of imagination to see that there is a sense in which ethnographers themselves are engaged in a process of 'world construction' when they analyse data and write research reports. Often this relativism has been used selectively, as a way of 'deconstructing' others' accounts. But recently there have been attempts to apply the idea more generally. We can see this in the constructivism of Guba, Lincoln, Smith and others (Smith, 1989; Guba, 1990) and in the beginnings of attempts to apply poststructuralist and postmodernist ideas to qualitative research (Clifford and

Marcus, 1986; Gubrium and Silverman, 1989; Lather, 1991). One effect of these sceptical and relativist interpretations of social research is to undermine the basis on which researchers can claim the relevance of their work to practise. The authority that researchers are able to claim in the intellectual marketplace is that they provide reliable knowledge of the world. Once the very possibility of such knowledge has been denied, the findings of research lose their distinctive value. Furthermore, relativism undermines political commitment. The case of Foucault is instructive: while he manages to retain an image of political radicalism in his work, this is only achieved by an implicit reliance on what he explicitly criticizes. While apparently abandoning the enlightenment project, he retains the central idea that knowledge is power; along with a residual, and in terms of his framework indefensible, belief in the value of resistance (Dews, 1986 and 1987).[22]

These two problems, respectively about the nature of policy making and practice and of research, are genuine and serious; though I think they have sometimes been exaggerated. As regards the first, while confident views about the capacity of theory to guide practice must certainly be abandoned, we should be careful not to go to the other extreme, celebrating irrationality and dismissing the value of research completely. Similarly, scepticism and relativism seem to me to be false conclusions drawn from genuine criticisms of positivism and naive realism (Hammersley, 1992). However, even a moderate view about both these issues has far reaching implications for the capacity of research to contribute to practice. Where once educational and political practice could be seen as open to 'rationalization' on the basis of scientific research founded on a method that guaranteed valid results, now we must recognize that politics and practice may be ontologically resistant to such 'rationalization', and also that the knowledge produced by research is always fallible. Furthermore, what research offers is not a God's eye view, but rather perspectives from particular angles, the appropriateness of which can be challenged. I do not believe that as educational researchers we have yet come to terms with the implications of these arguments for our work.

Conclusion

In the course of this chapter I have highlighted some problems with the enlightenment thinking that has shaped ideas about the relationship between research and social and political practice. It no longer seems possible, if it ever was, simultaneously to pursue the goals of contributing to disciplinary knowledge and serving educational policy making and practice, while at the same time framing research within some all-embracing political philosophy. Attempts to justify this rest on functionalist or Hegelian ideas that have come to be unconvincing, and there are no obvious alternatives. In addition, I considered some arguments about the nature of policy making and practice and the character of the knowledge produced by research that also pose a threat to the enlightenment paradigm. While I do not accept the extreme versions of these arguments, I believe they raise serious difficulties about the role of research, difficulties that are highlighted for educational researchers at the present time by the circumstances I outlined at the beginning of this chapter. In our situation we may, more than usually, feel a practical need to exert what resistance we can against current policy trends. If it were true that our research could produce practically applicable theories that are guided by a cogent political perspective, all soundly based on a methodology that guaranteed validity, we would be well-placed to use (and would be justified in using) our research to promote that resistance. But if we take account of the problems I have discussed in this chapter, our basis for doing this is weakened considerably, if not completely undercut. We need to rethink the role of educational research in these new conditions, and this may mean questioning much that we have previously taken for granted about the nature of research and its relationship to politics and educational practice.

Notes

1 I am taking the term 'ethnography' to refer to qualitative research in general. Indeed, much of the argument presented here applies to educational research as a whole.

2 For one of the earliest ethnographic critiques, see Cicourel *et al.* (1974).

3 I am not implying that the education reforms are all being instituted in the manner, or with the effects, intended by the government. See Ball and Bowe (1992) for an account of the micro-political processes involved.

4 See Bulmer (1982) for a useful discussion and for references.

5 Habermas's work has been concerned with explicating the philosophical and political justification for this model (for a useful account, see Holub (1991)).

6 For a brief account of this approach, an approach whose influence was not limited to educational research and whose history can be traced back into the nineteenth century, see Halsey *et al.* (1980) Chapter 1. See also Glass (1950) and Westergaard (1979), and Smith and Smith (1992).

7 Sociology was not defined narrowly but in large part by contrast with biological, psychological, and economic approaches.

8 Dennis and Halsey (1988) refer to the political ideals that motivated their research as ethical socialism, which they see as exemplified in the writings of Hobhouse. Orwell, Marshall and above all Tawney.

9 The introduction to Halsey, Floud and Anderson (1961) gives a clear sense of this technological functionalism. For a critique of American versions of technological functionalism, see Goldthorpe (1967). It is worth pointing out that Halsey *et al.*, did not see the relationship beween technology and social development, or that between education and economy, as simple and unmediated. And their functionalism seems to have been inherited as much from Marx as from structural functionalism. On Marx's functionalism, see Cohen (1978).

10 I am using the term 'enlightenment conception' here in a slightly different sense to Bulmer (1982). All three of the models I outlined in the previous section draw on enlightenment thinking, of course, but the position adopted by the political arithmeticians is a paradigm case. For a useful summary of enlightenment ideas, see Brinton (1967).

11 See Young and Whitty (1977) for a useful account by key protagonists. I will use the term 'new sociology of education' broadly to refer to the whole range of new trends that emerged in the early 1970s, not just those to be found at the London Institute of Education. See Atkinson *et al.* (1993).

12 This was anticipated in Hargreaves' book *Social Relations in a Secondary School*; see his final chapter (Hargreaves, 1967). The influential work of Hargreaves and of Lacey (1970) which preceded the new sociology, stemmed from a different source: the Manchester school of social anthropology, on which see Frankenberg (1981).

13 For an explication in the field of antiracist research, see Troyna and Carrington (1989).

14 These developments were not part of the sociology of education, strictly speaking, but there was a strong mutual influence.

15 Notably marxist work of various kinds as well as that of writers like Mills (1959) and Gouldner (1970 and 1973).

16 For some reflections on this question of the target audience for the new sociology of education and its relation to practice, see Whitty (1985).

17 See McCarney (1990). Closely related was criticism of the work of critical sociologists for not being accessible to practitioners because it is written in a language that does not address them. See the comment by Young in Nisbet and Broadfoot (1980, p. 44) and Saraga (1992). Again, this is a general problem within western Marxism; see Anderson (1976, pp. 53–4).

18 For useful discussions of these issues in the field of education, see Taylor (1973) and Nisbet and Broadfoot (1980).

19 We find this, for example, in the writings of Schwab (1969), Hirst (1983), Schön (1983 and 1987), and Carr (1987).

20 This picture of the character of teaching is of course compatible with an appreciative interactionist stance; but, interestingly, interactionist ethnography has often adopted a much more ambivalent attitude towards the classroom practices of teachers (see for instance Woods, 1977 and Hargreaves, 1978). In fact, the only sort of empirical work that is consistently appreciative is that of the ethnomethodologists (such as Payne and Cuff, 1982).

21 This is at the core of Marx's work, being a reaction against the element in Hegelianism that sees theory as reconciling us with the world; see Plant 1973. For a general discussion of the Hegelian and marxist background to critical ethnography, see Hammersley (1992, Chapter 6).

22 What this scepticism and relativism amount to in large part, of course, is a rejection of the model of science. But, as Lepenies (1980) points out, the most significant feature of the present intellectual crisis is that there seems to be no new alternative waiting in the wings to take over from science; there are only old and discredited ones such as religion or literature.

References

ALTHUSSER, L. (1971) 'Ideology and ideological state apparatuses', *Lenin and Philosophy and Other Essays*, London, New Left Books.

ANDERSON, P. (1976) *Considerations on Western Marxism*, London, New Left Books.

ARNOT, M. and WHITTY, G. (1982) 'From reproduction to transformation: recent radical perspectives on the curriculum from the USA,' *British Journal of Sociology of Education*, 3, 1, pp. 93–103.

ATKINSON, P., DELAMONT, S. and HAMMERSLEY, M. (1993) 'Qualitative research traditions: A British response', in HAMMERSLEY, M. (Ed) *Educational Research: Current Issues*, London, Paul Chapman.

BALL, S.J. and BOWE, R. (1992) 'Subject departments and the "implementation" of National Curriculum policy: An overview of the issues', *Journal of Curriculum Studies*, 24, 2, pp. 97–115.

BERGER, P. and LUCKMANN, T. (1967) *The Social Construction of Reality*, Harmondsworth, Penguin.

BOWLES, S. and GINTIS, H. (1976) *Schooling in Capitalist America*. London, Routledge and Kegan Paul.

BLUMER, H. (1966) 'Sociological implications of the thought of George Herbert Mead', *American Journal of Sociology*, 71, pp. 535–44.

BRINTON, C. (1967) 'Enlightenment', in EDWARDS, P. (Ed) *The Encyclopedia of Philosophy*, New York, Macmillan.

BULMER, M. (1982) *The Uses of Social Research*, London, Allen and Unwin.

CARR, W. (1987) 'What is an educational practice', *Journal of Philosophy of Education*, 21, 2, pp. 163–75.

CARR, W. and KEMMIS, S. (1986) *Becoming Critical*, Lewes, Falmer Press.

CICOUREL, A.V., JENNINGS, K., JENNINGS, S., LEITER, K., MACKAY, R., MEHAN, H. and ROTH, D. (1974) *Language Use and School Performance*, New York, Academic Press.

CLIFFORD, J. and MARCUS, G. (1986) *Writing Culture: The Poetics and Politics of Ethnography*, Berkeley, University of California Press.

COHEN, G.A. (1978) *Karl Marx's Theory of History*, Oxford, Clarendon Press.

DENNIS, N. and HALSEY, A.H. (1988) *English Ethical Socialism*, Oxford, Oxford University Press.

DEWS, P. (1986) 'The nouvelle philosophie and Foucault', in GANE, M. (Ed) *Towards a Critique of Foucault*, London, Routledge and Kegan Paul.

DEWS, P. (1987) *The Logics of Disintegration: Post-structuralist Thought and the Claims of Critical Theory*, London, Verso.

ELLIOTT, J. (1991a) *Action Research for Educational Change*, Buckingham, Open University Press.

ELLIOTT, J. (1991b) 'Changing contexts for educational evaluation: The challenge for methodology', *Studies in Educational Evaluation*, 17, 2, pp. 215–38.

FINCH, J. (1985) 'Social policy and education: Problems and possibilities of using qualitative research', in BURGESS, R.G. (Ed) *Issues in Educational Research*, Lewes, Falmer Press.

FINCH, J. (1986) *Research and Policy: The Uses of Qualitative Methods in Social and Educational Research*, London, Falmer Press.

FLOUD, J. and HALSEY, A.H. (1956) 'English secondary schools and the supply of labour', *The Yearbook of Education, 1956*, London, Evans Brothers Ltd.

FRANKENBERG, R. (1981) 'Introduction', in FRANKENBERG, R. (Ed) *Custom and Conflict in British Society*, Manchester, Manchester University Press.

GIPPS, C. (1993) 'The profession of educational research', *British Educational Research Journal*, 19, 1, pp. 3–16.

GLASS, D.V. (1950) 'The application of social research', *British Journal of Sociology*, 1, pp. 17–30.

GOLDTHORPE, J.H. (1967) 'Social stratification in industrial society', in BEDIX, R. and LIPSET, S.M. (Eds) *Class, Status, and Power, Second Edition*, London, Routledge and Kegan Paul.

GOULDNER, A. (1970) *The Coming Crisis of Western Sociology*, New York, Oxford University Press.

GOULDNER, A. (1973) *For Sociology: Renewal and Critique in Sociology Today*, London, Allen Lane.

GREGORY, R. (1989) 'Political rationality or "incrementalism"? Charles E. Lindblom's enduring contribution to public policy making theory', *Policy and Politics*, 17, 2, pp. 139–53.

GUBA, E. (Ed) (1990) *The Paradigm Dialog*, Newbury Park, Sage.

GUBRIUM, J. and SILVERMAN, D. (Eds) (1989) *The Politics of Field Research*, London, Sage.

HALSEY, A.H. (1982) 'Provincials and professionals: The British post-war sociologists', *Archives Europeennes de Sociologie*, XXIII, 1, pp. 150–75.

HALSEY, A.H., FLOUD, J. and ANDERSON, C.A. (1961) *Education, Economy and Society*, New York, Free Press.

HALSEY, A.H., HEATH, A.F. and RIDGE, J.M. (1980) *Origins and Destinations*, Oxford, Oxford University Press.

HAMILTON, D., JENKINS, D., KING, C., MacDONALD, B. and PARLETT, M. (1977) *Beyond the Numbers Game*, London, Macmillan.

HAMMERSLEY, M. (1981) 'The outsider's advantage: Reply to McNamara', *British Educational Research Journal*, 7, 2, pp. 167–71.

HAMMERSLEY, M. (1992) *What's Wrong with Ethnography?*, London, Routledge.

HAMMERSLEY, M. (1993b) On the teacher as researcher', *Educational Action Research*, 1, 3.

HAMMERSLEY, M. and WOODS, P. (Eds) (1984) *Life in School: The Sociology of Pupil Culture*, Milton Keynes, Open University Press.

HARGREAVES, D.H. (1967) *Social Relations in a Secondary School*, London, Rouledge and Kegan Paul.

HARGREAVES, A. (1978) 'The significance of classroom coping strategies', in BARTON, L. and MEIGHAN, R. (Eds) *Sociological Interpretations of Schooling and Classrooms: A Reappraisal*, Driffield, Nafferton.

HARGREAVES, A. (1980) 'Synthesis and the study of strategies: A project for the sociological imagination', in WOODS, P. (Ed) *Pupil Strategies*, London, Croom Helm.

HARGREAVES, A. and WOODS, P. (Eds) (1984) *Classrooms and Staffrooms: The Sociology of Teachers and Teaching*, Milton Keynes, Open University Press.

HIRST, P.H. (1983) 'Educational theory', in HIRST, P.H. (Ed) *Educational Theory and its Foundation Disciplines*, London, Routledge and Kegan Paul.

HOLUB, R.C. (1991) *Jurgen Habermas: Critic in the Public Sphere*, London, Routledge.

HUSTLER, D., CASSIDY, A. and CUFF, E.C. (Eds) (1986) *Action Research in Classrooms and Schools*, London, Allen and Unwin.

KEDDIE, N. (1971) 'Classroom knowledge', in YOUNG, M.F.D. (Ed) *Knowledge and Control*, London, Collier-Macmillan.

LACEY, C. (1970) *Hightown Grammar*, Manchester, Manchester University Press.

LATHER, P. (1991) *Getting Smart: Feminist Research and Pedagogy With/in the Postmodern*, New York, Routledge.

LEPENIES, W. (1980) 'The critique of learning and science, and the crisis of orientation', *Social Science Information*, 19, 1, pp. 1–37.

LINDBLOM, C. and COHEN, D. (1979) *Usable Knowledge: Social Science and Social Problem-Solving*, New Haven, Yale University Press.

McCARNEY, J. (1990) *Social Theory and the Crisis of Marxism*, London, Verso.

McNAMARA, D. (1980) 'The outsider's arrogance: The failure of participant observers to understand classroom events', *British Educational research Journal*, 6, 2, pp. 113–25.

MILLS, C.W. (1959) *The Sociological Imagination*, New York, Oxford University Press.

NISBET, J. and BROADFOOT, P. (1980) *The Impact of Research on Policy and Practice in Education*, Aberdeen, Aberdeen University Press.

NIXON, J. (Ed) (1981) *A Teachers' Guide to Action Research*, London, Grant McIntyre.

PAYNE, G.C.F. and CUFF, E.C. (Eds) (1982) *Doing Teaching: The Practical Management of Classrooms*, London, Batsford.

PLANT, R. (1973) *Hegel*, London, Allen and Unwin.

POLLARD, A. (1984) 'Ethnography and social policy for classroom practice', in BARTON, L. and WALKER, S. (Eds) *Social Crisis and Educational Research*, London, Croom Helm.

ROTHSCHILD, LORD (1971) 'The organisation and management of government R and D', in *A Framework for Government Research and Development*, Cmnd. 4184, London, HMSO.

SARAGA, J. (1992) 'Thwarted talent' (review of H. Giroux's Border Crossings), *Times Educational Supplement*, June 5, p. 34.

SCHÖN, D. (1983) *The Reflective Practitioner*, London, Temple Smith.

SCHÖN, D. (1987) *Educating the Reflective Practitioner*, San Francisco, Jossey Bass.

SCHWAB, J. (1969) 'The practical: A language for curriculum', *School Review*, 78, 1, pp. 1–23.

SHARP, R. (1982) 'Self-contained ethnography, or a science of phenomenal forms', *Boston University Journal of Education*, 164, 1, pp. 48–63.

SHARP, R. and GREEN A. (1975) *Education and Social Control*, London, Routledge and Kegan Paul.

SIMONS, H. (1987) *Getting to Know Schools in a Democracy*, London, Falmer Press.

SMITH, G. and SMITH, T. (1992) 'From social research to educational policy: 10/65 to the Education Reform Act 1988', in CROUCH, C. and HEATH, A. (Eds) *Social Research and Social Reform: Esssays in Honour of A.H. Halsey*, Oxford, Oxford University Press.

SMITH, J.K. (1989) *The Nature of Social and Educational Inquiry*, Norwood, NJ, Ablex.

STENHOUSE, L. (1975) *An Introduction to Curriculum Research and Development*, London, Heinemann.

TAYLOR, W. (1973) 'Knowledge and research', in TAYLOR, W. (Ed) *Research Perspectives in Education*, London, Routledge and Kegan Paul.

TROYNA, B. and CARRINGTON, B. (1989) 'Whose side are we on? Ethical dilemmas in research on "race" and education', in BURGESS, R.G. (Ed) *The Ethics of Educational Research*, Lewes, Falmer Press.

WEISS, C, and BUCUVALAS, M. (1980) *Social Science Research and Decision Making*, New York, Columbia University Press.

WESTERGAARD, J. (1979) 'In memory of David Glass', *Sociology*, 13, 2, pp. 173–7.

WHITTY, G. (1977) 'Sociology and the problem of radical educational change: notes towards a reconceptualisation of the "new" sociology of education', in YOUNG, M.F.D. and WHITTY, G. (Eds) *Society, State and Schooling*, Ranklin, Falmer Press.

WHITTY, G. (1985) *Sociology and School Knowledge*, London, Methuen.

WILLIS, P. (1977) *Learning to Labour*, Aldershot, Gower.

WOODS, P. (1977) 'Teaching for survival', in WOODS, P. and HAMMERSLEY, M. (Eds) *School Experience*, London, Croom Helm.

WOODS, P. (1986) *Inside Schools: Ethnography in Educational Research*, London, Routledge and Kegan Paul.

WOODS, P. and POLLARD, A. (Eds) (1988) *Sociology and Teaching: A New Challenge for the Sociology of Education*, London, Croom Helm.

YOUNG, M.F.D. (Ed) (1971) *Knowledge and Control*, London, Collier Macmillan.

YOUNG, M.F.D. and WHITTY, G. (Eds) (1977) 'Introduction' in *Society, State and Schooling: Readings on the Possibilities for Radical Education*, London, Falmer Press.

Chapter 11

Why Didn't You Use a Survey so You Could Generalize Your Findings?: Methodological Issues in a Multiple Site Case Study of School Governing Bodies after the 1988 Education Reform Act

Rosemary Deem and Kevin J. Brehony

Introduction

What challenges are presented by carrying out qualitative case-study research on an aspect of current educational policy which is itself still developing? Do the richness, depth and explanatory potential of the data derived from qualitative research justify the investment in time and energy involved? Can a case-study strategy, defined by Yin as an empirical inquiry that: 'investigates a contemporary phenomenon within its real-life context; when the boundaries between phenomenon and context are not clearly evident; and in which multiple sources of evidence are used' (Yin, 1989, p. 23), offer anything of value both to theoreticians in social science *and* those interested in critically appraising educational reform? Or does the use of case-study strategies merely yield idiosyncratic data which are easily dismissed by critics on the grounds that the findings are 'unrepresentative'?

In 1993 we completed a four-year study about the impact of recent English educational reforms on the social processes of primary and secondary school governance. The case we investigated was that of the English local education authority maintained school governing body in the late 1980s and early 1990s. The research fieldwork consisted mainly of an in-depth, multiple-site investigation of a small number of governing bodies from two different LEAs. Although we were interested in critically assessing policy changes surrounding lay participation in the administration of state-maintained schools, we also had wider theoretical interests about the nature of educational organizations, decision-making processes involving lay people and professionals, power relations between headteachers and governors, the complexities of gender, ethnicity and social class as demonstrated in the workings of governing bodies and issues about democratic participation and citizenship as evidenced by service on voluntary bodies. We thought this range of interests was better addressed by a qualitative case-study approach rather than a more quantitative survey. The research data which our study generated have proved to be fascinating, extensive and controversial.[1] Part of the controversy has related not only to our findings, which are critical of recent government educational policy but also our methods. Those who do not accept our conclusions, rather than contest our interpretation of the data, are wont to point instead to the small size of our 'sample' of governing bodies (Holdsworth, 1993).

Why School Governors?

This is a question that many people have asked us! Prior to the late 1980s the study of school governance was of interest only to those concerned with the practicalities of school management and administration and those wishing to analyse chains of accountability within publicly funded education systems. Few sociologists had shown any curiosity about school governance and the topic played only a minor role in most studies of educational policy. We wanted to demonstrate that these omissions and absences should and could be rectified and that it was possible to carry out valid policy-relevant research on the basis of a mainly qualitative, multiple-site research strategy.[2]

The project which we undertook between 1988 and 1993 arose out of a complex blend of biographical, theoretical, methodological and political factors. Our interest in school governors began well before the 1986 No 2 Education Act and the 1988 Education Reform Act which marked the legislative beginnings of late twentieth-century school reform in England and Wales. We had both become LEA-nominated school governors in the early 1980s. As a result we became curious about the power relations of governing bodies. Why were so many governors white and middle-class? How did teachers and headteachers come to terms with the presence in their administrative midst of lay people whose educational and other expertise or lack of it seemed largely to be left to chance? Why did some chairs of governors exercise enormous influence and others none? Why did some parents seem to regard LEA-nominated governors as being 'too political' and why in turn did LEA governors sometimes seem to regard parent representatives as inferior to themselves?

In the early 1980s, governors' formal responsibilities were ill-defined but included oversight of the curriculum and general organization of the school. The 1980 Education Act made parent representation in LEA-maintained governing bodies a legal requirement. Prior to this many governing bodies were dominated by party political governors, although in some LEAs the participation of parents and other community members was encouraged. In 1986 a new Education Act (No 2) was passed, increasing the numbers of parents and coopted governors and decreasing LEA representation. The Act also gave new responsibilities to governing bodies. These included involvement in headteacher appointments, writing annual reports for parents and holding meetings to discuss these, deciding whether school sex education should be offered, establishing a secular curriculum policy, and keeping the curriculum free from political bias. When in the aftermath of the 1987 General Election a new Education Bill was proposed in order to achieve fundamental reforms of the schooling system, its funding and governance, the impact of further radical changes on governing bodies seemed likely to be considerable, coming so soon after the changes introduced by the 1986 Act.

During the 1980s both of us had been doing work which proved relevant to the governors project. Deem wrote and co-wrote a number of Open University units on school governance and management (Open University, 1981, 1988, 1989) and did research with Lesley Holly and Norma Sherratt on gender issues in Milton Keynes secondary schools, as well as editing two books on aspects of gender inequality in education (Deem, 1980, 1984). Brehony spent much of the early 1980s working on a doctoral thesis about the progressive child-centred ideology represented in the Froebel movement in nineteenth century and that movement's attempts to transform elementary education (Brehony, 1988). Among the many issues he considered were lay representatives on school boards and school managers, as well as the social composition and decision-making processes of the Consultative Committee of the Board of Education (Brehony, 1994).

Putting Out the Pilot Boat — An Exploratory Voyage into School Governance

Our decision to use a case study did not predetermine other aspects of our method; as Yin (1989) notes, case study is a research strategy rather than a particular technique. Prior to embarking on our own study we began to look at what research on governors had already been carried out or was in progress. There was not a great deal, although there was a large body of literature which purported to offer practical help to school governors. There was a Sheffield-based study by Bacon (1978), concerned with issues of participation and accountability, but this predated recent changes. The National Foundation for Educational Research (NFER) was being commissioned by the then Department of Education and Science (DES) to undertake surveys of issues like the social composition of the new bodies and we did not wish to replicate this work, which has subsequently proved useful in enabling us to set our research in a broader national context (Streatfield and Jefferies, 1989; Keys and Fernandes, 1990; Baginsky *et al.*, 1991). We found Kogan *et al.*'s (1984) study of school governance extremely valuable both as a piece of research in its own right and as a source of ideas about theoretical perspectives and methodology. The Kogan research team had undertaken a form of case-study analysis involving attendance at governing-body meetings. We soon realized that only qualitative research could help us learn about the processes of reformed school governance. The work of Golby and Brigley (1989), based on a case-study strategy utilizing qualitative data and focusing mainly on parent governors, was also helpful in confirming our decision to do qualitative research. We struggled to find ways of recognizing the relations of power internal to each governing body, including those to do with class, ethnicity and gender. Ethnicity and gender were largely uncharted territory so far as previous governing body research was concerned.

Formal meetings, along with subcommittees and appointment panels, are the major means by which governing body collective responsibilities are exercised. Early on we decided that these would form a significant focus for our research. This would involve us attending meetings as observers, taking extensive notes, devising a system for doing this, involving obtaining details about the discussions and the key participants, and collecting documents connected with the proceedings of the meetings. However, the increasing autonomy of governing bodies from LEAs, even in the more limited form offered by the 1986 Act, looked as though this might reduce the usefulness of relying on LEA officers as key respondents in the same way as the Kogan *et al.* (1984) study, although we did plan to have informal contact with relevant LEA employees. Our decision to focus on the micro-level of the individual governing bodies suggested that we would also need to interview governors and headteachers. However, during the first phase of our research we could not undertake more than a few interviews because of time and resource constraints. We decided instead to collect a limited range of questionnaire data about governors' background and reasons for becoming governors and to rely on informal discussions at the beginning and end of meetings as another source of information. Here we were perhaps departing from the tradition of some qualitative researchers in using triangulation to check 'the perceptions of one actor in a specific situation against those of other actors in the same situation' (Hopkins Bollington and Hewett, 1989, p. 66) because what we did was to check the perceptions of the same actors in different contexts: inside the meetings, outside them, and in questionnaires. We accepted too that there were some aspects of school governance which would not be readily accessible to us — private pre-meeting discussions, telephone calls, informal meetings of some governors in the pub — and about which we would not be able to say anything. Similarly, we knew that whatever the extent of our observation of meetings, we would inevitably be selective in what we noted.

The Selection of Cases for Study

In the summer of 1988 we established some firm plans for our research fieldwork. Timing was critical as the first governing bodies to be established under the provisions of the 1986 Education Act were to commence their four-year term of office in September 1988. We wanted to look at governing bodies over a reasonable period of time and thought that three terms would take us through from the beginning of one school year to its end and give us a good idea of the range of issues and concerns which confronted governing bodies operating under the newly revised regulations and legislation. We decided to choose sixteen governing bodies (this became fifteen as one rejected us at the last minute and it was not possible to get a suitable replacement in time) in two different LEAs, the latter selected partly for pragmatic reasons to do with access and our geographical location but also because they provided a useful contrast in terms of their policies towards schools and governing bodies. Here we took account of Hammersley and Atkinson's (1983) point that although using a larger number of instances and sites might allow more confidence about findings, it does not resolve the issue about representativeness of findings since 'the universe of cases being sampled is infinite, comprising all the cases . . . that have occurred, or will occur in the future. We cannot be sure that a random sample of the cases currently available for study would be representative of this universe' (Hammersley and Atkinson, p. 44). We did not expect our data to be widely generalizable in a statistical sense; our primary purpose was to progress from interpretive description through to theoretical analysis.

We tried to search for critical cases within the confines of our two LEAs and after discussion with LEA officers and heads, we used a cross-section of types of schools and catchment areas which would enable us to make internal and frequent comparisons of the themes and concerns of the project. Our interest in social class and ethnicity also indicated that we should include governing bodies of schools in a variety of different catchment areas and with pupil intakes which differed in their social composition. Such a strategy also permitted us to contrast different data from various social groupings within individual governing bodies in relation to established theory about social divisions, which Yin (1989) terms 'theoretical replication'. We did not know whether variations between primary and secondary school governing bodies would prove to be crucial so we decided to include both. Our concern with the coping strategies of governors led us to seek information from LEA officers about how the governing bodies of particular schools had operated prior to autumn 1988. We excluded selective schools because the majority of state-maintained primary and secondary schools in England are non-selective. We did not include church schools because their composition and powers were less drastically altered by the 1986 Education Act. The critical case approach proved useful both during the study and in the final analysis of data at the completion of fieldwork. Hammersley, Scarth and Webb (1985) refer to the use of critical cases as the comparative method. Burgess, Pole, Evans and Priestly (1993) also note how their multi-site study of Record of Achievement in four Warwickshire secondary schools allowed considerable cross-case analysis which would not have been possible in a single-site study. Like both these teams, we found that what we were comparing changed over the duration of our research.

Having secured travel funds, we sought to identify governing bodies which fitted our critical case criteria and would permit us access to their meetings. We wanted to be in a position to research the first formal meetings of the governing bodies concerned, a vital moment in the governors' enactment of their responsibilities. After choosing schools, we sent explanatory letters to headteachers and acting chairpersons of governing bodies (the chairpersons proper could not be elected until the first meeting) asking them to pass these onto other newly elected/nominated governors as those names became available. The governing bodies concerned then had the option of holding a brief discussion before the official start of their first meetings to decide whether or not to let us in. In fifteen schools this approach proved successful and we commenced our fieldwork in October 1988. We each had our 'own' governing bodies whose meetings we attended but we tried to ensure that we had the opportunity to visit the other governing bodies on some occasions; this was helpful not only in confirming that we had some measure of agreement about what we were observing, how and why but subsequently in assimilating new members of the research team. At meetings we drew seating plans, took extensive long-hand notes of the discussions, noted the duration of agenda items and kept details about who spoke and on what. In due course these notes were sifted and major components of them transferred to a computer database.

Once we began our fieldwork, further issues began to emerge from our initial observations and thoughts, including the nature of the organizational culture of governing bodies and their decision-making processes, and the changing nature of the relationship between governing bodies and their LEAs, as the financial arrangements for school budgeting began to be radically altered under the provisions of Local Management of Schools (LMS).

Research Design and Case Study

Yin's (1989) definition of case study talks of it as an appropriate strategy when the phenomenon to be studied is in a real-life context and the boundaries between phenomenon and context not clearly defined. The phenomenon we were investigating was very much within a 'real-life context' and the boundaries between phenomenon and context were far from visible. If the school is seen as part of the governing body's immediate context are governors part of the school's organizational structure or not? Blurred boundaries are also prominent in the mapping of a governing body in relation to the whole education-reform policy of the State. At certain levels of abstraction, for instance, the making of decisions about how the governing body should organize itself to achieve maximum effectiveness, in this wider context is relatively unimportant. But in other discussions, e.g., raising admission numbers or making staff redundant, the context merges into a much larger whole constituted by national and LEA policies about delegated budgets and formula funding and informed by ideologies of markets, choice and standards. In this latter instance the governing bodies become a case of those policies, whereas in the former they are a case of governing bodies. In a similar way, when we sought to elucidate the flows of power within a governing body, already sensitized to the operation of gender, class and ethnicity, we were treating instances of racist and sexist behaviour as a case of the sum total of cases which constitute a society or social formation, itself a case abstracted from global society. Thus even though the micro-level of interaction within the governing body was our unit of analysis, the boundaries between it and the other levels frequently became blurred. Yin's final definitional category, that of multiple sources of evidence is more straightforward; such sources of evidence are essential if the description is to be in any way rich and if the theoretical ambitions of the case-study design are to be realized.

Even if we accept Yin's definition of case-study, there are many other potential areas of disagreement amongst those engaged in qualitative work of this sort. We regard those models of research design which plot a series of stages in a logical or linear order as problematic, especially in a multi-site project. Others have also noted the disadvantages of this kind of approach (Burgess, 1984). However, Eisenhardt (1989) suggests in her attempt to describe how theory may be induced from case study, that once research questions have been refined, the next move is to 'enter the field' and subsequently 'analyse data' (Eisenhardt, 1989, p. 533). Such a formulation inadequately represents what is a far more complex and multi-linear process. This is particularly the case in research spread over several years and where the pace of policy change is considerable, as issues and questions which could not have even been formulated at the start of the research, inevitable arise. However our stance can present problems when writing final reports to funding agencies who may have a more linear view of the research process and who also assume that you will only research that which you set out to research. Had we done this, we would have missed many opportunities for theoretical advancement and would have persisted with lines of enquiry (such as governor training) which were not likely to prove fruitful in the overall context of the study.

What Is the Role of Theory in Qualitative Case-study Research?

We depart significantly from the view (Hammersley, 1985 and 1992a) that case-study research ought properly to be concerned with theory testing and deduction rather than induction. We did begin our study with some theoretical notions which we wanted to explore. These included the idea that social relations and interaction based on class, 'race' and gender affect actors in a variety of social settings (Deem, 1989 and 1991; Deem, Brehony and Hemmings, 1992). We also wanted to explore whether the Kogan *et al.* (1984) model of school governing bodies, which saw them as being highly dependent on the political culture of their LEAs and the ethos of their schools, was still operational. Other theoretical concerns emerged from our observations of meetings, including our development of Weick's concept of organizational loose coupling (Weick, 1976; and Orton and Weick, 1990). We tried to apply loose coupling to governing bodies and their schools as a means of understanding the semi-detached yet responsive relationship between the two (Deem, 1993b; Deem and Brehony, 1993). Other emergent theoretical concerns have been our interest in different perspectives on decision-making (Brehony and Deem, 1990; Deem and Brehony, 1993), our concern to contrast a discourse of public interest and accountability in education with that of a market and consumer-driven discourse (Deem, 1994a) and our endeavours to set our study of school governance in a wider cross-cultural context focusing on globalization and democratic participation of lay people in school administration (Brehony and Deem, 1992; Deem, 1993a; Deem, 1994b). All of these theoretical developments have been arrived at inductively, as a result of our immersion in our data, a process other qualitative researchers have also found useful (Hopkins, Bollington and Hewitt, 1989).

The Emergence of the Longitudinal Study

By Easter 1989, as we entered what was intended to be the final term of our pilot study, many changes to governors' responsibilities were still in process. These included delegated budgets, *de facto* governing-body control over the hiring and firing of staff, the potential to embark on the opting out process, and overseeing of the National Curriculum, all under the provisions of the 1988 Education Reform Act. The data we had already gathered suggested that we would gain from a longer period of observation and document collection. Thus, to take one example, we attempted an analysis of decision-making by our fifteen governing bodies in relation to their development of policy on charging for optional extras (Brehony and Deem, 1990). We realized that such an analysis would be strengthened greatly by being applied to a wider range of topics and debates. In addition the reforms that we were researching were themselves still developing. However, by mid-1989 we had also realized that fifteen governing bodies was too large a number to study intensively and thought that we could retain important contrasts by reducing this number to ten.

We applied for Economic and Social Research Council funding in 1989 for a further three-year study. Our ESRC funding did not commence until February 1990, so we continued our pilot study of fifteen governing bodies until December 1989. We then reduced the number of governing bodies being studied to ten. In April 1990 Sue Hemmings joined the research team. By then several of our governing bodies had acquired an elaborate network of sub-committees and working groups (made possible by a 1989 change to the regulations under which governing bodies operated). Some of these we planned to observe since we wanted to compare what went on in the smaller groups with what occurred in formal meetings of the whole governing body. Interviews with heads, governing body chairs and chairs of subcommittees also became a full part of the main project, as did a questionnaire to all the governors in the ten governing bodies in the summer of 1992, asking them to reflect back on their experiences as governors over their full period of office. In addition we followed through from short-listing to the final interview panel stage, three headship appointments. As a result of recruiting Suzanne New to the project team in February 1992 as a replacement for Sue Hemmings who had resigned for personal reasons, the final stage of the research also looked at teacher governors and their response to the changing composition and responsibilities of lay governors (New, 1993a, 1993b). The latter would have been excluded if we had followed a linear model of research or if we had felt able only to use theory in a deductive manner.

Ethnography, Qualitative Methods and Case-study Research

The research described here is certainly qualitative but is it also ethnographic? In our view it is important that the terms qualitative research, case study and ethnography are not used as though they were the same phenomenon. Several authors, including Hammersley (1992a) and Yin (1989), have pointed out that case study and ethnography are not the exclusive preserve of the qualitative researcher. Indeed although much of our research data is qualitative, we have also collected and used quantitative data as for example, in some elements of the questionnaire and the usage made of File Maker Pro software, in the analysis of meetings.

How is ethnographic research defined? Writers seem divided into two camps; those who say they have done ethnographic work without defining it at all (see for example Mirza, 1992; and Bowe, Ball and Gold, 1992) and those who provide definitions of what they understand by the term. Whilst recognizing that an endless search for definitions can be self-defeating, it does seem important to operate with at least a working definition. For some researchers, ethnography seems coterminous with description of actors' accounts (e.g., Smith and Keith, 1976), though this leaves unanswered the charge that description is always interpreted by the researcher (Stanley and Wise, 1993). Hammersley, Scarth and Webb (1985) suggest that many accounts of ethnography 'fuse description and the generation of theory. The goal of ethnography is often portrayed as "presenting a theoretical account" of an institution or culture' (p. 48). Certainly we would not see ourselves as simply presenting a theoretical account of the activities of school governors. Presenting a descriptive account of the processes at work in governing bodies has also been important since so much has changed in the context and responsibilities of governors over the period of our study. This might not satisfy Hammersley (1992a) who argues that too much ethnography is descriptive and not enough if it tests theory or is concerned with measurement, since being theoretically informed is not the same as testing theory. Perhaps, however, Hammersley, in trying to develop a gold standard for ethnographic research, represents not what ethnography is but what he would like it to be.[3]

Another view of ethnography is presented by Hitchcock and Hughes (1989). It includes providing a cultural description of a group and its activities from the viewpoint of the actors themselves, outlining the features constitutive of membership of that group describing, analysing group patterns of social interaction and developing theory. Hitchcock and Hughes suggest that 'an ethnography . . . becomes the realization of the fieldwork experiences and encounters, formalizing . . . the overt or covert involvement of the researcher in a particular setting and the information obtained resulting in a written report or document, the 'ethnography'. (Hitchcock and Hughes, 1989, p. 53)

Whilst we would accept some aspects of this definition as descriptive of our research, that study does not conform to the notion of ethnography as a description of activities from the viewpoint of actors. We do report those views but also interpret and analyse them, rather than adopting the style used by some qualitative researchers, who present their data as long chunks of transcript, interspersed by the occasional comment from the researcher (Smith and Keith, 1976; Bowe, Ball and Gold, 1992). Thus our research conforms neither to Hammersley's definition of ethnography nor that of Hitchcock and Hughes. Accordingly we would prefer to retain for our project only the descriptors 'qualitative research' and 'case study'.

The Validity of Qualitative Case-study Research

The definition of research as qualitative case study gives rise to many epistemological problems. The issue of the validity of case-study research, especially in policy-relevant areas, is a topic which excites not only professional social scientists but also the lay person who hears of the findings of case-study projects. It would be possible to take the view that qualitative research can never be as valid, or indeed as reliable (in the sense that others cannot replicate it exactly) as quantitative research. As Schofield (1993) points out, many qualitative researchers are interested in theory or in illumination and illustration rather than in empirical generalizability and will use quantitative methods if they wish to engage in such generalization. However, the differences between qualitative and quantitative research can be exaggerated and many researchers now see fewer polarities between the two than was previously the case (Bryman, 1988; Brannen, 1992). Indeed we found that although we used qualitative methods, this did not preclude us from collecting and analysing some of our data in quantitative ways, which allowed us to make case-study-wide generalizations about the sites and processes we were studying. Validity can be crudely defined as the extent to which the data we collect relates to and can answer the research questions asked.

Hopkins, Bollington and Hewett (1989) argue that it is useful to link different aspects of validity to features of the methods used. Thus using multiple sources of evidence, knowing what is being looked for and having key informants review drafts are amongst the suggestions. These authors argue that the integrity of the research can be assisted by collecting data at different points in time, seeking alternative explanations, using clear and rigorous analysis and undertaking triangulation. External validity can be ensured by multi-site design and by replication. Though these points are useful, like most models of research design, they represent an ideal type which is rarely conformed with completely. We have undertaken some of the things mentioned by Hopkins *et al.* Concerns about internal validity were dealt with by using a mix of methods in the same research context, comparing accounts from the same actors in different meetings, via questionnaires and in interviews, scrutinizing the same events and issues on different sites, through the eyes of different actors and through the comparison of research notes with documentary sources used by the case-study governing bodies. We also fed back our intermediate findings and publications to the research governing bodies (we are exploring ways of doing this for the study conclusions as most of the governing bodies we studied no longer have membership at all comparable to that at the time of completion of fieldwork). External validity we have tried to tackle by setting our research in the context of other contemporary research on educational and social-policy change and by using a range of theoretical approaches.

These endeavours, however, only deal with validity at a fairly technical level. Underlying the discussion of validity and qualitative research are another set of more philosophical and epistemological concerns. Many of these deal with what is termed realism. Hammersley (1992a) suggests that naive realism, which assumes that as researchers we can simply describe what we see, is untenable because reality is never reproduced; we can only provide selections from it. Moreover, Hammersley claims, reality is unknowable, so there is no yardstick against which to measure our descriptions and explanations. This is a complex debate which is dealt with very systematically by Sayer (1992). We find Sayer's arguments in favour of a realist approach in social science more convincing than Hammersley's stance against it though naive realism is certainly problematic.

The issue of theory testing is another issue with deep epistemological roots. Hammersley (1992b) questions the validity of studies which are purely or largely concerned with description, or theory development, rather than with testing theory. However, theory development is very important for research on educational policy, perhaps more so than theory testing. The latter notion assumes that useful and relevant theory already exists whereas we believe that the sociological study of educational policy remains theoretically underdeveloped. Hammersley's arguments about the centrality of theory testing (Hammersley and Atkinson, 1983; Hammersley, 1985, 1992b) seem to focus principally around the theory of differentiation and polarization as tested in the works of Hargreaves (1967), Lacey (1970) and Ball (1981), which is a very limited conception of the role of theory in educational research. For us the view held by Tsoukas (1989), an advocate of realist epistemology, is more helpful. Tsoukas argues that explanatory case studies are epistemologically valid because they: 'are concerned with the clarification of structures and their associated generative mechanisms, which have been contingently capable of producing the observed phenomena' (Tsoukas, 1989, p. 556). Perhaps then, validity is best regarded as something which is to be worked towards rather than fully achieved.

Audience, Purpose and Level of Abstraction in Policy Research

These are important issues for researchers studying education reform. Hammersley (1992a) argues that the contribution of research to practice is necessarily small and that it should not try to be multi-purpose, serving the needs of both practitioners and the research community. Even if we accepted this view, which we do not, it would be difficult to implement in relation to research on education reform, where the topicality of the issues inevitably lead most researchers into being featured in the national press (e.g., Holdsworth, 1993), being interviewed on television or radio and speaking to practitioner audiences. This does not mean that the research has no validity or interest for the research community, since the means of presenting data which are used in a popular format will differ from its presentation to an academic audience. Nor does presentation of findings in a popular form mean that no theoretical advances have been made in their research. Hammersley's position appears based on his underlying belief that scientific inquiry should not be concerned with changing the world, which forms one basis of his critique of feminist methodology (Hammersley, 1992b). If this belief is challenged, then multi-functionality remains possible and must remain a significant element of research on educational policy.

Against this concern about functions lies another critique of small-scale and case-study research on policy and the possible audiences for such research, this time emanating from Ozga (1990). Ozga argues that small-scale case studies in educational policy are of little use unless they also take into account macro-concepts and entities like the State, because only thus can the contradictory aspects of education reform be revealed. But are abstract theories of the State, which can never be fully empirically developed or tested, the only means of revealing contradictory elements of policy making? If the implication is that every piece of case-study research in education should be accompanied by a contribution to the theory of the State or its conceptual equivalent at similar levels of abstraction, then this is problematic; it both devalues qualitative case study as a method and privileges macro-level theory over everything else.

There is also however another important issue about audience and function and that is the question of critically informed cross-cultural analysis of educational policy. One way of providing the wider context that Ozga seeks whilst simultaneously exposing the contradictory nature of educational policy, is to examine the educational reform process in different countries. Whilst it is not uncommon to find UK writers analysing educational reform in one other country (Grace, 1991) or within the different countries of the UK (McPherson and Raab, 1988), wider comparisons of policy are rare. This in itself is not surprising because detailed comparative work is expensive, conceptually difficult and logistically complex. Nevertheless, if we are to say anything about the possible structural determinants of similar processes of educational reform in different countries, such comparison must be undertaken. A beginning can be made by using theoretically informed, speculative comparison across different countries, something we have attempted recently in comparing school governance in England, Scotland and Catalunya (Brehony and Deem, 1992; Deem, 1993b, 1994b).

Conclusion

We have endeavoured to justify our theoretical, methodological and epistemological reasons for choosing a particular set of research strategies for a policy relevant study of school governing bodies in a period of educational reform. We have also explained the long genesis of the research theme and design and noted its lack of resemblance to the neat stages envisaged by some writers (Eisenhardt, 1989). The longitudinal, multiple-site, case-study approach has proved to be a very fruitful one for our project and we do not regret the mix of analytic induction and deduction which has characterized our theoretical approach. We could not have generated the amount and extent of our data or explanations had we felt confined to testing existing theory, constrained to examine our findings only through the lens of abstract theories of the State or obliged to conduct a large-scale survey.

Whilst principally considering the methodological issues we have confronted in our own research, we have tried to situate these dilemmas within current debates about case-study method, qualitative research, ethnography and validity. However, we have also been mindful of the need to tackle issues which all those engaged in research on education reform are likely to encounter: questions about levels of analysis, theoretical frames of reference, purpose, audience and policy relevance. There are many concerns raised here which cannot be resolved by individual researchers or even by the research community as a whole. But we should like to emphasize our view that it is important for researchers engaged in policy relevant research to discuss openly their concerns about methodological and epistemological issues. In the current climate of research assessment exercises and intense competition for research resources, it is tempting for some to keep quiet about doubts, revealing only polished and glossy accounts of their work. But this approach would result not only in a rejection of the peer review that is so much more central to research excellence than a whole string of performance indicators; it would also ensure that methodological concerns become mostly or only the preserve of those not engaged principally in empirical research. Should this become the norm, research on educational policy would suffer and the whole social science research community would be the poorer.

Notes

1 The research was funded by a grant from the Economic and Social Research Council (R000 23 1799) from 1990–3. The pilot stage from 1988–9 was funded by the Research Committee of the Open University School of Education and the Department of Education Studies and Management, Bulmershe College of Higher Education, to which we are most grateful. We would also like to express our gratitude to the governing bodies and LEAs involved in the study for their cooperation in making the research possible. Thanks to Robert Burgess for his very helpful comments on an earlier version of this chapter and also participants in the ESRC-funded seminar in July 1992 whose contributions we found most useful.

2 We use the term policy relevant to mean that elements of the research findings are intended to have some resonance for policy analysts, illuminating aspects of current policy and providing some possible pointers to future policy. However, the project did not have as its main *raison d'être* the generation of data useful to those managing and/or administering schools or those overseeing such administration and management at the national and local level. We would not therefore regard our research as policy-led and the questions to which we were seeking answers were in the main theoretical ones derived from social science literature and thought.

3 We are indebted to Robert Burgess for suggesting this concept in relation to certain views about ethnography.

References

BACON, A. (1978) *Public Accountability and the Schooling System*, London, and Row.
BAGINSKY, M., BAKER, L. and CLEAVE, S. (1991) *Towards Effective Partnership in School Governance*, Slough, NFER.
BALL, S. (1981) *Beachside Comprehensive*, Cambridge University Press.
BALL, S. (1987) *The Micro-politics of the School*, London, Methuen.
BOWE, R., BALL, S. and GOLD, A. (1992) *Reforming Education and Changing Schools*, London, Routledge.
BRANNEN, J. (1992) (Ed) *Mixing Methods*, London, Sage.
BREHONY, K.J. (1988) 'The Froebel Movement and State Schooling 1880–1914: A Study in Educational Ideology', Unpublished Ph.D thesis, the Open University, Milton Keynes.
BREHONY, K.J. (1994) 'The "school masters parliament": The origins and formation of the consultative committee of the board of education', *History of Education*, June.
BREHONY, K.J. and DEEM, R. (1991) 'Charging for free education: An exploration of a debate in school governing bodies', *Journal of Education Policy*, 5, 4, pp. 333–45.
BREHONY, K.J. and DEEM, R. (1992) 'The participating citizen: A comparative view from education', Paper presented to British Sociological Association Annual Conference, University of Kent, April.

BREHONY, K.J. and DEEM, R. (1993) 'Governing bodies and LEAs: Who shall inherit the earth?', *Local Government Studies*, 19, 1, pp. 56–76.

BRYMAN, A. (1988) *Quantity and Quality in Social Research*, London, Unwin Hyman.

BURGESS, R.G. (1984) (Ed) *The Research Process in Educational Settings*, Lewes, Falmer Press.

BURGESS, R.G., POLE, C., EVANS, K. and PRIESTLEY, C. (1993) 'Four Studies from one or one study from four: Multi-site case study research', in BRYMAN, A. and BURGESS, R.G. (Eds) *Analysing Qualitative Data*, London, Routledge.

DEEM, R. (1980) (Ed) *Schooling for Women's Work*, London, Routledge.

DEEM, R. (1984) (Ed) *Co-education Reconsidered*, Milton Keynes, Open University Press.

DEEM, R. (1989) 'The new school governing bodies: are 'race' and gender on the agenda?', *Gender and Education*, 1, 3, pp. 247–60.

DEEM, R. (1990) 'The reform of school governing bodies: The power of the consumer over the producer?', in FLUDE, M. and HAMMER, M. (Eds) *The Education Reform Act 1988; its origins and implications*, London, Falmer Press.

DEEM, R. (1991) 'Governing by gender? School governing bodies after the education reform act', in ABBOTT, P. and WALLACE, C. (Eds) *Gender, Power and Sexuality*, London, Macmillan.

DEEM, R. (1993a) 'Educational reform and school governing bodies in England 1986–1992: Old dogs, new tricks or new dogs, new tricks?', in PREEDY, M., GLATTER, R. and LEVACIC, R. (Eds) *Managing the Effective School*, London, Paul Chapman.

DEEM, R. (1993b) 'The challenge of working with governors' Module 2, part 5, 'The School in its environment', Open University Course E326, *Managing Schools: Challenge and Response*, Walton Hall, the Open University.

DEEM, R. (1994a) 'School governing bodies — public concerns or private interests?', in SCOTT, D. (Ed) *Accountability and Control in Educational Settings*, London, Cassell.

DEEM, R. (1994b) 'Free marketeers or good citizens? Education policy and lay participation in the administration of schools', *British Journal of Educational Studies*, 42, 1, pp. 23–37.

DEEM, R. and BREHONY, K.J. (1991) 'Governing bodies and Local Education Authorities: Relationships, contradictions and tensions', in GOLBY, M. (Ed) *Exeter Papers in School Governorship No 3*, Tiverton, Devon, Fairway Publications.

DEEM, R. and BREHONY, K.J. (1993) 'Consumers and Educational Professionals in the Organisation and Administration of Schools: Partnership or conflict?', *Educational Studies*, 19, 3, pp. 339–55.

DEEM, R., BREHONY, K.J. and HEMMINGS, S. (1992) 'Social Justice, social divisions and the governing of schools', in GILL, D., MAYOR, B. and BLAIR, M. (Eds) *Racism and Education: Structures and Strategies*, London, Sage.

EISENHARDT, K. (1989) 'Building theories from case study research', *Academy of Management Review*, 14, 4, pp. 532–50.

GOLBY, M. and BRIGLEY, S. (1989) *Parents as School Governors*, Tiverton, Devon, Fairway Publications.

GRACE, G. (1991) 'Welfare Labourism versus the New Right: The struggle in New Zealand's education policy', *International Studies in Sociology of Education*, 1, pp. 25–42.

HAMMERSLEY, M. (1985) 'From ethnography to theory: A programme and paradigm in the sociology of education', *Sociology*, 19, 2, pp. 244–59.

HAMMERSLEY, M. (1992a) *What's Wrong with Ethnography?*, London, Routledge.

HAMMERSLEY, M. (1992b) 'On feminist methodology', *Sociology*, 26, 2, pp. 187–206.

HAMMERSLEY, M. and ATKINSON, P. (1983) *Ethnography Principles in Practice*, London, Tavistock Books.

HAMMERSLEY, M., SCARTH, J. and WEBB, S. (1985) 'Developing and testing theory: The case of research on pupil learning and examinations', in BURGESS, R.G. *Issues in Educational Research*, London, Falmer Press.

HARGREAVES, D. (1967) *Social Relations in a Secondary School*, London, Routledge.

HITCHCOCK, G. and HUGHES, D. (1989) *Research and the Teacher*, London, Routledge.

HOLDSWORTH, N. (1993) Governors 'display racist attitudes', *Times Educational Supplement*, 23 April, p. 7.

HOPKINS, D., BOLLINGTON, R. and HEWETT, D. (1989) 'Growing up with qualitative research and evaluation', *Evaluation and Research in Education*, 3, 2, pp. 61–79.

KEYS, W. and FERNANDES, C. (1990) *A Survey of School Governing Bodies*, Slough, NFER.

KOGAN, M., JOHNSON, D., PACKWOOD, T. and WHITTAKER, T. (1984) *School Governing Bodies*, London, Heinemann.

LACEY, C. (1970) *High Town Grammar*, Manchester, Manchester University Press.

MCPHERSON, A. and RAAB, C. (1988) *Governing Education: A Sociology of Policy Since 1945*, Edinburgh University Press.

MIRZA, H.S. (1992) *Young, Female and Black*, London, Routledge.

NEW, S. (1993a) 'This is the teacher here: Governing bodies and the teacher voice', *Journal of Teacher Development*, 2, 2, pp. 70–80.

NEW, S. (1993b) 'The token teacher: School governing bodies and teacher representation', *International Studies in the Sociology of Education*, 3, 1, pp. 69–90.

OPEN UNIVERSITY (1981) DEEM, R. and FERGUSSON, R., Unit 15 'Parents, pupils and teachers: the politics of schools', E353 *Society, Education and the State*, Milton Keynes, Open University Educational Enterprises.

OPEN UNIVERSITY (1988) BURGESS, R.G. and DEEM, R., Unit S1/2, 'Schools at work; organisation, practices and culture', EP228, *Frameworks for Teaching*, Milton Keynes, Open University Educational Enterprises.

OPEN UNIVERSITY (1989) DEEM, R., Unit 18, 'The control of schools', E208, *Exploring Educational Issues*, Milton Keynes, Open University Educational Enterprises.

ORTON, J.D. and WEICK, K.E. (1990) 'Loosely coupled systems: A reconceptualisation', *Academy of Management Review*, 15, 2, pp. 203–23.

OZGA, J. (1990) 'Policy research and policy theory: A comment on Fitz and Halpin', *Journal of Education Policy*, 5, 4, pp. 359–62.

SAYER, A. (1992) *Method in Social Science: A Realist Approach*, London, Routledge.

SCHOFIELD, J. (1993) 'Increasing the generalisability of qualitative research', in HAMMERSLEY, M. (Ed) *Social Research: Philosophy, Politics and Practice*, London, Sage.

SMITH, L. and KEITH, P.M. (1976) *Anatomy of Educational Innovation*, New York, John Wiley.

STANLEY, L. and WISE, S. (1993) *Breaking Out Again*, London, Routledge.

STREATFIELD, D. and JEFFERIES, G. (1989) *Reconstitution of School Governing Bodies*: Survey 2, Slough: National Foundation for Educational Research.

TSOUKAS, H. (1989) 'The validity of idiographic research explanations', *Academy of Management Review*, 14, 4, pp. 551–61.

WEICK, K.E. (1976) 'Educational organisations as loosely coupled systems', *Administrative Science Quarterly*, 21, pp. 1–19.

YIN, R. (1989) *Case Study Research*, London, Sage.

Chapter 12

Students' Secondary School Careers: Research in a Climate of 'Moving Perspectives'

Gwen Wallace, Jean Rudduck and Susan Harris

The research discussed in this chapter is a four-year longitudinal qualitative study of students' careers in three comprehensive schools (1991–5). The value of the concept of 'career', as Goffman (1959, p. 119) points out, is its 'two-sidedness': one side is linked to the development of image of self, self-identity and sense of future, while the other concerns the progress of the individual through institutional time and his or her movement within the hierarchical structure of the institution (see Harris and Rudduck, 1993, p. 230). Interest-ingly, when Hughes first wrote about the concept of career in 1937 (discussed in Cicourel and Kitsuse, 1971; Esland, 1971) he highlighted the 'moving perspective' in which persons orient themselves with reference to the social order. In studying students' in-school careers in the 1990s, we have not only the 'moving perspective' of the students themselves but also the unprecedented degree of turbulence affecting the educational 'social order' and each school's place within it. We want, therefore, to underline the deliberate ambiguity of the title: 'school career' is not only about students; it is also about schools — and the ways in which changes at school level are redefining the structure of opportunity and achievement for students.

We are helped in our task by the consistency of message across the gov-ernment's post–1988 portfolio of policy initiatives, and the general agreement among its critics about the broad pattern of effects. Our argument is that as the Secretary of State for Education pursues a market policy based on divers-ity and choice, schools as institutions and students as individuals are subject to parallel processes of reorientation and reidentification. In each case, we find an intensification of the process of differentiation and a move towards catego-rizing the performance of both school and student in a more public manner.

Context 1: Schools, Schooling and Competitive Markets

The highly visible nature of current policy making on schooling, the extent to which it challenges the balance of power between central government, local authority and school established by the 1944 Education Act, and the controversies it has generated all provide an unusual historical moment for examining the effects of policy changes on schools and on students' experiences of schooling. Ball (1993c, pp. 205–9) characterizes it as a return to 'curricular fundamentalism' and to an 'education of deference'.

It is assumed that 'good' schools will rank highly in their league and that parents will choose the best. By funding the schools according to age-weighted student numbers, it is further assumed that good schools will get better and bad schools close down for lack of customers — unless they are rescued by the 'Education Associations' set up by the 1993 Education Act to 'turn round' an HMI generated 'hit list' of failing schools (see Simon and Chitty, 1993, pp. 70–3).

Ball makes the point (1993a, p. 10) that 'the stress is on winners' — in short, that market theories represent middle-class rather than working-class interests, with accompanying 'fractioning along ethnic, religious and gender lines' (p. 16). Corbett (1993, p. 18) echoes this view in the comment that the 'philosophy of "choice and diversity" is driving a well-known wedge between the strong and the weak'. And Codd, writing about parallel trends in New Zealand, says that in the utilitarian-led, market culture, 'a preferred good such as education is distributed so as to gain optimal average benefits for all, even if the least advantaged become worse off' (1993, p. 81).

Context 2: The General Impact of Government Policy on the Research Schools

Our three research schools were chosen partly because senior management had appeared confident and positive about their future. Nevertheless, in these schools — as is likely in many comprehensive schools across the country — there is evidence of uncertainty of identity and of internal division as heads and teachers assess the goodness of fit between the values that the school has sought to endorse and the values that underpin new national policy. Local Management of Schools may promise greater freedom, but the constraints and pressures are strong. Ball (1993b, pp. 106, 111) points to an 'over-determined and over-regulated' situation, where teachers are enmeshed in overlapping webs of control — the statutory curriculum, the market and the new monitoring structures, all of which, he argues, serve to bring teachers' values more closely in line with their interests. Carter (1993, p. 151) echoes this statement, referring to the way in which, in a climate of structured competition, we can all become vulnerable to the 'technologies of the self that align individual aspirations with dominant political perspectives'.

As yet we are in the early stages of analysing our first two years of data (from the 1991–2 and 1992–3 interviews with students and teachers) and we are aware that our schools are only now beginning to feel the full effects of formula funding as transitional arrangements are phased out. Nevertheless, we are beginning to see how government policy is creating tensions that are tending to be resolved through increasing differentiation at the level of the school and the student.

Two of our schools, already below target last year, have lost further students this year to rival comprehensives and to a City Technology College. This loss will reduce the Spring 1994 budget in one school by about £80,000. The school may well lose more students from the middle-class neighbourhoods in what was previously its 'catchment area' not only at the primary–secondary transfer but also in 'sideways' moves in later years. This process is exacerbated when, because numbers are below target, the school is obliged to take students excluded on behavioural grounds by schools. The effect of this is also to create a gender imbalance. Students excluded for behavioural problems tend to be boys; students moving out have often been girls. Although the school is unlikely to become unviable as it serves a large, socially mixed area, with many parents who are likely to go on regarding it as their 'local' school, it is having to face the prospect of developing new policies to deal with the larger numbers of potentially disruptive boys. It is also about to lose Section 11 money, previously available to schools with significant proportions of children from ethnic-minority groups.

As a result of the loss of revenue, the senior-management team negotiated three voluntary redundancies in 1993 — including the departure of one pastoral post holder. The governing board is now working on criteria for compulsory redundancy in 1994, taking into account the need for coherent curriculum planning: with voluntary redundancy some areas can become understaffed while others remain overstaffed. The head predicts the loss of a member of the senior-management team during the next two years and the head will also have to teach. Aware of the likelihood of continuing problems with recruitment, the school is trying to generate a market niche by developing specialist provision in the arts. At the same time as staff are having to support the larger numbers of young male students with behavioural problems they could find themselves stretched by the constant need, not only to achieve highly in the league tables of attendance and achievement, but also by having to mount regular public performances.

In another of our three schools, in contrast, it is oversubscription that is creating the problems. Despite the head's commitment to developing a new culture, the old grammar-school image dies hard and is, ironically, the basis of its present surge in popularity among a socially broader segment of local population. With its rising numbers the school is likely to find it difficult to maintain the quality of its resources and facilities.

The constant worries about finance in all three schools mean that it is difficult for staff to plan long-term; all feel that the situation is, in some way or another, unreliable and precarious. As one headteacher explained (November 1992):

It's corrosive of good planning, it's corrosive of morale to be constantly worried about the cost of things. And it is profoundly uncomfortable to have in the back, well at the front, of your mind all the time 'what's the cost of this activity?'

Considerable effort, across the three schools, is going into public-relations exercises to attract parents of prospective students. It is apparent that some primary schools are developing clear 'brand name' loyalties to particular secondary schools. For instance, the attempts of one of our schools to attract students from a former 'feeder' primary school were rebuffed by the head who favoured a different secondary school. These allegiances, which signal, publicly, a commitment to particular values and their continuity at secondary level, are serving to differentiate the market of choice quite sharply. For two of our research schools, the close proximity of 'rival' comprehensives and of a City Technology College is a constant and visible reminder of the two-edged sword of competition; there are winners and there are losers.

Context 3: The National Reforms and Students' School Careers

We are following eighty students through their last four years of secondary schooling (Y8 to Y11). The students were 12 when the research started in 1991 and will be 16 when it ends. On the advice of the participating schools, we involved one form group in each of the three schools. We interview the students individually once a term. We also interview form and year tutors once a term, and the headteacher of each school, members of the senior-management teams, and those teachers who are regularly in contact with the research students, once or twice a year. All the interviews are recorded and transcribed.

The cohort of students that we chose to study have a significant place in the history of government reform; they would have been the first to experience the national programme of reported assessments in the core subjects during the Summer of 1993. In the event, following widespread boycott by teachers, the national programme was only patchily implemented across the country. Some schools chose to set tests — either the government's or their own — so that they could report on student progress to parents but the results were not, in the main, forwarded to the Secretary of State who was unable, as a result, to publish comparative data on achievements in different schools at Key Stage 3.

There seems to be a common pattern across students' experiences of schooling that is affecting their sense of self as learners and their sense of futures: it is the intensification of categorizing and labelling. The national concern to match level of attainment to teaching leads logically to an increase in setting, and the attainment tests are the main mechanisms for differentiation, although, in the longer-term, the differentiation between schools, may prove even more significant. Option choices can also serve as a device for differentiation rather than as a means of respecting students' wish, at 14 years, to have some control over their learning agenda.

In Summer 1993 our students were at the end of Year 9 — a year which they characterized as the year of 'sats 'n options' (see Harris, Rudduck and Wallace, 1994). In fact, options were more limited than they had been in previous years, both because of the requirements of the National Curriculum and because of staffing constraints. In one school students had to choose between business studies (which is thought worthy of the brightest students) and a new Youth Award Scheme which leads not to GCSE but to a school certificate and which is seen as appropriate for students not expected to reach GCSE standard. In two of the three schools, teachers were concerned to guide students towards 'appropriate' courses (in terms of their perceived ability or capacity for sustained effort) and to reorient students who made 'inappropriate' choices. In the third — the smallest — where choice was most limited but where the options were more equal in status, students had, ironically, greater autonomy in making their choices.

While senior management and teachers are trying to make sense of the new requirements in relation to their own values and their schools' chances of survival, students are, on the whole, less aware of the way the changes are affecting them. Successive cohorts of students move through the structures for organizing learning that prevail at the time without any real sense of the force of policy changes. Their only basis for comparison are the recollections of older friends and siblings, and even if they hear that there *are* changes they are unlikely to comprehend their significance for their identities as learners and for their life chances. Students' awareness of change is more likely to be built up out of evidence of teachers' anxiety and pressure and out of the patches of information that teachers offer them directly — but since few have a framework that allows them to make sense of such information, it does not feed a critical understanding.

Simon reminds us that a National Curriculm Council report called for 'the setting of pupils according to ability where this is practicable' but, he adds, the report did 'not give one single reason nor any rationale to support the recommendation' (Simon, 1993, p. 37). Sadly, however, teachers across all three schools, even those with values and traditions that were in opposition to grouping by ability, felt that the SATs would prove to be a back door to the introduction or reintroduction of widespread setting or streaming. As one teacher said:

> I actually think it's on the way back. And I think Sats will make it happen . . . It's quite obvious that SATs are a filtering device . . . It's such a monster to administer and run that it's easier to set. And that could well happen not for any educational reason but because it's easier to do it and cheaper. (English teacher)

One of the pastoral staff elsewhere was actively questioning whether setting earlier would not be of benefit to students, given the way many students in Year 10 were welcoming their escape from the year group. Indeed, she believed, behaviour had been improved by the setting and option process. Given that many of the arguments for keeping the class group together centred on its function as a socially supportive system, she was beginning to wonder if, in practice, rather than provide support, it generated the kinds of internicine feuds and conflicts more common in families.

The Protocols and Risks of Conducting a Long Term Research Relationship in the Present Climate

It is within the contexts outline above, marked, both centrally and locally, by turbulence, that we are trying to pursue a longitudinal-based study. Conducting a longitudinal study is an inherently complex research task, whether the main instrument is a questionnaire or interview. Conducting such a study in the present climate adds to the complications.

Let us, first, briefly rehearse the more or less routine problems of our methodology. We do not have real concerns about sample continuity and loss in that our students are a captive group. We have had an occasional 'sideways' move and some unwitting evasions — the one or two students whose families move away from the area during the period of the research, or the long term non-attender in one school whose occasional days of presence have not so far coincided with any of our fieldwork visits. Equally, however, we have had additions to our cohorts: a student who returned, having once chosen to move elsewhere, and a student repeating Year 10 who had had a disastrous career in another school. These undoubtedly have an effect on the groups we are interviewing and are included for that reason. They also may provide a sharper perspective, contrasting their current experience with that in another school.

We have not had any unanticipated problems in eliciting 'usable responses' although we need to consider how far these are influenced by the way our subjects view us. We are aware that we entered as 'outsiders', strangers to the particular schools (though not to schools as such) and we acknowledge that researchers are not a normal part of the everyday world of school. Hence we had to negotiate a role both with staff and students. Students came to us, on site and with the agreement of their tutors to be interviewed. For the first interviews in Year 8 we asked them to come in small friendship groups of twos and threes so that they might talk to us freely, in 'conversational encounters' (Powney and Watts, 1987). In Year 9 we interviewed them individually and in our current round, at the start of Year 10, we are again interviewing in pairs. Our experience is that both methods have advantages and disadvantages. Some individuals clearly relish the opportunity to talk about themselves on a one-to-one basis, although not all students are equally confident. Similarly, the friendship groups can work differently for different students. In one instance in the Year 10 interviews, two friends have provided graphic, mutually supportive, accounts of recent racial harassment in the school catchment area. In other groups we have had open disagreements, with friends taking alternative perspectives and debating them quite heatedly in response to our questions. And again, we have had situations where one partner dominated, and inhibited a less assertive friend from expressing a view. In analysing our data, we have to take into account this diversity across individuals and groups.

On our first encounters, and at subsequent interviews, it was important to us to explain to all students that we were interviewing in two other schools, as well as their own, and that we would be talking to them three times a year over a four-year period. We told them we were writing a book about their experiences as they went through school; that we wanted to know what *they* felt about it all, so we could tell others, but that whatever they said would not be passed back to teachers or others in any way that could be attributable to particular individuals.

On each occasion, students have been reminded of our intentions in advance of our visits. Our experience suggests that their relationships with their form tutors are good enough for complaints to be voiced should they object to our presence. Indeed, as the project progresses, we are more likely to be greeted as familiar faces and asked when we will be back. On each visit we cover a common, loosely structured schedule. However, each of us brings different qualities to our respective schools and the point remains that it is the diversity of responses which is noteworthy. Different students treat us differently and, in spite of our attempts at presenting ourselves as 'writers of a book about them', have different concepts of our role. One student, for example, who had transferred into a class group from another school, took a complaint about a member of staff to her pastoral tutor, and with reference to our interview added the comment, 'I told that inspector about him'. On other occasions, we have been used by students as confidents and counsellors, sometimes with the expectation that we have the power to intervene in a crisis. One of us, for example, was asked to prevent two girls, who were close friends, from being split up. Another was told about a teacher's behaviour which subsequently (and without our intervention) became a matter for a disciplinary tribunal. On another occasion we were caused some heart-searching when we faced the possibilities that, from different schools, we were getting evidence which could imply in one case child abuse and in the other illegal drug use. In the event these matters were made public elsewhere and resolved without our intervention. The ethical *and* legal issues they raised for us are akin to those of the photographer who is uncertain whether to take the picture as it is or intervene to forestall predicted, undesirable consequences. What we conclude from this is that some students see us, at present, as having some authority to influence events on their behalf. We must therefore take into account their perception of us as 'participants' as well as observers.

It is not usual to see analogies between interviewing as a research method and participant observation. Yet the continuum which participant-observation represents fits quite well with our experience of conducting interviews with students on a longitudinal project where we have promised feedback to staff. It is worth considering the two ends of this continuum separately.

The Interviewer As 'Observer'

We shall stay, for the present, with our data-gathering roles as 'observers' in the broadest sense. If we consider the ethical and methodological issues surrounding the gathering of data from on-site interviews with students, we must acknowledge that we are negotiating much of the time without the students' full involvement. In this sense the students (who are, in structural terms, the 'objects' of schooling) may be seen as no more than the 'objects' of our study. The interviews are scheduled to suit the school and the researcher not the individual student, and students can have their bad days — when they feel upset about something that has happened at school or at home, or when they have a sore throat, or when they are tired after playing a match and might not feel like talking to us.

Even so, we would wish to counter Denscombe and Aubrook's (1992) ethical reservations about the voluntary nature of students participation in research, at least where the major tool is the interview. Although we accept that the 'voluntariness' of *any* student participation in a school-based study may be doubted at a general level, the evidence from our data — available both from the tape transcripts and in our observations of body language and general rapport at interview — suggests that our students *have* felt able to respond to our questions with rather more sense of voluntariness than they apparently felt in Denscombe's study when a questionnaire was administered to them at their desks by their teachers. This sense of voluntariness shows in the varying degrees of willingness and enthusiasm in responding to specific issues both within a single interview and between students. In itself we suggest that the quality and length of responses constitutes evidence that some matters engage students more willingly and more personally than others. Unsurprisingly, matters of complaint evoke the most heartfelt responses. For example, in one school, the loss of most of their physical education lessons and the curtailing of school trips, because of the demands of the National Curriculum and assessments were a source of grievance. Two students expressed the view that they were being 'cleaned up' as the school tried to improve its image and force them into uniforms; others felt strongly about queueing for lunches which cost so much when they finally reached their turn that they could not afford to satisfy their hunger, 'so we go out now'.

Comments on boring lessons spent copying teachers' notes from blackboards, and lessons structured round worksheets or lessons with unprepared teachers were frequent enough to allow us to identify practices which encourage disengagement from classroom learning. On the other hand, we met with great enthusiasm for many lessons. Students readily discriminated between lessons they enjoyed, where they were engaged with the subject matter and felt they learned, and lessons where they may have had to 'work hard' but learned little:

> S: Well in English last year all we did was write in books, copying paragraphs. In English this year we, like, read books. I enjoyed that. Now we're doing a bit of writing — we're doing something on survival which I enjoy. It's like you're in a plane and it crashes in a jungle, an island, and it blows up and you need all your . . . it's got a list of things like salt tablets and everything, and parachute, and you have to list what goes first from one to fifteen. Y8/F

The contrast, we believe, is between subjects or lessons which elicit evidence of personal engagement and lessons where students are struggling to express what they are doing and are having to rely on teachers' words. Contrast this reply with the student quoted above: 'Well we're learning about a long topic called "reaction" and that will last us, well we started it in September and it will last us.'

Here is another example where a student is struggling to find his own words:

> Well I enjoy science because you do a lot of chemicals and that. But in Year 8 you just use a power pack or something and get a battery and do a light or something but now as soon as you get older into another form you get to do chemicals and things like that. Y9/M

We have yet to analyze these issues further but we are beginning to speculate that the distinction made by Gramsci (1971) between 'common-sense knowledge' and 'philosophical knowledge' may be applied, by extension, to the differences between students' and teachers' knowledge about learning.

We have also to decide how far monosyllabic responses from students suggest the respondent has neither a (perhaps imperfect) understanding of the teachers' explanations nor a 'common-sense' interpretation with which to address our concerns. We think that we can tell, when in interview, a student is thinking things through for himself or herself; the words have a vitality and spirit of their own. Alternatively, we are sometimes aware that we have aroused some personal embarrassment over, for example, a question on test results or their placing in a particular set. When we sense embarrassment, on occasions, we try to change the emphasis. On these occasions we have to make a judgment, based on the quality of our rapport with individuals, about when to try to get behind the reticence, and when to let a matter drop.

Of course, it takes time to build up a relationship of trust — students know now that we are interested in what they have to say, that we do not tell teachers what they say, that we are not part of any official 'surveillance' mechanism, and that their encounters with us will not affect the way that they are perceived or treated in school.

Our general case remains that students did not see the interviews as schoolwork in the sense that Denscombe suggested was the case when students were required to complete questionnaires, at their desks, under teacher direction. Whilst we would not claim that we have an ideal situation, we would suggest that the nature of our contact and long-term relationship means students are more likely to see the interviews as a regular *escape* from lessons and an opportunity to talk to a sympathetic adult in a way not readily available at any other time. This in itself is becoming problematic in one school where teachers are reluctant to allow their students the time out of class to participate in the interviews because it is seen as disruptive of the hard-pressed timetable for GCSE.

We have more problems when we consider what we might feed back to our students. As 'observers' of their progress through four years of schooling, our promise is that they will contribute to a book which will make their experiences heard. The nature of the exercise is such that any benefits such a narrative might offer, in terms of changed practices, will not benefit them. Even more, we are not in a position to intervene directly on behalf of individuals (though they may believe we can) without betraying confidences. At a general level, even immediate feedback to heads and teachers is unlikely to be reflected in changes of school policy soon enough to affect the circumstances of particular students, although it may do so.

An alternative view would urge us to provide direct feedback to students. Apart from the difficulties this creates in requiring extended contact time, feeding back to students what they said in a previous interview for verification in the next has no point in a study where we expect to document students' *changing* perspectives over time in response both to greater maturity and changing circumstances. However, here again a longitudinal study, where we have the chance to get to know the students we are interviewing and share their hopes and fears, does allow us to check back with them precisely on those changing perspectives. Thus, for example, we can discuss with them how far their option choices in Year 9 live up to their expectations in Year 10 in a way which demonstrates a very real interest in what they have told us already.

Although our main source of data is the interview, we know that we cannot rely solely on this to paint a full picture of students' life in school. Students' perspectives are limited both by the boundaries of each individual's experiences and the discourses each has available to communicate and interpret those experiences to us — and of course, his or her willingness at any one moment to do so, as we have seen above. We supplement the data from student interviews with written records — the reports that accompany students from their primary to secondary school, which they may not know exist, and which often 'fix' a reputation in advance — and the regular records that the secondary school maintains; we have access to registers of attendance, to lists of awards won, and to notes of behaviours that have led to trouble. We also have access to documents such as students' Records of Achievement and school reports as well as statements of school policy.

Interpreting the relationships between the personal and the impersonal data in our analyses can be a problem, since the latter are structured into systems in ways that are only vaguely understood by students, even when the likely effects on their own school careers are, to us as observers, quite striking. One methodological issue centres, therefore, on how we select from, and balance, these different sources. The complexity is enhanced at the level of the individual by the structural imbalances surrounding race and gender. We are also aware in talking to students, to teachers and to school managers that what we are offered in interview are sometimes contradictory ways of describing and explaining the same event. We have to take into account therefore the way that position in the school's social order can colour perception of a situation, as well as the expectations of some speakers that *their* account will be regarded as the official or authentic one!

These are, in the main, the routine problems of longitudinal and interview-based studies where students are the main focus and source of data. However, there are some additional concerns that seem to us to relate directly to the current political context.

The Interviewer As 'Participant'

We are working with three schools over a long period of time — almost five years if we include the preliminary negotiations and the discussion of the final report. We must therefore ensure that the schools maintain confidence in us as researchers and goodwill towards the purposes of the study. The last two years have been times of enormous pressure for teachers who have tried to maintain programme continuity for students while making constant adjustments to their content and approach as new and detailed policies are introduced — and then, quite often, changed (a pattern that has led to the government's education department being dubbed 'The Ministry of U-Turns'; *TES*, 20 August 1993). Teachers do not have much time to think; they are preoccupied with keeping up on a day-to-day basis and with looking ahead in an uncertain world to safeguard the futures of their schools. The strain often shows, both in terms of stress-related absences and in terms of their having to apologize to their students for being on a 'short fuse'. In such circumstances, having to arrange and take part in interviews for researchers could easily be seen as yet another burden.

We need then to address our role as 'quasi-participants' and the issues this raises for the research. It is here, rather than in our roles as interview observers, that most of the ethical dilemmas arise, given our claim that the 'voluntary' nature of student participation in contributing useful data is built into the interview situation.

We are not attempting to be 'flies on walls'. We are intermittent visitors whose arrival is announced in the daily newsheets. Yet there is a sense in which we come to our schools as researchers with something to offer: each of us has taken on board an issue that our fieldwork school is concerned with so that it feels that it has a stake in the research; we offer feedback sessions to the head and whichever colleagues he or she chooses to invite; we may be able to use our wider knowledge of the system to make constructive educational links for the school; we try to respond positively to invitations to speak at local in-service events organized by teachers in our schools. We are now half-way through the research and some teachers have said that interviewing students and inviting them to talk about their learning seems to be having a beneficial effect. We also have reason to believe that students feel that what they say is worth listening to and we know we are prompting them to think about their work, something which busy teachers may have little time for. Overall, we are generally seen as, at worst, not damaging and, at most, a source of insight and understanding for the school. One teacher recently reported back to us that a student had returned to class to announce that 'QQSE is great Miss' (QQSE being the Centre for Qualitative and Quantitative Studies in Education at Sheffield University).

Nonetheless, attempts to provide feedback to schools raises questions about how we select what we tell to whom. We are conscious of the dangers of modifying our analyses and interpretations with our audience in mind. So far we have fed back *general issues* of relevance to all the schools and we have been able to do this with a degree of detachment which has engaged our audiences, without making them defensive in the face of data which can sometimes appear to blame schools rather than to analyse issues. At the same time, we know that, particularly in the present climate, research about schools is a potentially significant instrument of shaping opinion — particularly at the local level where changes in reputation can quickly affect a school's recruit-ment and therefore its confidence. We are also aware that we are operating in a national climate in which research has been deliberately 'downsized' by the government. In some way we have to demonstrate to participating teachers that our research addresses issues that are relevant to schools, and that what we write will make sense to schools and will not damage any individual in any of the schools involved in the study.

In order to build and sustain trust, at the start of the research we con-structed a collection of information about the project, including careful guar-antees about confidentiality and anonymity. Each school has a copy and although, now, they are unlikely to refer to the documents, they were import-ant at the beginning, and for our part we have continued to respect the prin-ciples that structured the agreement. We aim to be as positive as we can in responding to the work of schools but we must not conspire to soften *general evidence* of, for instance, bullying, or the negative effects on some students of the return to setting, or evidence of insensitivity towards and harassment of students from ethnic minorities. Nonetheless, we have promised anonymity to our respondents and can find ourselves recipients of data which are difficult to report without leaving open the possibility of our sources being identified. As researchers, we believe we must resolve the tension between accountability to those who supply us with data: the students, teachers and heads; and accountability, as researchers, for the quality of our reports. Ultimately, this involves us in value judgments as issues arise, and, we can only justify those in open dialogue with our respective audiences. The values we hold create dilemmas in that we wish to be 'true' to all our sources, without divulging them and without compromising the integrity of our interpretations. So far, we believe we have managed to walk the tightrope that these constraints imply. Given the complexity of conducting a longitudinal study in the current educational climate we have few, if any precedents to guide us in our interpretations.

Above all, we do not go into schools, as Philip Jackson says researchers tend to do, 'looking for trouble' — for trouble is often more interesting to write — and read — about than the virtues or positive regularities of school life, the 'ordinary stuff': 'The natural temptation . . . is to seek out the dramatic, the troublesome, the unexpected, leaving behind the mundane or the ordinary, the run of the mill' (Jackson, 1990, pp. 158, 160). We are aware that on-site school researchers are, at the present time, when so many schools are vulnerable, holders of a risky store of information. We are careful in the way we report the research, both orally and in writing, and we try to be fair to schools as well as to students. We try to see the three schools as caught in a web that others have spun and while there are of course many aspects of their policies and practices that they are fully responsible for, and have control over, external pressures are obliging them to go down some avenues that they find uncongenial.

The Final Analysis

In the end we will have more than 700 transcribed student interviews covering four years of their student experiences in a context of changing educational policy. We will also have interview data from key adult figures in our students' school careers and documentary evidence of their progress, some of which dates back to nursery school. We are also considering how we might collect students' own reflections of the four-year period when they complete their schooling and are also hoping to extend the project to get reflective interviews from their parents.

With this quantity of data (not all of which will be equally valuable), we hope to be able to do two kinds of analysis. We are coding our transcripts for computer analysis and recording contextual changes as they arise. We hope firstly to be able to explore the way in which national change impacts on individual schools and it turn how this affects individual students' experiences of school. Secondly, we have to trace selected individual student 'careers' through documentary, biographical and autobiographical evidence with the aim of discovering those 'critical incidents' in their life histories which oriented them towards particular patterns of choice and affected their 'life chances'.

References

BALL, S.J. (1993a) 'Education, markets, choice and social class: The market as a class strategy in the U.K. and the U.S.A., *British Journal of Sociology of Education*, 14, 1, pp. 3–13.

BALL, S.J. (1993b) 'Education policy: Power relations and teachers' work', *British Journal of Educational Studies*, 41, 2, pp. 106–21.

BALL, S.J. (1993c) 'Education, Majorism and "the curriculum of the dead" ', *Curriculum Studies*, 1, 2, pp. 195–214.

BOWE, R. and BALL, S.J. (1992) 'Parents, Privilege and the Education Market Place', Paper presented at the 19th Annual Conference of the British Educational Research Association, Stirling University, September 1993.

CARTER, B. (1993) 'Losing the common touch: A post-modern politics of the curriculum? (essay review)', *Curriculum Studies*, 1, 1, pp. 149–56.

CICOUREL, A.V. and KITSUSE, J.I. (1971) 'The social organisation of the high school and deviant adolescent careers', in COSIN, B.R., DALE, I.R., ESLAND, G.M. and SWIFT, D.F. (Eds) *School and Society*, London, Routledge and Kegan Paul.

CODD, J.A. (1993) 'Equity and choice: The paradox of New Zealand educational reform', *Curriculum studies*, 1, 1, pp. 75–90.

CORBETT, A. (1993) 'The peculiarity of the British', in CHITTY, C. and SIMON, B. (Eds) *Education Answers Back*, London, Lawrence and Wishart.

DENSCOMBE, M. and AUBROOK, L. (1992) 'It's just another piece of schoolwork', *British Educational Research Journal*, 18, 2, pp. 113–31.

ESLAND, G.M. (1971) 'Teaching and learning as the organization of knowledge', in YOUNG, M.F.D. (Ed) *Knowledge and Control*, London, Collier-Macmillan.

GOFFMAN, E. (1959) 'The moral career of the mental patient', *Psychiatry*, 22, May.

GRAMSCI, A. (1971) *Selections from Prison Notebooks* (edited and translated by HOARE, O. and SMITH, N.G.), London, Lawrence and Wishart.

HARRIS, S. and RUDDUCK, J. (1993) 'Establishing the seriousness of learning in the early years of secondary schooling', *British Journal of Educational Psychology*, 63, pp. 322–36.

HARRIS, S., RUDDUCK, J. and WALLACE, G. (1994) 'Sats "n" options', in HUGHES, M. (Ed) *Teaching & Learning in Changing Times*, London; Blackwell.

JACKSON, P. (1990) 'Looking for trouble: Or the place of the ordinary in educational studies', in EISNER, E.W. and PESHKIN, A. (Eds) *Qualitative Inquiry in Education. The Continuing Debate*, Columbia, Teachers College Press.

POWNEY, J. and WATTS, M. (1987) *Interviewing in Educational Research*, London, Routledge and Kegan Paul.

SIMON, B. (1993) 'A return to streaming?', *Forum*, 35, 2, pp. 36–8.

SIMON, B. and CHITTY, C. (1993) *SOS: Save Our Schools*, London, Lawrence and Wishart.

Chapter 13

Researching Parents after the 1988 Education Reform Act

Martin Hughes

Overview

This chapter will describe some of the methodological and ethical issues which I encountered in carrying out research on parents in the context of current educational reforms.[1] The chapter starts by outlining the central role which parents have been given within these reforms, and looks at some of the assumptions underlying this role. Two studies are then briefly described which have aimed to provide evidence with which to examine some of these assumptions. The first study, funded by the Leverhulme Trust, was a longitudinal study of parents' views as their children moved through Key Stage 1 (5–7 years). The second study, funded by the ESRC, examined the effects of assessment at Key Stage 1 on parents, teachers and classroom practice. The rest of the chapter describes and discusses some of the methodological and ethical issues raised by this research. These issues fall into three main areas: those concerned with locating and identifying parents, those concerned with longitudinal research on parents, and those concerned with disseminating research findings. The chapter concludes by raising wider issues such as sensitivity, empowerment and voice.

Why Research Parents?

Parents have been given a central role to play within the current educational reforms. The explicit market philosophy which underlies these reforms assumes that education is to be regarded as a commodity, that schools and teachers are the 'providers' of this commodity, and that parents are the 'customers' or 'consumers'. The parents' role in the educational market-place is to make considered choices between schools on the basis of publicly available information, such as a school's performance in national examinations or on standardized assessment results. The underlying assumption is that schools will have to raise their standards, and make public the fact that they have done so, or parents will take their custom elsewhere.

This new role for parents as 'consumers of education' differs markedly from other ways in which parents have frequently been perceived. For example, there is a long tradition within the British education system whereby parents (or at least, particular groups of parents) are seen primarily as 'problems'. That is, they are considered to possess certain attitudes, or bring up their children in certain ways, which make it difficult, if not impossible, for schools to do their job properly (see Docking, 1990). As a consequence, teachers may come to feel they are engaged in an uphill struggle against the adverse effects of the home environment. More recently, teachers have been encouraged to see parents primarily as 'partners' with whom they can share the task of educating their children: this is exemplified by the rapid growth in parent-reading schemes such as PACT (Griffiths and Hamilton, 1984) or parent-maths schemes such as IMPACT. It remains to be seen how far the new role of parents as consumers fits with either of these alternative perceptions of parents. Indeed, the tension between these different parental roles is a major unresolved issue.

The idea that parents should be seen as consumers of education emerged in the writings of various Right-Wing educationalists in the late 1970s and 1980s (Cox and Boyson, 1977; Flew, 1987; Sexton, 1987). The underlying argument of these writers was that schools had become 'producer-dominated', that egalitarian ideas and progressive teaching methods had taken over, and that educational standards had fallen as a result. The proposed remedy was to 'free' schools from the control of local and central authorities, and make them more accountable to market forces. The likely effects this might have on schools were made starkly clear in the following passage from the Hillgate Group (1986):

> Their survival should depend on their ability to satisfy their customers. And their principal customers are parents, who should therefore be free to place their custom where they wish, in order that educational institutions should be shaped, controlled and nourished by their demand . . . Schools will have to work to stay in business, and the worse their results, the more likely they will be to go to the wall. (Hillgate Group, 1986, pp. 7 and 16)

Such ideas exerted a major influence on the 1988 ERA, which as well as introducing the National Curriculum and standardized assessment, also sought to increase parental choice and established the Local Management of Schools. The importance of parental choice, and of parents' rights to information about schools, were further emphasized in subsequent documents, such as the Parent's Charter (DES, 1991) and the Education White Paper 'Choice and Diversity' (DFE, 1992). By the early 1990s, the idea that informed parental choice should be the major vehicle for raising educational standards had become firmly located at the heart of government policy.

Given the central role which parents have been asked to play in the current reforms, it might reasonably be assumed that many of the reforms, and particularly those which seek to empower parents, have arisen from a groundswell of popular demand among parents for such changes. But in fact, the reality is very different: parents have been given little role in the shaping and refining of recent legislation. Rather, it has been taken as a self-evident certainty that the reforms are what parents want. As the Secretary of State for Education, John Patten, commented when he launched the 1992 White Paper:

> Our proposals are radical, sensible and in tune with what parents want. This is above all a common sense White Paper. (Patten, *TES*, 7 August 1992)

Like the rest of the current reforms, the 1992 White Paper rests on a whole series of unsupported assumptions about what parents want and how they will behave. Thus it is widely assumed that parents are dissatisfied with the standards which currently prevail in state education; that they approve of the National Curriculum and standardized assessment; that they are happy with their new role as consumers of education; and that they will in practice choose schools purely on the basis of published academic results. Similarly, it is assumed that schools are sensitive to what their parents or prospective parents want, and that they will accommodate themselves to parental wishes. Yet there is little firm evidence on which to base such assumptions.

Our Research on Parents

The overall aim of our research on parents has been to look critically at some of these assumptions about their role in the current reforms. The research has focused on Key Stage 1, as this is the stage where the reforms have so far had their greatest impact. To date, two main studies have been carried out.

The first study, entitled 'Parents and the National Curriculum', was funded by the Leverhulme Trust from 1989 to 1992. This study — which was carried out with Felicity Wikeley and Tricia Nash — aimed to examine parents' views as the reforms were first introduced at Key Stage 1, and to look at how their views changed as the reforms unfolded in practice. The project therefore used a longitudinal design, and followed a group of around 150 children who started Key Stage 1 in 1989. These children were subsequently among the first group of 7-year-olds to undergo standardized assessment in 1991. Their parents were interviewed face-to-face in the Autumn terms of 1989, 1990 and 1991, and by telephone in the Summer terms of 1991 and 1992. The interviews covered topics such as parents' conceptions of themselves as consumers, parents' choice of school, parents' satisfaction with the school, parents' attitude towards the National Curriculum, parents' knowledge about what goes on in school, and parents' experience of assessment and their attitude towards it. Initial findings from this research were made available in two interim reports (Hughes, Wikeley and Nash, 1990, 1991), and the full findings were reported in Hughes, Wikeley and Nash (1994).

The second study, entitled 'Parents and Assessment at Key Stage 1', was funded by the ESRC from 1991–4 as part of the Initiative on 'Innovation and Change in Education: The Quality of Teaching and Learning'. This project — which was carried out with Charles Desforges and Cathie Holden — focused on the assessment and reporting procedures for 7-year-olds at the end of Key Stage 1. Our aims were two-fold: first, to look at the effect which assessment and reporting were having on parents' views, teachers' views and classroom practice, and secondly to look at the effect which parents' views were having in turn on the assessment and reporting procedures. Two cohorts of around 120 children each were followed through the 1991 and 1992 SATs, and interviews were carried out with their parents and teachers both before and after the SATs. Observations were also carried out in the children's classrooms before the 1991 SATs and after the 1992 SATs. Findings from the 1991 cohort were published in Holden, Hughes and Desforges (1993) and in Desforges, Hughes and Holden (1994a), while findings from the 1992 cohort are to be published in Desforges, Hughes and Holden (1994b) and in Hughes, Desforges and Holden (1994).

Two general points about our methodology should be noted at the outset. First, we have operated primarily in a quantitative mode. In both studies, our sample size was sufficiently large for us to carry out statistical analyses of the data — for example, of changes in parents' attitudes over time, or between particular subgroups of parents within the sample. However, we have also carried out various qualitative analyses of the data — for example, in analysing parents' responses to particular questions — and we have generated some critical case studies — for example, of parents who moved school in the course of each study. This mixture of quantitative and qualitative approaches is not unproblematic, but it has allowed us to approach our data from a number of different directions.

The second general point is that our research has focused almost entirely on interviews with parents and teachers. We have thus gained considerable insight into their perceptions, attitudes and opinions. However, we have virtually nothing to say about their behaviour — apart from when this has been reported to us. In the Leverhulme study, for example, we asked parents in each interview how far they saw themselves as 'consumers' with regard to their children's education. Over the three years of the study, we found a significant increase in the extent to which parents described themselves in this way. However, we were unable to say whether these changes in parents' self-ascription were associated with any change in their behaviour with regard to their children's schools. In other words, we cannot say whether parents *acted* more like consumers — whatever this might mean — over the period of the study.

Locating and Defining Parents

One of the main methodological problems we have encountered is concerned with locating and defining parents. At one level this is primarily a practical problem to do with raising a suitable sample for study. At the same time it is also a conceptual problem in that it raises the question of what exactly is meant by the term 'parent'.

One of the main problems in locating a sample of parents is that they are a much more disparate group than teachers or pupils, who are two of the main groups studied by educational researchers. Compared with parents, teachers and pupils are relatively easy to locate — they can usually be found in schools, and in reasonably large numbers at that. Parents, on the other hand, tend to be scattered over a wide geographical area, and need to be tracked down in ones and twos. Moreover, while teachers and pupils carry out most of their business in relatively public settings, parents are essentially private individuals — or rather, one is dealing with the private rather than the public part of their lives. As a result, the whole business of negotiating agreement for an interview is often much more complicated and time-consuming than it is for teachers or pupils.

In our research we have adopted three different approaches towards locating a sample of parents. In the Leverhulme study we first identified eleven contrasting schools in the South West of England which were prepared to take part in the study. We then wrote individual letters to the parents of all pupils starting Year 1 in Autumn 1989, except that in the three largest schools we only used children from one class in that year group. The letter explained that we were carrying out research on parents' views about the new National Curriculum, and that we would like to interview them in their own homes. The letter gave parents the opportunity to decline if they so wished, although only 6 per cent of parents did so at this point.

The ESRC study involved a slightly different design, although again we approached the parents through their children's schools. In this study our sample of schools was slightly larger (twenty in each cohort) and was drawn from a wider geographical area (London and Bristol as well as the South West). For each cohort, we wanted to study six Year 2 children from each school — a boy and a girl of low, medium and high attainment. For the 1991 cohort we asked the Year 2 teachers to choose the sample for us. However, we had reservations about this approach, as we suspected that in some schools the teachers were selecting parents who were better known to them and whom they felt would be cooperative. We therefore decided for the 1992 cohort to select the six children ourselves, drawing on information about attainment which was provided by their teachers. As with the Leverhulme study, the parents in each cohort were written to individually and asked if they would take part in the study. Again, around 5 per cent of parents declined to do so.

Even when parents agreed to take part in the study, our problems in locating them for an interview had often only just begun. Some parents were extremely elusive. Letters were not answered, appointments were not kept, or notes were pinned to the front door explaining that some unexpected event had occurred to prevent the interview taking place. Others were simply very busy, so that interviews had to be fitted in at odd times of the day, such as during their lunch-breaks from work, or while they were simultaneously doing some housework, feeding a younger child, and looking after the neighbour's sick dog. One parent, from an ethnic-minority group, wanted to take part in the research but her husband disapproved; she could therefore only be interviewed when her husband was not around. As can be imagined, collecting data in such circumstances requires a considerable amount of patience, flexibility and resourcefulness.

One major decision that has to be made when researching parents is whether to collect data from the mother, the father or from both parents — and if the latter, whether together or separately. This decision raises some problematic issues about what exactly is meant by the term 'parent' — issues which tend to be ignored in public statements about the role of parents in education. One approach, for example, is to regard the child's mother and father as two unrelated and independent individuals, and to interview them individually on separate occasions. Another approach is to regard them as interchangeable individuals, and to interview one or the other, depending on who happens to be available. A third approach is to regard them as a single entity, and to interview them together as a pair. Each of these approaches, of course, assumes a two-parent family with mother and father living together, whereas in reality one encounters a number of alternative family arrangements. Parents may have separated, divorced, remarried, or be living with another partner. In such circumstances, the non-custodial parent may have little to do with their child's education, while the step-parent or new partner may be much more centrally involved.

Clearly, this is a complex and sensitive area in which to be treading. Our approach was the same for both studies. First, we decided only to interview one parent from each family — primarily on the grounds that we had insufficient resources to interview both parents, but also because we were unclear how far data collected from both parents could be regarded as independent for the purposes of analysis. However, we decided not to object if the other parent (or step-parent, partner or indeed anyone else) wanted to be present at the interview. Our second decision was to let each family decide for itself which parent would be interviewed. In practice, we usually ended up interviewing the parent who was most available during the day or early evening — our preferred interviewing times. This also had the advantage that we usually interviewed the parent who had most day-to-day contact with the school. In both studies this meant that we mostly interviewed the mother alone, sometimes the father alone, and occasionally some combination of mother, father, step-parent, partner or friend. Having established who would be interviewed on the first occasion, our aim on subsequent occasions was to reinterview the same person as far as possible.

Martin Hughes

Researching Parents Over Time

In both studies we were interested in changes to parents' views over a period of time. The period was somewhat longer in the Leverhulme study than in the ESRC study (three years compared with six months or less), but the methodological problems were essentially the same.

One major problem for any longitudinal study is that of attrition to the sample over time. Parents may move to a new area, or their circumstances may change so they are no longer available for further interviews, or the novelty of being in a research study may simply wear off. This problem was clearly most acute for the Leverhulme study with its longer time-scale. Nevertheless, we were still pleasantly surprised that over the entire period of the study only twelve families out of the original 138 (9 per cent) were lost to the study. Six families moved out of the area, while the other six became 'noncontactable' for various reasons. In one case, for example, the mother left home and the father did not reply to our requests for an interview; in another case the mother was in considerable distress as her elder son had been killed in a car accident; while in a third case the family simply disappeared from their temporary accommodation and were never seen again.

There are probably two reasons for this relatively small loss to the sample. First, the study took place in the south-west of England, which has a more stable population than some other parts of the country. Secondly, and more importantly perhaps, the interviews were clearly seen by the parents as being something which they valued. The interviews usually lasted at least an hour, and sometimes much longer, and during this time parents were able to talk at length on a matter of major importance to them — their children's education. Indeed, anyone who considers that parents are disinterested or apathetic would be well-advised to spend an hour or two interviewing them in their own homes on this topic.

In both studies we were careful to ensure that each parent was reinterviewed by the same interviewer who had interviewed them initially. Our impression was that parents expected to see the same interviewer again, and would not have been quite so open if a new interviewer had appeared instead. But it was also an important part of the methodology of both studies that we repeated back to parents in later interviews what they had said in previous interviews. If this had been done by a different interviewer it would not only have seemed less natural, but it could also have been regarded as a breach of confidentiality.

This practice of repeating back to parents what they had said on earlier occasions requires some elaboration. We first adopted it on the Leverhulme study as we were interested in the issue of reliability; we were concerned that there might be no correlation at all between parents' response to a particular question on one occasion and their response on another. We thought it possible that parents would look puzzled when confronted by their previous answer, or make comments along the lines of 'did I really say that?'. In fact, this virtually never happened. Parents appeared to accept what we repeated back to them as a reliable account of what they had felt at the time, and then used it as a basis for considering how far (if at all) their views had changed in the intervening period. In addition, if the parents had changed their views, this technique encouraged them to add some sort of explanation as to why the change had occurred.

A further methodological problem in longitudinal research is that the research process itself may have a distorting effect on what is being researched. This is a problem, of course, in any kind of research, but it seems particularly acute in longitudinal research. Our concern was that by repeatedly asking parents about current developments in education, we might have been making them unusually sensitive to those developments. This could merely have increased their interest in what was going on, but it could conceivably have resulted in their taking some action — such as confronting the school on a particular issue or moving their child to another school — purely because of our research.

In the Leverhulme study we tried to investigate this possibility by asking parents at the end of the final interview what effect they felt our research had had on them and on their interaction with the school. The most common response, given by nearly half the parents, was that the interviews had made them think more deeply about the issues involved. At the same time, very few parents felt that being involved in the research had changed the way they had actually behaved. The following comments were typical of many:

> I think it has just made me sit back and think about it, but it hasn't changed anything. I've always had good communication with the school.

> It's made me give more thought to the National Curriculum. Because I know you're coming asking questions, I try to take it in more. But it hasn't changed my behaviour.

> It's made me think more about the questions I've never asked at the school. It's made me think more about the work my child's doing.

One parent described his feelings in rather different terms. He was a senior teacher at another school, and felt strongly critical of some aspects of the reforms. Our interviews provided him with an opportunity to express some of these feelings:

> I feel much better after your interviews. It's like having a confessional or a therapeutic session. It saves me having to write to the Education Minister.

The parents' claims that the interviews had not significantly affected their behaviour were supported by comments made by the headteachers of the eleven schools at the end of the Leverhulme study. The heads said they had received little or no feedback from parents about the research, apart from the occasional comment that they had found it 'interesting' or 'useful'. The heads also claimed that the research had had no observable effect on the interaction between parents and the school, although one head did say it had made her more aware of the need to keep parents informed.

It seems reasonable to conclude that our research had not had a major effect on the parents' behaviour or on their interaction with the school. At the same time, it seems to have made them more thoughtful and aware of the issues involved. While it could be argued that this casts doubt on the validity of our findings, we prefer to take the view that these parents' opinions should be treated with greater respect precisely because they *are* the product of thought and reflection, rather than a glib response produced on the spur of the moment.

Disseminating Research on Parents

The final set of issues with which I wish to deal are concerned with disseminating the outcomes of research. In theory, this process is relatively unproblematic: researchers simply identify the main 'findings' of their research, and present them in a form appropriate for the audience being addressed. In practice, of course, matters are not so straightforward, particularly when the research is concerned with a politically sensitive area.

This point is well illustrated by our findings on parental satisfaction with their children's schools. As we saw earlier, it is widely assumed that parents are generally dissatisfied with their children's schools, and with the educational standards which prevail in them. This assumption of widespread parental dissatisfaction is frequently fuelled by statements from politicians and by attacks in the media on standards in state education. Not surprisingly, many teachers have come to believe these assumptions, and feel that parents are highly dissatisfied with their performance as teachers.

Our research suggests that levels of parental satisfaction depend very much on what exactly parents are being asked about. In both the Leverhulme and the ESRC studies we asked parents how happy they were with their own child's school. In each study we found that around 85–90 per cent of parents were basically happy with their children's schools, and that the proportion who were not happy was around 5 per cent or less. The Leverhulme study also found that 85–90 per cent of parents thought that the teachers at their child's school were 'doing a good job'. These figures all indicate that there are high levels of parental satisfaction with their own children's schools. At the same time, both studies found much greater levels of dissatisfaction when parents were asked about standards in state education more generally. In the Leverhulme study over half the parents said they were 'concerned' about standards in state education, while in the ESRC study parents were more likely to say that standards were falling than that they were rising or staying the same.

These findings point to a possible disassociation between parents' views regarding their own child's school, where their judgments are presumably based on first-hand experience, and their views about the state system more generally, where their judgments are presumably much more dependent on media accounts. At the same time, they present a serious ethical problem for the dissemination process, in that different parts of the findings could be used as ammunition for very different political positions. For example, if one wanted to be supportive of teachers, it would be relatively easy to emphasize the widespread parental satisfaction with their own child's school, and ignore their wider concerns. Alternatively, if one wanted to be critical of state education, one might focus primarily on parents' wider concerns and ignore their more immediate satisfaction.

In our own dissemination activities we have always aimed to maintain a balanced perspective, and wherever possible presented both sets of data. However, it has been interesting to note the different reactions which these findings have received from different audiences. When speaking to groups of teachers, for example, there is always a great deal of interest in our finding that parents are mostly satisfied with their own children's schools. Indeed, we have frequently found that once we have communicated these particular findings, teachers become much more relaxed and receptive towards some of our other findings, which are potentially more critical of schools. In contrast, our dealings with the media suggest there is little interest for them in our findings of parental satisfaction, and much more interest in parents' criticisms of schools. 'Good news', it would seem, does not make good news.

The final point I want to make concerns the methods used for dissemination. Because we are dealing with a topic of high policy relevance, we have wanted to disseminate our findings as quickly as possible. Inevitably, this has led us to look beyond the conventional academic method of publishing in refereed journals. One method we developed on the Leverhulme project was to produce short interim reports and make them widely available to the media, to various teacher and parent organizations, to academics and to practitioners. This method has been reasonably successful, in that our interim reports appear to have reached a wide audience. Moreover, such reports can be produced relatively quickly. Our first interim report, for example, was based on data collected in the Autumn term of 1989, analysed in the Spring term of 1990, and written and produced in the Summer term. However, despite the speed with which our interim reports have been produced, we still compare very poorly with professional opinon-poll organizations such as Mori or Gallup.

This point was brought home to us particularly clearly in the Spring of 1993. During this period, high levels of opposition to SATs amongst teachers and parents had placed considerable political pressure on the then Secretary of State for Education, John Patten. For a few weeks there was intense media interest in the issue. Both the *Daily Telegraph* and the *Independent* commissioned opinion polls in which over 1000 parents were asked for their views on assessment. The organizations conducting these opinion polls were able to collect their data and report back in a matter of days. I was contacted at the time by an educational journalist who wanted to know whether I had any comparable data to add to the picture. In fact, our most recent data at that time were from the 1992 cohort of the ESRC study. While these data were relatively fresh from our own data-analysis process, they were based on only 120 parents and nearly nine months out of date. Although our findings were duly reported in the journalist's paper, it is perhaps not surprising that they received much less attention than the findings of the commissioned opinion polls.

The conclusion I want to draw from such experiences is not that academics should not get involved in researching and disseminating potentially controversial topics where their findings might shape public opinion or influence government policy. Rather, it is to raise the question of whether the methods by which academics normally carry out, analyse and report research are the most appropriate for engaging in that kind of public debate (see Mortimore, 1991, for further discussion of these issues).

Conclusion

In this chapter I have discussed a number of methodological and ethical issues which have been raised by our research on parents. I have described problems in locating and identifying parents, in studying parents in a longitudinal manner, and in the dissemination of findings. In each of these areas I have given some indication of the sensitivity required to carry out research with this particular group.

The notion of *sensitivity* in social research has recently been considered in some depth by Renzatti and Lee (1993). At the heart of their definition is the idea of threat. Thus they suggest that:

> A sensitive topic is one that potentially poses for those involved a substantial threat, the emergence of which renders problematic for the researcher and/or the researched the collection, holding and/or dissemination of research data.

While this definition is a useful starting point in considering the notion of sensitivity, our experience suggests that it may need some expansion. In particular, attention needs to be given to the nature of the supposed 'threat', and whether groups outside the researcher and/or the researched might become threatened by the findings of the research. Thus we felt it important to stress to parents that everything they said was confidential, and that nothing would be reported back to their child's school. For some parents, though, the anxiety was not so much that they themselves might feel threatened if the school became aware of their views, but that their child might suffer in some way. As one parent graphically put it: 'At present if I moan and groan it will be a rod for my daughter's back.'

We also became aware while conducting our research that there are two further groups who might feel threatened by its possible outcomes. The first group are teachers, who are frequently — and no doubt understandably — defensive about possible criticisms of their practice which might emerge from research on parents. As indicated earlier, sessions disseminating our findings to teachers are often characterized by high levels of anxiety on the part of the teachers; these anxiety levels tend to be radically reduced once our findings of overall parental satisfaction have been reported. The second group who might feel threatened are those politicians and policy makers who have placed parents in a central position in the current reforms. Such groups might well view our findings with some trepidation, as they call into question many of the assumptions which they have made about parents when formulating policy.

While the notions of sensitivity and threat are clearly relevant to our research on parents, other notions are relevant too. One of these is the *insider–outsider* distinction. Several chapters in the book are concerned with the perceptions of those — such as teachers and pupils — who are essentially experiencing the current reforms from the *inside*: for these groups, the reforms impinge directly on their day-to-day lives in schools. Parents, in contrast, remain very much on the *outside*. Unlike teachers and pupils, their daily concerns are not directly shaped by current educational policy; in addition, parents frequently lack the necessary information or knowledge with which to evaluate what is happening in their children's schools. Yet these matters are not ones of indifference to them for they have a strong emotional stake in their children's education. Indeed, the overall impression gained from many of our interviews is of a highly concerned but somewhat bewildered group, trying to make sense from the outside of what is happening on the inside of their children's schools.

Finally, research on parents is directly relevant to notions of *empowerment* and *voice*. As was indicated at the start of the chapter, our research on parents was originally prompted by the central role they have been given in the current educational reforms. As the then Secretary of State for Education, Kenneth Baker, said to a conference of parents soon after the Education Reform Act was passed:

> I have given you more power than you have ever had, or ever dreamed of (cited in Docking, 1990, p. 79)

Yet, despite the rhetoric, our research provides little evidence for this empowerment. Certainly, most parents do not see themselves in a position of power — although there are signs of a growing awareness of this in a small minority of parents (see Hughes, Wikeley, Nash, 1994, Chapter 4). Rather, our research brought home to us the parents' relative lack of power in relation to the educational professionals. In addition, we became increasingly aware of their lack of an effective voice. Despite the presence of parent governors and Parent–Teacher Asociations, many parents still feel there are few opportunities for them to voice their views on educational issues, and in particular, on the changes which are directly affecting their children's lives.

I have on occasion described our research on parents as 'giving voice' to a relatively powerless group who lack an effective means of communicating their concerns to those in power. Such a claim has been criticized on the grounds that it is both patronizing and beyond the remit of academic researchers. While these criticisms should not be dismissed lightly, it should also be noted that such claims to be 'giving voice' to parents come not from our own aspirations but from many of the parents themselves. I leave the final comment on our research to one such parent:

> I'm glad you're doing this research. It gives credence to the fact that not everyone is happy with the National Curriculum and what's going on . . . I'm glad of the opportunity to find out the opinion of parents who have never really been asked. No political party ever asked us if we wanted what they've done.

Note

1   The research described here was supported by grant no. F144P from the Leverhulme Trust and by grant no. X208252007 from the ESRC. I am grateful to Felicity Wikeley and Cathie Holden, and to the participants at the ESRC research seminar series, for their comments on an earlier version of this chapter. I should make clear, however, that the views expressed here are my own.

References

Cox, C.B. and Boyson, R. (Eds) (1977) *Black Paper 1977*, London, Temple Smith.
Department for Education (1992) *Choice and Diversity: A New Framework for Schools* (Education White Paper), London, HMSO.
Department of Education and Science (1991) *The Parent's Charter*, London, DES.
Desforges, C., Hughes, M. and Holden, C. (1994a) 'Parents' and teachers' perceptions of assessment at Key Stage One', in Hughes, M. (Ed) *Perceptions of Teaching and Learning*, Clevedon, Multilingual Matters.
Desforges, C., Hughes, M. and Holden, C. (1994b) 'Parents and assessment at Key Stage One', *Research Papers in Education*, 9, 2, pp. 133–58.
Docking, J.M. (1990) *Primary Schools and Parents*, London, Hodder and Stoughton.
Flew, A. (1987) *Power to the Parents*, London, Sherwood Press.
Griffiths, A. and Hamilton, D. (1984) *Parent, Teacher, Child*, London Methuen.
Hillgate Group (1986) *Whose Schools? A Radical Manifesto*, London, Claridge Press.
Holden, C., Hughes, M. and Desforges, C.W. (1993) 'What do parents want from assessment?', *Education 3–13*, 21, pp. 3–7.
Hughes, M., Desforges, C. and Holden, C. (1994) 'Parents, teachers and assessment at Key Stage One', in Hughes, M. (Ed) *The Quality of Teaching and Learning*, Oxford, Basil Blackwell.

HUGHES, M., WIKELEY, F. and NASH, T. (1990) *Parents and the National Curriculum: An Interim Report*, University of Exeter, School of Education.
HUGHES, M., WIKELEY, F. and NASH, T. (1991) *Parents and SATs: A Second Interim Report*, University of Exeter, School of Education.
HUGHES, M., WIKELEY, F. and NASH, T. (1994) *Parents and their Children's Schools*, Oxford, Basil Blackwell.
MERTTENS, R. and VASS, J. (1990) *Sharing Maths Cultures*, London, Falmer Press.
MORTIMORE, P. (1991) 'The front page or yesterday's news: The reception of educational research', in WALFORD, G. (Ed) *Doing Educational Research* London, Routledge.
RENZATTI, C. and LEE, R. (1993) (Eds) *Researching Sensitive Issues*, London, Sage.
SEXTON, S. (1987) *Our Schools — A Radical Policy*, London, IEA Education Unit.

Chapter 14

Practice and Prospects in Education Policy Research

David Halpin

Introduction

Looking across the chapters of this book, a number of recurring themes and issues are raised and explored. One of the most prominent is the broad commitment of all of the contributors to qualitative, sometimes specifically ethnographic, approaches to the study of education policy which, in some cases, are allied to quantitative methods of data gathering. Another, though to a much lesser extent, is the social-scientific perspective through which many of their analyses of education policy are generated. Finally, several chapters point up the increasingly significant role that contemporary social and political theory plays in developing explanations of the education policy-making process.

Qualitative Studies of Education Policy

The favoured status which many education policy analysts give to qualitative methodologies predates considerably the publication of this book. Qualitative research strategies in the social sciences generally have wide currency because no one seriously doubts that what people say, think and do are better understood if their words, perceptions and actions are located in, and articulated with, specific contexts. Hence the importance which most of the contributors to this collection place on interviewing people and observing and recording their behaviour in particular settings. Indeed the naive charge that qualitative researchers simply report their own and their respondents' subjective perceptions fails to appreciate that the ideas people think and act with, and the presuppositions researchers routinely draw on in the course of data gathering, structure and help reproduce the very social worlds within which both respondents and investigators live and work.

This said, qualitative approaches to the investigation of education policy need to avoid the risk of only telling us a great deal about the fine-grain detail of the assumptive worlds of policy makers and the contexts in which their policies are implemented and very little about the effects that certain policies have in terms of improving or making things worse. To be sure, many of the authors in this collection demonstrate how interpretation of their qualitative-data sources provides significant insight into the impact and consequences of education policy. However, the problem, as Pettigrew's chapter observes, is that the 'makers' of education policy, more often than not, prefer outcomes to be reported in quantitative terms which they judge to be more trustworthy and capable of replication. One consequence of this particular attitude is that the interpretive approaches favoured by many education policy analysts often inform very well the thinking of members of their intellectual communities, but fail to penetrate the minds of policy makers who are seeking answers to more prosaic, but nonetheless important, questions about the relative merits of different proposals for reform and improvement. It is not simply, after Hammersley in this volume, that the assumptions behind recent educational reform are at odds with the methodological orientation of qualitative research; rather, it is that the primary *interests* respectively of the makers and researchers of education policy do not overlap sufficiently, the former being preoccupied with defending and trying to make policies work, the latter with theorizing and explaining their significance.

Theorizing Education Policy

At this point, however, we are confronted by a paradox. For while many education policy researchers are committed to theorizing events and explaining their significance, education policy studies, *per se*, has yet to become established as a field of enquiry generally renowned for theoretical sophistication. As Ball and Shilling argue, 'the vast majority of studies of education policy . . . have something to say to those affected by such policies, but are largely devoid of any explanatory or sociological interest' (1994, p. 2). Like Dale's contribution to this volume, Ball and Shilling invite education policy researchers to produce analyses which have greater theoretical and explanatory import. In their case this is achieved via an exploration of the significance of recent developments in contemporary social theory, in particular those that illuminate aspects of postmodern society which stress the importance of consumerism and enterprise and the globalization of information systems. However, as Henry (1993) has cautioned, such theoretical eclecticism may have its own intellectual limitations if the final result looks more like an accumulation of interesting insights, albeit cleverly integrated, than a thoroughgoing theorization of why education policy takes the form it does at particular times, and why its impact is more likely to have certain effects than others. Presumably this is why Raab in this volume stresses the importance of implementation research (see also Fitz, Halpin and Power, 1994). Hence, too, the continuing attractiveness of state-centred theory for the explanation of education policy, as reflected, not only in Ozga and Gewirtz's chapter in this book, but also the complementary critiques offered elsewhere by Hatcher and Troyna (1994), Henry (1993) and Lingard (1993).

Of course, it is easy at this point to be persuaded that the study of education policy is simply a branch of the sociology of education. Certainly, as Barry Troyna points out in Chapter 1, this is what he and I took mostly for granted in our thinking about the shape and content of the seminar series. But this surely was an unfortunate sleight of hand on both our parts to the extent that education policy studies cannot legitimately be equated with the sociology of education policy. As Raab, Hughes, Pettigrew and Wallace, Rudduck and Harris in this collection in particular demonstrate, empirical approaches to the study of education policy do not have to be explicitly sociological before they can be either insightful or informative. Alongside sociologists, historians, psychologists, economists, political scientists, anthropologists, evaluators and those who deliberately transcend disciplinary boundaries may have much to contribute to our understanding of the sources, nature and effects of education policy. By seeming to downgrade the importance of their contribution to the deliberations of the seminar series, we may therefore have been guilty, to use one of Dale's strictures, of our own particular brand of 'disciplinary parochialism'.

Dale in this volume, and Gerald Grace (1991) and Jenny Ozga (1990) elsewhere, are anxious that, by seeking to answer the sorts of questions posed by policy makers, education policy researchers run the risk of suspending their critical faculties in favour of mere 'problem-solving'. There is the possibility, too, as Pettigrew's chapter reminds us, that researchers who choose to work closely with policy makers may find they are constrained to investigate and report only uncontroversial aspects or surface features of policy.

These are important intellectual health warnings. Even so, they should not distract education policy researchers from developing research designs that seek to answer some fundamental questions about the actual outcomes of government legislation. In this connection, one helpful strategy (as utilised by Whitty, *et al.* in their study (1993) of the City Technolgy College (CTC) initiative and recycled in Halpin and Fitz's (1990) investigation of the Grant Maintained (GM) Schools policy) is to test empirically the claims made on behalf of particular policies by their architects and advocates. In other words, to draw on these particular examples, to ask if CTCs do act as significant catalytic agents in promoting technology education throughout the school service; to ask whether a high concentration of GM schools in particular localities increases parental choice; to ask if the self-governance entailed in opting out and the local management of schools leads to measurable improvements in the use and distribution of material and human resources; to ask if schools are more successful in fostering improved levels of pupil attainment if they are managed along institutional autonomous lines. As a social scientist seeking, in his case, sociological explanations of policy, Dale would probably interpret such questions as mere 'problem-solving' ones. But, as I have stressed, there are other legitimate, non-sociological, ways of investigating and evaluating policy which have the potential for increasing our understanding of what sorts of initiatives in education are more or less likely to work, if only in their own terms. Clearly such approaches are capable of generating theory, though not necessarily of the kind envisaged by either Dale or Ball and Shilling. But, then, why should they be allowed to define what theory is of most value in this context?

From Boom to Decline in Education Policy Research?

Besides confirming the pre-eminence of qualitative-research methodologies and the significance of social theory, many of the chapters in this collection, but most notably Barry Troyna's, testify to the resurgence and enlargement of interest in the study of education policy and of the role of the 1988 Education Reform Act in helping this process along. Indeed, the late 1980s and early 1990s were periods during which education policy researchers found unprecedented support for their ideas in terms of research-council funding. While it is never sensible to describe any period as a 'golden' one, it is likely that many education researchers, unlike teachers in schools, will look back on recent times as ones in which they found plenty of welcome new work to do and the resources to undertake it. However, as Pettigrew's chapter depressingly points up, serious threats loom on the horizon, most notably in the form of the constraints that sponsors are increasingly imposing on researchers as a condition for the granting of external funds.

At the time of writing, there are further fears that the 1993 Education Bill will consolidate this process through the narrowing of education-research activity on studies which, broadly speaking, support rather than interrogate policy, thus confirming Dale's anxieties about the present state of education policy research. Indeed, many other education policy analysts consider that the measure in the Bill to channel the funding of educational research through a new Teacher Training Agency (TTA) will restrict their freedom to conduct research and damage the quality of rational discourse about education.

Their concerns in this connection derive from the fact that the TTA is likely to be made up entirely of members appointed by the Secretary of State and that the research grants it allocates will be subject in each case to such terms and conditions as the funding agency think fit. Up to now, education research has been funded through the higher education funding councils which safeguard academic freedom via the process of peer review. By removing this safeguard, there is the danger that researchers in education seeking external funding will be free neither to pursue what they consider as significant issues for enquiry nor to publish the results of investigations which do not 'fit' comfortably with government-policy priorities and commitments. During the Second Reading of the Bill, these fears were brushed aside by Baroness

Blatch, the then Minister of State, who confidently reassured her critics that academic freedom would 'remain the same under the TTA'. But, as the General Secretary of the British Education Research Association, Michael Bassey (1993), observed subsequently, 'if this is to be the case, why not leave educational research under the administration of the Higher Education Funding Council . . . (a body which) . . . has the experience of how to do this and has demonstrated its competence.'

Power and Education Policy Research

As Barry Troyna's and a number of other chapters highlight, issues of power, of which the likely workings of the TTA is a particularly glaring example, significantly articulate with the business of doing research on government-initiated education policy. The claims made on behalf of such research — that it has the potential to 'empower' both the researchers and the researched and therefore inform the policy process itself — are not taken for granted by any of our contributors.

The informal contracts which researchers draw up with institutions and individual respondents, both to protect their sources and to gain access and approval, also exhibit interesting dynamics of power. There is still a tendency, to negotiate issues of access only with leading figures like headteachers and to leave those with no ascribed status, most notably children, in a position where they have little option but to cooperate. In fact, apart from Hughes' and Wallace, Ruddack and Harris' chapters, the relative lack of power of lay people in the research process is one that receives insufficient attention in this book and others like it.

Relatedly, the micro-politics of research projects is hardly touched on either, except at the end of Troyna's opening chapter. What I am referring to here are analyses of the power struggles that routinely occur within research teams, usually involving tenured directors and non-established research officer 'subordinates' over such issues as the intellectual ownership of ideas and the direction of work in hand, both of which affect crucially what is undertaken and how it is finally reported. Reading some of the accounts in this volume one might be forgiven for thinking that such struggles either do not take place or that when they do they have little or no relevance to methodological issues and final outcomes, when, of course, they must impact on both.

Comparative Education Policy Research

Another noteworthy absence in this collection is any analysis of education policy written from a comparative perspective, though a number of contributors, notably Dale and Deem and Brehony, make strong appeals for more work of this sort. However, in doing so, they are concerned to castigate those theoretically crude cross-national policy analyses which make facile juxtapositions between policies developed in different national contexts that appear to be alike but which, on close inspection, only have a very superficial family resemblance. An example of this tendency is the uncomplicated way in which some advocates of the self-governing principle in school management 'compare' the British GM schools policy with the Charter Schools legislation in the USA (see, for example, Wohlstetter and Anderson, 1994). In such work, the assumption is that because each policy embraces the general idea of institutional autonomy they must have comparable characteristics on the ground. But nothing could be further from the truth in this case to the extent that the GM schools policy and the Charter Schools legislation interpret the principle of self-governing status for schools in very different and contrasting ways. For example, Charter Schools are experimental institutions set up by contract for a fixed term (see: Datnow *et al.*, 1994); GM schools, on the other hand, are constrained by the central State in so many ways that it is difficult for them to be innovative, least of all leading edge, establishments (see Power, Halpin and Fitz, 1994).

There are other fundamental differences, but they need not concern us now; the point is that a proper comparison of GM and Charter Schools ought to begin (after Dale in this volume) by first rendering unfamiliar the national system of provision from out of which each policy orginates and then disassembling the 'problems' the system is alleged to have and for which self-governing schools are seen as one solution (see Halpin and Troyna, 1994). As Dale (1992) has argued elsewhere: 'Only rarely are we offered a comparative analysis that has the virtue of demonstrating that things . . . could be otherwise and consequently requiring us to make problematic rather than taking for granted, not only the ideas themselves . . . but also the particular sets of historical, social, political and economic conditions under which one or other interpretation of those ideas become installed' (p. 209).

This, of course, is not an issue particular to the study of education policy. On the contrary, as Dale demonstrates, it can be applied to other social movements with equal effect. Thus, while feminism is concerned with the conditions and rights of women, the actual forms taken by feminist thought and action owe a very great deal to the political traditions of the countries in which they are created (Bassnett, 1986). Similarly, it appears that the central tenets of New Right thinking and their translation into policies for educational reform have been interpreted differently in different national contexts. In this connection, Dale and Ozga's (1993) comparative study of the impact of 1980s education reform in New Zealand and England and Wales raises important questions about the role of New Right ideas in forming recent education policy. Briefly, what they argue is that, while the recent school reform measures of New Zealand and England and Wales exhibit ideological similarity (they both, for example, stress deregulation, devolution of power and consumer choice), their respective direction does not. Specifically, Dale and Ozga point out that whereas neo-liberal and neo-conservative strands of New Right thinking underpin the education reforms in England and Wales (especially their local management of schools and National Curriculum policies) 'conservatism played little, if any, part in [New Zealand's] . . . where the emphasis was [more] on the reform of the role of the state and of public administration, informed by particular strands of neo-liberal thought.'

This conclusion can be applied with equal conviction, albeit with a slightly different inflection, to the circumstances of recent school reform in the US and Britain. Notwithstanding the core-curriculum measures entailed in President Bush's National Goals initiative, US education reform in the 1980s was chiefly about restructuring, that is to say, creating new school choice systems, including the introduction of education voucher programmes. True, some neo-conservative emphases are reflected in USA education policy deliberations in this period, particularly in the case of New Right religious groups (e.g., 'the Moral Majority') that objected to the kinds of subjects taught, and books used, in public schools. However, such neo-conservative criticisms did not hold centre stage. Rather, as in New Zealand, on those occasions when the New Right in the US mobilized behind specific school reform initiatives, it was mostly neo-liberal argument that held sway, particularly in debates about the relationship between deregulation and school improvement, but also in discussions of ways of reining in and limiting future spending on education, and welfare generally.

In this light, and notwithstanding the contrasting interpretations of 'self-governance', 'feminism' and aspects of New Right thinking, it may be worth considering the work of those education policy theorists, like Kenway, Bigum and Fitzclarence (1993), who draw attention to the importance of modern global-communication systems and the potential they have for dissolving boundaries between nation states and between national and local contexts. In these circumstances, there may be a strong case for investigating the nature, pattern and direction of information flows and how these influence the scale and pace of education policy take-up. Dale's (1992) conception of 'carriers' of education policy and Finegold, McFarland and Richardson's (1992) notion of the 'borrowing agent' are moves in this direction inasmuch as they both form part of analyses which seek to explore the processes which lead to universalizing tendencies in educational reform.

A key aspect of this process is the general internationalization which has taken place among the world's academic and policy communities. The extent of education policy 'borrowing' (or 'modelling', 'transfer', 'diffusion', appropriation' and 'copying') is both under-researched and inadequately theorized. The work of Robertson and Waltman (1992) is exceptional in this context, representing a major achievement in the development of a subtle analytic framework for understanding this process which, among other things, helps to categorize the extent and type of trans-Atlantic education policy transfer that has occurred in recent times and the factors which make it more or less likely. More of this work will undoubtedly be undertaken in the field of education policy research in the years ahead. Regrettably, unlike other themes, it is only anticipated and advocated in this volume.

References

BALL, S.J. and SHILLING, C. (1994) 'At the cross-roads: Education policy studies', *British Journal of Educational Studies*, 42, 1, pp. 1–5.

BASSEY, M. (1993) 'Agency ties will hit education research', *Times Higher Education Supplement*, 31 December, p. 9.

BASSNETT, S. (1986) *Feminist Experience: The Women's Movement in Four Countries*, London, Allen and Unwin.

DALE, R. (1992) 'Recovering from a pyrrhic victory? Quality, relevance and impact in the sociology of education', in ARNOT, M. and BARTON, L. (Eds) *Voicing Concerns: Sociological Perspectives on Contemporary Education Reforms*, Wallingford, Triangle Books.

DALE, R. and OZGA, J. (1993) 'Two hemispheres — both New Right? 1980s education reform in New Zealand and England and Wales', in LINGARD, R., KNIGHT, J. and PORTER, P. (Eds) *Schooling Reform in Hard Times*, London, Falmer Press.

FINEGOLD, D., McFARLAND, L. and RICHARDSON, W. (1992) 'Introduction', *Oxford Studies in Comparative Education*, 2, 2, pp. 7–24.

FITZ, J., HALPIN, D. and POWER, S. (1993) *Education in the Market Place: Grant Maintained Schools*, London, Kogan Page.

FITZ, J., HALPIN, D. and POWER, S. (1994) 'Implementation research and education policy: practice and prospects', *British Journal of Educational Studies*, 42, 1, pp. 53–69.

GRACE, G. (1991) 'Welfare labourism versus the New Right: The struggle in New Zealand's education policy', *International Studies in Sociology of Education*, 1, pp. 25–42.

HALPIN, D. and FITZ, J. (1990) 'Researching grant-maintained schools', *Journal of Education Policy*, 5, 2, pp. 167–80.

HALPIN, D. and TROYNA, B. (1994) 'Lessons in school reform from Great Britain?: The politics of education policy borrowing', Paper presented at the Annual Meeting of the American Educational Research Association, New Orleans, April.

HATCHER, R. and TROYNA, B. (1994) 'The policy cycle: A Ball by Ball account', *Journal of Education Policy*, 9, 2, pp. 155–70.

HENRY, M. (1993) 'What is policy? A response to Stephen Ball', *Discourse*, 14, 1, pp. 102–5.

KENWAY, J., BIGUM, C. and FITZCLARENCE, L. (1993) 'Marketing education in a postmodern world', *Journal of Education Policy*, 8, 2, pp. 105–22.

LINGARD, B. (1993) 'The changing state of policy production in education: Some Australian reflections on the state of policy sociology', *International Studies in Sociology of Education*, 3, 1, pp. 25–47.

OZGA, J. (1990) 'Policy research and policy theory: A comment on Halpin and Fitz', *Journal of Education Policy*, 5, 4, pp. 359–62.

POWER, S., HALPIN, D. and FITZ, J. (1994) 'The grant-maintained schools policy: The English experience of education self-governance', Paper presented at the Annual Meeting of the American Educational Research Association, New Orleans, April.

ROBERTSON, D.B. and WALTMAN, J.L. (1992) 'The politics of policy borrowing', *Oxford Studies in Comparative Education*, 2, 2, pp. 25–55.

David Halpin

WHITTY, G., EDWARDS, T. and GEWIRTZ, S. (1993) *Specialization and Choice in Urban Education: The City Technology Experiment*, London, Routledge.

WOHLSTETTER, P. and ANDERSON, L. (1994) 'What can US Charter schools learn from England's grant-maintained schools?', *Phi Delta Kappan*, 75, 6, pp. 486–91.

Evaluation and Research — Project Outline (Chapter 4)

Evaluation and Research is a two-year project (1 June 1991–30 May 1992 and 1 November 1992–31 October 1993) funded by the ESRC. It is based at the Centre for Applied Research and Evaluation and is being conducted by Nigel Norris and May Pettigrew. Four key questions form the basis of the research:

- Has the research community's increasing commitment to social applied research and evaluation work meant diminished public access to the knowledge generated by the community?
- What kinds of contractual obligations are drawn up between funding agencies and applied research and evaluations and what kind of relationships between the parties to the contract emerge as a consequence?
- Are methodological and ethical compromises entailed in commissioned applied research and evaluative inquiry and, if so, what justifications are offered by researchers for them?
- What strategies have developed in different research groups to take account of the changing political circumstances of social inquiry?

The database of the project so far derives from interviews with over sixty researchers, most of them in senior positions, within the educational research and other social-research communities such as health, organizational behaviour, sociology, criminology and social administration. From these key informants and from other sources, the project has additionally collected a range of contracts from the main government departments and agencies that commission research. In addition, a review of the literature and relevant documentation has been conducted to establish what is already known about the conditions of applied research and evaluative enquiry with respect to the questions outlined above.

Notes on Contributors

Stephen J Ball is Professor of Education in the Centre for Educational Studies, King's College, London, where he was previously Lecturer in Urban Education and University of London and Reader in the Sociology of Education. His interests are particularly centred on education and social class, conflict in education and ethnographic research methods. His recent research has been focused upon aspects of education policy, organisational responses to change, markets in education, policy discourses, and the importation of the values and methods of business into public education. He has also recently been involved in research into the impact of childhood cancer on families and the role of palliative care education in Colleges of Nursing. His recent books include *Politics and Policy Making in Education* (Routledge, 1990); *Reforming Education and Changing Schools* (with Richard Bowe and Anne Gold; Routledge, 1992) and *Education Reform: Critical and Post-Structural Perspectives* (Open University Press, 1994).

Kevin J Brehony is a Senior Lecturer in Education at the University of Reading. Formerly a primary school teacher in the West Midlands, he gained a PhD from the Open University for a thesis on the Froebel Movement. As well as work in historical sociology concerned with child centred ideologies, he has also published several articles on school governors and education policy. He teaches and coordinates an MA entitled 'School and Society' and a module on qualitative research for the Research Methods programme. He is currently carrying out research on the Montessori movement.

Robert Burgess is Director of CEDAR (Centre for Educational Development, Appraisal and Research) and Professor of Sociology at the University of Warwick. His main teaching and research interests are in social research methodology and the sociology of education. He has written ethnographic studies of secondary schools and is currently working on case studies of schools and higher education. His main publications include: *Experiencing Comprehensive Education* (1983); *In the Field: An Introduction to Field Research* (1984); *Education, Schools and Schooling* (1985); *Sociology, Education and Schools* (1986); *Schools at Work* (1988 with Rosemary Deem) and *Implementing In-Service Education and Training* (1993 with John Connor, Sheila Galloway, Marlene Morrison and Malcolm Newton), together with fourteen edited volumes on qualitative methods and education. He was recently President of the British Sociological Association and is currently President of the Association for the Teaching of the Social Sciences. He was a member of the ESRC Training Board and is currently a member of the ESRC Research Resources Board.

Roger Dale is Professor and Head of the Department of Education, University of Auckland. His main interest is in the political sociology of education, an area in which he has published several papers and books including, *The State and Education Policy* and *The TVEI Story: Policy, Practice and Preparation for Work. Producing Tomorrow's Schools*, a book on the education reforms in New Zealand (with John Codd and Liz Gordon), will shortly be published by Auckland University Press. He is currently engaged on writing *Learning Choice*, a political sociological account of educational markets.

Rosemary Deem is Professor of Educational Research and Dean of the Faculty of Social Sciences at Lancaster University, where she teaches qualitative methods on the Faculty Research Training Programme. She has published widely on gender and education, women and leisure, and the governance of education, and with Kevin J Brehony was co-director of the ESRC funded project, *The Reform of School Governing Bodies* from 1990–1993. She is currently planning some research on women and holidays and writing a book on feminist methodology.

Sharon Gewirtz is a Researcher at King's College, London. Her current research is on parental choice and market forces in education and the culture and values of schooling. She has published mainly in the field of education policy and is co-author of *Specialisation and Choice in Urban Education* (Routledge, 1993) and the forthcoming *Markets, Choice and Equity in Education* (Open University Press).

David Halpin is a Lecturer in Education Policy and School Management at the University of Warwick Institute of Education. His research interests include self-governing schools, comprehensive education, the secondary school curriculum and the education policy making process. He has published widely on aspects of each of these areas including a book (with John Fitz and Sally Power) on opting out, *Grant-Maintained Schools: Education in the Market Place.* He is also Joint Editor of the *British Journal of Educational Studies*.

Martyn Hammersley is Reader in Educational and Social Research in the School of Education, Open University. In recent years most of his work has been concerned with the methodological issues surrounding social research. He has written several books: (with Paul Atkinson) *Ethnography: principles in practice* (Tavistock, 1983 second edition, 1994); *The Dilemma of Qualitative Method* (Routledge, 1989); *Classroom Ethnography* (Open University Press, 1990); *Reading Ethnographic Research* (Longman, 1991) and *What's Wrong with Ethnography?* (Routledge, 1992).

Susan Harris graduated in Sociology and History at Aberdeen University in 1985. She went on to complete her PhD research on 'Careers Teachers' at Nottingham University. She is currently a Research Fellow in the Division of Education, Sheffield University, where she is working on an ESRC qualitative study of students' experiences of teaching and learning. Her interests are in the sociology of education, gender, careers education and guidance and careers teachers' careers. She has written various articles on careers teachers and their marginal position in school. At present she is collaboratively writing a book on students' experiences of school.

Martin Hughes is Reader in Education at the University of Exeter. He has researched and written widely on the development and education of young children. His books include, *Young Children Learning* (with Barbara Tizard, 1984); *Children and Number* (1986) and *Parents and their Children's Schools* (with Felicity Wikeley and Tricia Nash, 1994). He is currently researching the effects of social interaction on learning, and the relationship between parents and schools. He is also co-ordinator of the ESRC Research Programme on 'Innovation and Change in Education: The Quality of Teaching and Learning'.

Jenny Ozga is Professor of Education Policy at Keele University. Before that she was Dean of Education at Bristol Polytechnic (now University of the West of England) and previously worked in the School of Education at the Open University. She has taught at the Department of Administration at Strathclyde University and was Senior Administrative Officer in the National Union of Teachers. Her main research interests are in education policy and in the study of teachers' work and teacher-state relations. She also researches and writes about gender and education management.

May Pettigrew is a Senior Research Associate in the Centre for Applied Research in Education, School of Education, University of East Anglia. In addition to her work on the contemporary conditions of social research, May Pettigrew has a broad range of interests in the area of applied research and evaluation in education. She is currently researching (with Maggie MacLure) the relations between the press, public knowledge and education policy and practice. She has recently conducted enquiries in environmental education and co-edited, *Evaluation and Innovation in Environmental Education* (OECD, 1994).

Charles D Raab is Senior Lecturer in the Department of Politics, University of Edinburgh. He has published many articles and contributions to books on education policy, and on methodological and theoretical issues. Under an ESRC grant, he is co-directing comparative research on the devolved management of schools in England and Wales and in Scotland. His book (with Andrew McPherson) *Governing Education: A Sociology of Policy Since 1945* (Edinburgh University Press, 1988) won the 1989 Annual Book Prize of the

Standing Conference on Studies in Education. He is a member of the International Advisory Board of the *Journal of Education Policy*.

Jean Rudduck was a founder member of the Centre for Applied Research in Education (CARE) at the University of East Anglia. In 1984 she moved from Norwich to be Professor of Education at Sheffield University. In January 1994 she was appointed Director of Research at Homerton College, Cambridge. She is interested in research which focuses on the experience and perspectives of students and teachers and which explores the process of change. Recent books include, *Developing a Gender Policy in Secondary Schools* (Open University Press, 1994) and *Innovation and Change: Individuals and Institutions* (Open University Press, 1991).

Beverley Skeggs now teaches Women's Studies at Lancaster University, having recently left the Centre for Women's Studies at York. From her earliest ethnographic research, Dr Skegg's work has concentrated on how power relations are lived. This focus comes from a desire to locate the sites and possibilities of social change. Her work analyses how young women, using the cultural resources to which they have access, construct their identities in relation to institutionalized constraints. The results of this work have been published in a variety of journals and will soon culminate in a book she is currently editing, *The Production of Feminist Cultural Theory*. She has also published *The Media* (with Joan Mundy, Nelson, 1992).

Barry Troyna holds a personal Readership and is Director of Research Development in the University of Warwick Institute of Education. He is editor of the *British Educational Research Journal* and on the editorial boards of the *Cambridge Journal of Education*, *Journal of Education Policy* and *Discourse*. His research and teaching interests focus on antiracist education, education policy and research methodology. His latest books include *Racism in Children's Lives* (with Richard Hatcher, Routledge, 1992) and *Racism and Education: Research Perspectives* (Open University Press, 1993).

Gwen Wallace is Reader in Policy and Sociology and Faculty Research Co-ordinator in the Faculty of Education, Humanities and Social Sciences at the University of Derby. She moved into higher education after thirteen years teaching in secondary schools. Her major research interests lie in the relationships between educational policy, classroom practices and school students' experiences of schooling. She co-ordinated the LMS Policy Task Group for the British Educational Research Association for three years and her publications include an annotated bibliography and three edited collections of papers on the subject.

Geoffrey Walford is a Senior Lecturer in Sociology and Education Policy at Aston Business School, Aston University, Birmingham. He has published over 80 academic articles and book chapters on such areas as private schooling, higher education and research methods. His books include, *Life in Public Schools* (Methuen, 1986); *Restructuring Universities: Politics and power in the management of change* (Routledge, 1987); *Privatization and Privilege in Education* (Routledge, 1990); *City Technology College* (with Henry Miller, Open University Press, 1991) and *Choice and Equity in Education* (Cassell, 1994). He has also edited several books on private education and on educational research methods.

Index

academic subject areas 27
Ainsworth, Alan 109–11, 116
Aldridge, Judith 8–9
Allison, L. 55–6
Althusser, Louis 108, 144
analysis, interactionist 17, 18, 24, 26
Apple, Michael 2
Archer, Margaret 34–5
assessment, in schools 174, 187, 193–4
   National Curriculum 43
   SATs 174, 187, 193–4
Aston 94, 105
audience 165–6

Bacon, A. 156
Baker, Kenneth 109, 114, 195
Ball, Stephen 9, 21, 23, 24, 25, 26, 36,
   171, 199, 201, 208
Bartlett, Will 3
Bassey, Michael 202
Becker, Howard 9
Bell, Colin 6, 62
Bernstein, E. 34
Bertaux, D. 127
Bhavani, K.K. 80
biology lesson 101
Black, Paul 43
Blatch, Baroness 201
Blumer, Herbert 147
Boelen, W.A.M. 7–8
Bonnett, Alastair 5
Bourdieu, P. 34, 111
Boyson, Sir Rhodes 114–17
Brinton, C. 149
British Educational Research Association
   x, 3, 47
Bulmer, M. 149
Burgess, Robert ix, x, 7, 167, 208–9

career
   building 62–4
   concept of 170
   students' in school 170–83

Carlisle, Mark 112, 113
Carter, B. 183
Carter, Ron 45, 46
case study strategy 154, 156–67
   multi-site 65–6, 154–67
   qualitative and quantitative 9, 94, 96,
   98–9, 103, 156, 160–5, 198–9, 201
censorship
   by research sponsors 44–53
   self- 123–4
Centre for Contemporary Cultural
   Studies 85
Charitable Status 52
Charter Schools, US 203
Choice and Diversity 75
City Technology Colleges 94–105, 200
Clarke, Kenneth 46
class, social 100, 102–3
classroom interaction 79
Codd, J.A. 171
Committee of Vice-Chancellors and
   Principals 51, 52
confidentiality 66, 124–5, 128–9
Conservative party education policy
   1–3, 19–20, 75, 76, 82, 85, 87,
   88–9, 95, 113–17
   see also government; Right, political
   faction
constructivism 147
contracts, research 42–53, 55–69
   careers and teams 62–4
   control 43–53, 123–4
   ethical issues 66–8
   funding and planning 58–61
   methodology 48–50, 64–6
control of sponsored research 43–53,
   123–4
Cooper, Philip 52
copyright 44, 49
Corbett, A. 171
Cox, Brian 115
Cox, Robert 39, 122, 123

213